A FAMILY GUIDE TO Parenting MUSICALLY

LISA HUISMAN KOOPS

OXFORD
UNIVERSITY PRESS

Oxford University Press is a department of the University of Oxford. It furthers
the University's objective of excellence in research, scholarship, and education
by publishing worldwide. Oxford is a registered trade mark of Oxford University
Press in the UK and certain other countries.

Published in the United States of America by Oxford University Press
198 Madison Avenue, New York, NY 10016, United States of America.

© Oxford University Press 2024

All rights reserved. No part of this publication may be reproduced, stored in
a retrieval system, or transmitted, in any form or by any means, without the
prior permission in writing of Oxford University Press, or as expressly permitted
by law, by license, or under terms agreed with the appropriate reproduction
rights organization. Inquiries concerning reproduction outside the scope of the
above should be sent to the Rights Department, Oxford University Press, at the
address above.

You must not circulate this work in any other form
and you must impose this same condition on any acquirer.

Library of Congress Cataloging-in-Publication Data
Names: Koops, Lisa, author.
Title: A family guide to parenting musically / Lisa Huisman Koops.
Description: [1.] | New York, NY : Oxford University Press, 2024. |
Includes bibliographical references and index.
Identifiers: LCCN 2024015215 (print) | LCCN 2024015216 (ebook) |
ISBN 9780197673607 (hardback) | ISBN 9780197673614 (paperback) |
ISBN 9780197673638 (epub) | ISBN 9780197673645 | ISBN 9780197673621
Subjects: LCSH: Music in the home. | Music—Social aspects. | Music and children. |
Parenting. | Music—Instruction and study—Parent participation.
Classification: LCC ML3916 .K679 2024 (print) | LCC ML3916 (ebook) |
DDC 780.23—dc23/eng/20240405
LC record available at https://lccn.loc.gov/2024015215
LC ebook record available at https://lccn.loc.gov/2024015216

DOI: 10.1093/oso/9780197673607.001.0001

The manufacturer's authorised representative in the EU for product safety is
Oxford University Press España S.A. of El Parque Empresarial San Fernando
de Henares, Avenida de Castilla, 2 – 28830 Madrid (www.oup.es/en or
product.safety@oup.com). OUP España S.A. also acts as importer into Spain
of products made by the manufacturer.

To my parents, Bonnie and Tom Huisman, and my parents-in-law, Esther and Rob Koops.

In gratitude for the many ways you parent musically and grandparent musically.

All my love.

CONTENTS

NOTE TO THE READER	xiii
ACKNOWLEDGMENTS	xv
LIST OF ACTIVITIES	xvii
ABOUT THE COMPANION WEBSITE	xxi

Introduction:	What Is "Parenting Musically" All About?	1
	What's at Stake?	2
	Reconsidering How We Think and Talk About Families and Music	3
	Four Main Ideas of *A Family Guide to Parenting Musically*	4
	Examining Assumptions in Books about Families and Music	5
	How to Use This Book	7
	Parenting Musically Podcast	8
	About Me	8

PART 1		MUSIC IS IMPORTANT	11
Chapter 1		Family Musicking Framework	13
	Reconsidering the Goals of Music in Family Life		13
	What Is Musical Parenting?		14
	What Is Parenting Musically?		14
	What Is Musicking?		15
	Family Musicking Framework		17
	Acknowledging Privilege and Resource Availability		21
	Use of Research in this Book		21
Chapter 2		You Are a Musical Family	24
	Musical Homes and Musical Families		24
	What Is Music Aptitude?		26
	Musicking as a Family		27

Chapter 3	**Celebrating Your Family's Musical Canon**	**30**
	What Is a Family Musical Canon?	30
	Family Musical Canon and the Long Game	32
Chapter 4	**Discovering New Music as a Family**	**35**
	Discovering and Expanding Your Family's Musical Preferences	35
	Research Connection: Global Music and Kids	36
Chapter 5	**Cherishing Your Additional Adults in Family Musicking**	**42**
	Be Present for the Ordinary Moments	42
	A Note to the Grandparents, Extended Family, and Friends	44
Chapter 6	**What Are Your Family's Musical Hopes and Dreams?**	**49**
	Identifying Your Family's Musical Hopes and Dreams	49
	When There Are Different Hopes and Dreams	52
	Building Relationships to Nurture Hopes and Dreams	53

PART 2	**MANY WAYS TO BE MUSICAL**	**59**
Chapter 7	**Sing with Your Kids**	**61**
	Benefits of Singing	62
	Can Adults Improve Their Singing Voices and Confidence?	63
	Children's Initial Singing Range and Your Comfortable Singing Range	64
	Singing through the Adolescent Voice Change	65
	Should My Child Take Vocal Lessons?	68
	Many Ways to Support Children's Voices	69
Chapter 8	**Music Listening Together**	**71**
	Listening IS Musicking!	71
	Benefits of Joint Music Listening	73
	The Magical Space of the Family Vehicle	74

Chapter 9	Found Sounds and Rhythm Bands	80
	Thinking Broadly About Instrument Playing	80
	Benefits of Playing Instruments	81
	Body Percussion	82
	Rhythm Instruments	82
	Found Sounds	84
	Recorders, and Other Noisy Things, in the Home	88

Chapter 10	Dance Parties Through the Decades	91
	Dancing IS Musicking!	91
	Benefits of Dancing	92
	Creative Movement and Laban Effort Elements	92
	Living Room Dance Parties	95
	Dancing Together as Kids Get Older	96
	Ways to Learn Dancing	98

Chapter 11	Creating Music, Creating Memories	100
	Creativity Comes Naturally . . . But How to Help It Stay?	100
	Benefits of Musical Creativity	102
	Producing Music	106
	The Importance of Modeling	108

PART 3	ALL HUMANS ARE MUSICAL	111
	Evaluating Research	111

Chapter 12	Music Before Birth	115
	Overview of Musical Development in Utero	115
	Will Your Baby Be Smarter if You Play Classical Music Before They Are Born?	116
	Shortcuts for Busy Expectant Parents	118

Chapter 13	Connecting with Your Infant Through Music (Birth to 12 Months)	119
	Overview of Musical Development, Birth to 12 Months	119
	Communicative Musicality	121
	Music and Your Child's Brain	122

Music in Routines with Infants	123
Music to Care for Yourself as a New Parent or Caregiver	126
Music and Relationships with Infants	127
Musical Toys	128

Chapter 14 Musicking Through the Day with Toddlers (Ages 12 to 36 Months) — 130

Overview of Musical Development, 12 to 36 Months	130
Connections Between Music and Language	134
Put Down Your Phone	135
Music in Routines with Toddlers	136
Music and Relationships with Toddlers	140

Chapter 15 Widening Musical Worlds with Preschoolers (Ages 3 to 5 Years) — 145

Overview of Musical Development, Ages 3 to 5	145
Considering Music Lessons in the Preschool Years	146
Musical Play	148
Music in Routines with Preschoolers	149
Music and Relationships with Preschoolers	150
Cultivating Interest in Musicians and Musical Cultures	151

Chapter 16 Uncovering Musical Interests with Early Elementary Age Children (Ages 5 to 9 Years) — 153

Overview of Musical Development, Kindergarten to 3rd Grade (Ages 5–9)	153
Music and Relationships with Early Elementary Age Children	155
Overview of General Music Teaching Methods	157

Chapter 17 Nurturing Musical Expression with Late Elementary Age Children (Ages 9 to 12 Years) — 163

Overview of Musical Development, 4th Through 6th Grade (Ages 9–12)	163
Recognize the Vast Potential: Meeting of Time + Skill!	164

Music and Other Learning	165
Choosing a Musical Instrument	166
Private Lessons?	167
Community Music Opportunities	167
Music in Routines and Relationships with Late Elementary Schoolers	168

PART 4 — EXPRESSING AGENCY AS A FAMILY WITH MUSIC — 171

Chapter 18 How to Participate in Early Childhood Music Experiences — 173

Early Childhood Music Experiences	173
When to Start	174
Choosing a Class	175
Paying for the Class	175
At the Class	176
After Class	177
Be an Advocate for Early Childhood Music in Your Community	177

Chapter 19 How to Help Your Child Choose an Instrument or Voice Part — 181

Three (of Many) Potential Paths to Starting an Instrument	181
Types of Ensembles Commonly Offered in Schools	182
Equity Note: School Music Participation for Children with Disabilities	183
Research on Instrument Selection	184
Roles of Child, Family, and Teacher in Instrument Selection	186
Promote Equity in Your School Music Program	187

Chapter 20 How to Help Your Child Develop Musical Skills — 191

Many Ways to Develop Musical Skills	191
"Teaching Themselves Music" and Learning Online	192
Learning from a Family Member or Friend	193

Group Instruction and Community Classes	193
Taking Lessons with a Teacher	194
Advocate General Music Programs in Elementary Schools	197

Chapter 21 How to Approach Musical Practice in Healthy Ways — 200

Finding Your Family Peace with Musical Practicing	200
Practice Principles	201
Scenario 1: "Am I scarring her for life?"	203
Scenario 2: Revisiting "Battle Hymn of the Tiger Mother"	205
Scenario 3: A Reminder About Music Aptitude	206
Scenario 4: Monitoring Your Relationship with Your Child	207
A Treasure Trove of Tricks and Tips	209
Strategies for the Rest of the Household	210

Chapter 22 How to Sustain Musical Involvement — 213

Musical Involvement for the "Long Game"	213
A Note About Regret	216
Psychology Related to Motivation	217
Modeling Musical Engagement	218
What Really Matters?	219

Epilogue: Parenting Musically and Musical Parenting in Context — 221

APPENDIX	225
NOTES	229
BIBLIOGRAPHY	245
FURTHER READING	259
INDEX	263

NOTE TO THE READER

Welcome! I'm so glad you are interested in incorporating music in family life. As you'll read in the coming chapters, I believe that music is important, there are many ways to be musical and all humans are musical. No matter what your own musical background is, you can create a musical home and weave music into your family's daily life. Throughout the book you'll see activities, links to audio recordings, and examples drawn from my podcast, also called *Parenting Musically*.

My hope is that this book will provide you with information and ideas as well as confidence to make music an important part of your family's daily life. I also hope that you will approach these ideas as starting points. Make the activities your own—adapt them to suit your family. Use the guiding questions to nurture your own curiosity about your children and music.

I love to teach—elementary general music students, families in an early childhood class, undergraduate students in music methods classes, and graduate students in philosophy of music education and research classes. I have also taught elementary classroom teachers who are not music majors and I have worked with children's librarians with a range of musical backgrounds. I drew on all of these experiences in creating this *Family Guide to Parenting Musically*. While reading this book you might even feel like a student in one of my university classes. This book can be the start or continuation of a process of weaving music into everyday life with intention and reflection.

All best,
Lisa

ACKNOWLEDGMENTS

This book is the culmination of 25 years of research and teaching in multiple settings with families and children. Heartfelt thanks to the families who have participated in research projects and Music and Movement classes with me over the last 20 years. I am deeply grateful for all you have taught me and the musical moments we have shared.

Thank you to my mentors and teachers. I learned many of the activity ideas included here from my graduate advisor Cynthia Crump Taggart and undergraduate mentor Dale Topp. My ethnomusicology-informed music education is shaped by mentors Michael Largey and Patricia Shehan Campbell. Music therapy awareness is thanks to friends Christine Leist and Deforia Lane. My open-hearted approach to "many right ways" comes from my parents, Tom and Bonnie Huisman. My commitment to writing clearly and plainly reflects what I learned from my German professor, Wally Bratt. I'm grateful to my many colleagues in the field of early childhood music education whose research and practice has shaped my work and this book.

Special thanks to my incredible, generous team of readers: Anastasia Tuckness, Aunt Barb Scott, Mom Bonnie Huisman, Samantha Webber, Justin Glanville, Lauren Dockery, Carol Scott-Kassner, Erin Hopkins, Linnea Koops, Julia Koops, Aimée Gaudette-Leblanc, and Elizabeth Tracy. Extra thanks to Stacey Kolthammer and Kelsey Giotta for their intense, insightful, thorough feedback on the text.

Gratitude to my colleagues and students at Case Western Reserve University for their support and interest in the project. Thank you to my chair, David Rothenberg; Associate Chair Nate Kruse; Dean Joy Ward and Interim Dean Lee Thompson for encouraging me in this project. To Davey Berris at MediaVision @ CWRU: thank you for your assistance with the sound recordings and with the *Parenting Musically* Podcast. To Ned Breznai, Colin McEwen, and David Hintz @ CWRU Marketing and Communications, thank you for the design and marketing assistance and encouragement.

I am thankful for financial support from Case Western Reserve University for this book in the form of a Manuscript Pre-Review Fund

Award as well as a CWRU Finish Line Fund Award. I am also grateful for CWRU's support of my podcast, *Parenting Musically*, through an ACES+ Advance Opportunity Grant (2021) and CWRU Emerging Horizons Initiative Disciplinary Award (2023).

Thanks to Michelle Moehler of Michelle Moehler Design for designing the cover art logo for this book, as well as logos and graphics for the *Parenting Musically* podcast.

At Oxford University Press, thanks to Norm Hirschy, Michelle Chen, Rada Radojicic, Amy Whitmer, Henry Wilkinson, and Patterson Lamb. Thanks also to the reviewers who read the manuscript on multiple occasions and provided formative feedback.

To all the musicians, researchers, and practitioners who participated in the *Parenting Musically* podcast, thank you for sharing your stories, insights, research, and advice for families. Thank you to Kelsey Giotta and Erin Hopkins for the social media and logistical support with the podcast.

To dear friends who walked alongside me, encouraged me, and brainstormed about this project, thanks: Jenn Carr, Tami Draves, Alison Lee, Christine Leist, Erica Steinweg, Leslie Szalay, and Ursula Rossman. I am so blessed by your friendship and support.

Thank you to my amazing husband, Jed, and terrific children, Linnea, Julia, Joshua, and Christopher (Kip). You continue to be my inspiration! Thank you for sharing your wisdom and experiences. To my parents, parents-in-law, brothers, sisters-in-law, brothers-in-law, nieces, and nephews: all the Huismans and Koopses and Campbells—I love you! Ephesians 3:20.

LIST OF ACTIVITIES

Activity 1:	Reflection Questions to Ask Regarding Musical Activities
Activity 2:	Mapping the Family Music Framework
Activity 3:	Encourage Your Child to Be Expressive Musically
Activity 4:	Family Music Bucket List
Activity 5:	Discover a Relative or Friend's Musical Canon
Activity 6:	Reminisce with Your Child About Musical Moments of Your Childhood
Activity 7:	Identify Music for Specific Emotions
Activity 8:	Become a Researcher of Musical Preferences
Activity 9:	Finding New Music
Activity 10:	Start with a Live Music Event
Activity 11:	Attend Free Concerts in Your Area
Activity 12:	Music and Dinner Around the World
Activity 13:	Making Meaningful Music Connections
Activity 14:	Go to a Music-Related Museum or Landmark
Activity 15:	For Grandparents, Extended Family, and Friends
Activity 16:	Map Your Family's Musical Web
Activity 17:	Thank Your Extra Adults
Activity 18:	Musical Hopes and Dreams Inventory
Activity 19:	Experiment with Range
Activity 20:	Blast from the Past—Listen to Your Voice on Home Movies
Activity 21:	Create an "Audio Photo Album"
Activity 22:	Explore Acoustical Spaces
Activity 23:	Keep a Listening Journal
Activity 24:	Where and When Does This Music Come From?
Activity 25:	Interview Grandparents and Elders About Music Listening
Activity 26:	Create a Soundtrack for a Picture Book Activity
Activity 27:	Found Sound Instrument Tidying Game
Activity 28:	Multi-Generational Jam Session
Activity 29:	Conducting

Activity 30:	Instruments at Playgrounds
Activity 31:	Laban Movement Activities
Activity 32:	Mirroring During Dance Party
Activity 33:	Learn a Dance from an Elder
Activity 34:	Create a Family Dance
Activity 35:	Hand Orchestra Thunderstorm
Activity 36:	ABA Composition
Activity 37:	Rhythm Round
Activity 38:	Create Loops
Activity 39:	Song-Writing
Activity 40:	Creating Digital Gifts for Family Members
Activity 41:	Your Music Playlist
Activity 42:	Look for Role Models
Activity 43:	Set Up a Digital Keepsake Account
Activity 44:	▶ "Where's ___?"
Activity 45:	▶ "Ah-choo!"
Activity 46:	Build a Playlist with Your Child
Activity 47:	Listen for "Little Songs"
Activity 48:	▶ Yoo-hoo!
Activity 49:	▶ "Hokey Poky What a Mess" Clean-Up Chant
Activity 50:	▶ Goodbye Song
Activity 51:	"Shake It Off" Boo-Boo Response
Activity 52:	Sing a Book
Activity 53:	▶ Making Soup
Activity 54:	Outdoor Concert
Activity 55:	Be an Early Childhood Music Researcher
Activity 56:	▶ Dinosaur Opera
Activity 57:	Nurture a Musical Passion
Activity 58:	Investigate Your Child's Musical Opportunities
Activity 59:	Create a Soundscape
Activity 60:	Found Sounds, Early Elementary Edition
Activity 61:	Instruments at a Museum
Activity 62:	Found Sound Instruments, Late Elementary Edition
Activity 63:	At-Home Music Class
Activity 64:	Attend an "Instrument Petting Zoo"
Activity 65:	Explore Your Child's Instrument Timbre (Sound Quality) Preference

Activity 66:	Be an Observer of Your Child's Motivation
Activity 67:	Consider Your Own Practicing History
Activity 68:	Make a List of Practice Strategies
Activity 69:	Keep a Parent Observation Journal of Practicing
Activity 70:	Write a Parenting Musically Manifesto

ABOUT THE COMPANION WEBSITE

www.oup.com/us/
familyguidetoparentingmusically

Oxford University Press has created a website to accompany *A Family Guide to Parenting Musically*. It includes audio examples recorded by the author and links to her podcast. These are indicated by the symbol ⓑ in the text.

Audio Links

a. D to A above Middle C
b. Grandma Bonnie's Lullaby, by Bonnie Huisman
c. Song with Repeated Syllables Instead of Words (tune: Quiet Me, by L. Koops)
d. Syllable Exploration
e. Yoo-Hoo
f. Where's _____? (Peek-a-Boo) (tune: Dana's Dance, by L. Koops)
g. Ah-Choo! (tune: Baby Bob's Boogie, by L. Koops)
h. Shoes Off, by Kim Tate
i. Goodbye Song (adapted from *Frere Jacques*, French folk song)
j. Hokey Poky, What a Mess: Clean Up chant by Jed Koops
k. Making Soup, including "Chip Chop" (American folk chant) (tune: Philip, by L. Koops)
l. By the Time I Get to Eight (American folk chant)
m. Dinosaur Opera

Podcast episodes

Episode 1, Ziggy Marley & Vanessa Bond
https://anchor.fm/parentingmusically/episodes/Episode-1-Ziggy-Marley--Vanessa-L--Bond-e1foteg

Episode 1.5, Lisa Koops, Musical parenting & parenting musically
https://podcasters.spotify.com/pod/show/parentingmusically/episodes/Episode-1-5-Lisa-Huisman-Koops--Musical-Parenting-and-Parenting-Musically-e1lrob5

Episode 2, Maggie Baird & Elizabeth Cassidy Parker
https://podcasters.spotify.com/pod/show/parentingmusically/episodes/Episode-2-Maggie-Baird--Elizabeth-Cassidy-Parker-e1fp08f

Episode 2.5, Lisa Koops, Adding relational musicking to the mix
https://podcasters.spotify.com/pod/dashboard/episode/e1lrtq8

Episode 3, Kenitha Roberts & Lisa Damour
https://podcasters.spotify.com/pod/show/parentingmusically/episodes/Episode-3-Kenitha-Roberts--Lisa-Damour-e1lrue5

Episode 4, Pua Pea & Claire Morison
https://podcasters.spotify.com/pod/show/parentingmusically/episodes/Episode-4-Pua-Pea--Claire-Morison-e1meicb

Episode 5, Making Music Lessons Work for Your Family with James Rhodes
https://podcasters.spotify.com/pod/show/parentingmusically/episodes/Episode-5-James-Rhodes-Bonus-Episode-Making-Music-Lessons-Work-for-Your-Family-e1qheca

Episode 7, Jason Hanley (Rock & Roll Hall of Fame)
https://podcasters.spotify.com/pod/show/parentingmusically/episodes/Episode-7-Jason-Hanley-Rock--Roll-Hall-of-Fame-e1vlgbn

Episode 8, Justin Andrews (Otis Redding Foundation) and David Thomspon (GlenOak High School)
https://podcasters.spotify.com/pod/show/parentingmusically/episodes/Episode-8-Justin-Andrews-Otis-Redding-Foundation--David-Thompson-GlenOak-High-School-e20duc8

Episode 9, Mandy Smith (Rock & Roll Hall of Fame)
https://podcasters.spotify.com/pod/show/parentingmusically/episodes/Episode-9-Mandy-Smith-Rock--Roll-Hall-of-Fame-e1vliuj

Episode 10, songstress jo, Nicole Ochenduski, and Nate Kruse (CWRU)
https://podcasters.spotify.com/pod/show/parentingmusically/episodes/Episode-10-songstress-jo--Nicole-Ochenduski--and-Nate-Kruse-CWRU-e219v7p

Episode 11, Chelsea Crowell, Rodney Crowell, and Laura Cirelli (University of Toronto)
https://podcasters.spotify.com/pod/show/parentingmusically/episodes/Episode-11-Chelsey-Crowell--Rodney-Crowell--and-Laura-Cirelli-University-of-Toronto-e21ohak

Episode 12, Risa & John Goehrke (Rock & Roll Hall of Fame)
https://podcasters.spotify.com/pod/show/parentingmusically/episodes/Episode-12-Risa--John-Goehrke-Rock--Roll-Hall-of-Fame-e227to4

Episode 13, JOHNNYSWIM and Beatriz Ilari (USC)
https://podcasters.spotify.com/pod/show/parentingmusically/episodes/Episode-13-JOHNNYSWIM-and-Beatriz-Ilari-USC-e22kptg

INTRODUCTION

WHAT IS "PARENTING MUSICALLY" ALL ABOUT?

> **CHAPTER PREVIEW**
> - Thinking about how you weave music into daily life is important. You are probably already doing more than you realize.
> - Families incorporate music into their lives in many different ways.
> - Musical engagement can have both musical and extramusical (areas other than music) goals. It can be more practical, more relational, or have blended purpose.
> - Identifying these elements can help you understand how music is working for your family.

Monica can hardly stop smiling as she snuggles her 8-month-old grandson Miles close for the first time. Born during the COVID-19 pandemic, Miles had seen and heard his grandparents during video calls but is now meeting them in person for the first time. Monica shifts Miles to her lap as she bounces him and sings "For the First Time in Forever," one of the favorite songs of the children she supervises in the elementary school lunchroom. As usual, she makes up new lyrics about seeing Miles for the first time. She watches him for signs of recognition—does he know her? Does he remember that she sang this song to him via video every week while they were waiting for the COVID-19 vaccine that would allow them to be together safely?

Bree's 2-and-a-half-year-old son, Holden, loves music. Anytime Bree plays music for him, Holden starts to bounce or dance. Holden was born prematurely, at 29 weeks gestation, and has language and motor developmental delays. He also has difficulty adapting to new social settings. Holden is part of a countywide early intervention program and receives physical, occupational, and speech therapy through that program. Bree wonders how they might incorporate more music into Holden's activities.

LaShanda's 12-year-old nephew, Ethan, has been playing violin since age 4. Ethan began with a Suzuki teacher and has experienced ups and downs along the way. There were some periods when he seemed to enjoy playing and practiced willingly. Other times he cried during practice and wanted to quit. LaShanda has encouraged Ethan to audition for the local symphony youth orchestra, but Ethan says he is not interested. LaShanda is concerned that Ethan might not be living up to his potential with violin. She also thinks sticking with the violin is important to Ethan's development of self-efficacy. As LaShanda listens to Ethan's lesson one week, she worries that she pushed Ethan too hard with the violin.

What's at Stake?

There are many ways that families interact musically, as shown in these vignettes. Weaving music into family life can have several benefits. For example, music can add joy to daily life and deepen family relationships. Incorporating music can help your child gain musical knowledge and skills. Including music in daily routines can enhance your child's extramusical (areas other than music) development and learning. Music can improve mood and strengthen relationships. And music can help you with some of your parenting tasks, from car seat buckling to teeth brushing to house cleaning to family bonding.

Music is an activity and an avenue available to everyone, not only those with special training. Many of the suggestions in this book are low cost or no cost. You are probably already including music in many ways in your parenting. Becoming more aware of what you are already doing can be a way to appreciate your own parenting (pat yourself on the back!). Awareness can also lead to ways to deepen or strengthen how we infuse music into home life. Finally, being aware of how your child is participating in music inside the home and beyond can help you to be in tune with what interactions are working and which might need to be altered.

The vignettes that open this introduction also bring up questions about children's musical development. Questions include the role of music in family relationships and how music relates to other spheres of children's lives. You can also see the complexity of family decision-making surrounding music and other activities. In this book, you will explore the purpose of various musical experiences, activities, or interactions. We will return to the vignettes in Chapter 1.

Reconsidering How We Think and Talk About Families and Music

A Family Guide to Parenting Musically is intended as a guide for family members and family friends who want to make music a part of their daily family life. The guide will also help you understand more about how music works in your children's lives. Throughout, I will refer to parents and family members. Please interpret this broadly to include any adult who is a part of a child's life—parents, bonus parents, stepparents, grandparents, aunts, uncles, cousins, neighbors, nannies, baby-sitters, and friends. This book is for all of us.

I hope this guide will help you:

- Gain insights about using music to make parenting a little (or a lot!) easier, more fun, and more meaningful.
- Expand your ideas about how to include music in family life.
- Put family flourishing at the center of discussions about musical involvement.
- Reflect on the assumptions you have about music and music education.

Some of the material written for families related to music can be overwhelming or pressure filled. Parents, teachers, and children can each have a different goal when it comes to music participation. Much of the prior research on musical parenting centers on a specific demographic (middle to upper-middle class). Finally, some messages about parents and music seem to indicate that there are better and worse approaches when it comes to raising kids with music.

That's where the idea of "Parenting Musically" was born. The focus in this guide is with the *entire* family and with *all* families.

This guidebook is not just for those who choose to participate in early childhood music classes or those who identify themselves as "musical." Here are the types of questions you can ponder as you read this guide:

- How is music a part of our daily lives?
- Would an extracurricular music opportunity add to our overall family flourishing, or would it be stressful?
- How can I use music to connect with my kids a little during our morning sprint to get ready for school and out the door?
- How do our kids see us engaging with music as grown-ups?

Some of the ideas in this book are based on a research study I carried out with eight families in the Cleveland, Ohio, area in 2018–2019.[1] I wrote about spending a year observing the eight families using music in daily life in the book *Parenting Musically*. In this guide, I also draw on additional research studies with families in early childhood music programs as well as studies by researchers around the globe. My experiences as an elementary music teacher, early childhood music teacher, and university music educator inform my work. Throughout the book if I identify a family by name (the Petersons, for example), that is a pseudonym, and the family was part of the research study for *Parenting Musically*. Examples that are not named are from other research studies or personal experience.

Four Main Ideas of *A Family Guide to Parenting Musically*

This book is based on four main beliefs:

- Music is important to families,
- All families are musical,
- There are many ways to be a musical family, and
- Families have agency (power, control, and authority) when it comes to creating musical homes and interacting with music in the community and schools.

The four assumptions align with the four sections of this book.

Part 1: Music Is Important. These chapters invite you to think about your ideas concerning music and family life.

Part 2: Many Ways to Be Musical. Here, I focus on five ways that we can be musical as families—singing, listening, moving, playing instruments, and creating.

Part 3: All Humans Are Musical. In these chapters I provide an overview of musical development for specific age groups, along with activity suggestions for each age group.

Part 4: Expressing Agency as a Family with Music. This section provides advice on how to navigate systems in the world of kids and music.

Examining Assumptions in Books about Families and Music

Many of the books related to music and families provide valuable information but are based on several unexamined, and potentially problematic, assumptions. The first is that Western classical music is more valuable and worthy of study than other forms of music. Those other forms include classical music originating from places outside of Western Europe, folk music from any culture, jazz, and popular music.

Stemming from the first assumption is the belief that elements of music-making that go along with Western classical music are also better than others. For example, some might think that reading music is more beneficial than learning music by ear. Others may say playing what is on a page is better than creating one's own variations. However, in many cultures around the world as well as close to home, music is primarily an aural tradition. Music may be composed or improvised and passed along aurally from one generation to the next. Being able to "play by ear" is an essential skill for many popular and folk musicians.

Another assumption found in some books is that there is one right way or just a few best ways to bring your child up musically. My research with families in Cleveland suggested just the opposite. Each family finds their own way to make music a part of their lives. This develops and changes over time and there are many pathways to musical fulfillment. Many music programs in schools are designed with the "one pathway" model, but others are starting to recognize a wider array of forms of music-making.

Most of all, I want you, the reader, to question anything you read or hear relating to music and children. What is an author or speaker assuming about music? What are they assuming about families? How are these assumptions shaping the message? What type of music or musical training are the researchers studying?

A few examples: you may have read that it is beneficial to play classical music, especially Mozart, for your child before birth. Perhaps you might feel a bit guilty if you did not do so. There is research documenting that newborns can recognize music they heard before birth. But there is currently no research suggesting that one form of music is better than another, nor are there conclusive studies on long-term effects of either hearing or not hearing music prenatally.[2]

Second, you might feel pressure to enroll your child in a caregiver-child music class because you think this is important to your child's early musical development. You might believe the class could have an impact on their cognitive or social development. I teach those types of classes and I brought several of my own children to the classes when they were little. The classes can be fun and provide ideas for how to interact with your child musically at home. But there is no body of research pointing to long-term impact of participation in early childhood music classes. There are many studies that examine the benefits of musical participation. However, the benefits of musical participation can be accessed in many ways, not only through tuition-based early childhood music programs.[3]

Third, your friends may have told you they heard that kids who are in high school music programs get higher SAT scores and stay out of trouble. These research studies tend to be correlational (one thing related to another, perhaps due to a third variable), not causal. We do not have parallel studies about the impact of participation in garage bands on SAT scores or how immersive listening to musical soundtracks can boost vocabulary. Research within music psychology and music education is just starting to look beyond situations centered in Western European art music or traditional school ensembles.[4]

All of these examples stem from living in a social system that has, for hundreds of years, valued Western classical music above other forms of music. Our society has also become increasingly specialized, assigning the role of music education to professionals in an early childhood or school classroom. This approach assumes that being musical requires a highly specialized skill set developed over many years. What if we rolled back those assumptions? What if we valued all musical traditions and provided ways for our children to learn them? What if we recognized every form of music making as valuable? In this book we will seek to do just that.

How to Use This Book

As you read *A Family Guide to Parenting Musically*, I hope you will be pleasantly surprised to discover that you are doing more than you think when it comes to music and your family life. Find the ideas in this book that fit easily and lightly into your existing rhythms and routines. Let this book help to make parenting more fun, more joyful, and even a little easier.

Feel free to skip around in this book according to the age of your children or the decisions you are making as a family about musical involvement. Be sure to read the two sections in Chapter 1, *Reconsidering the Goals of Music in Family Life* and *Family Musicking Framework* to understand the frameworks that I will use throughout the book. The chapters that follow are much shorter. The index at the end of the book is detailed and can help you find topics of interest or usefulness.

Many activities are scattered throughout the book. They are numbered and included in an Activity List in the front of the book. The numbers provide a way to organize them—you do not need to do the activities in order, and you do not need to do all of them! Audio examples and podcasts are marked with this symbol ⏵ and are included in a separate list. The audio examples and podcast links are found on this companion website: www.oup.com/us/familyguidetoparentingmusically.

I encourage you to write in this book! As you read, if something reminds you of something you did as a child, or a sweet story about one of your own children musicking, jot a note in the margin. You'll notice I do not include many specific examples of songs or pieces with activities. This is intentional—I want you to use or find music that is meaningful to your family. My goal is for you to learn the process of parenting musically and then apply it creatively to your own family.

Parenting Musically Podcast

The *Parenting Musically* podcast is a related resource for readers. Seasons of this podcast are in collaboration with cultural institutions such as the GRAMMY Museum and Rock & Roll Hall of Fame. In each podcast, I interview well-known artists or their parents, followed by responses from music education or music therapy researchers or practitioners. I have included quotes and themes from podcast episodes throughout the book, along with links to the episodes. If you are interested in hearing more about the topic referenced, check out the full episode. You can find all of the episodes at https://podcasters.spotify.com/pod/show/parentingmusically or by searching for "Parenting Musically" on your favorite podcast platform. You can follow the show and interact with me on Facebook and Instagram.

About Me

I am a music educator living in the Cleveland, Ohio, area. I taught general music in an elementary school before attending graduate school to become a university music educator. For my dissertation, I studied how children in The Gambia, West Africa, learn music informally from one another. My research since then has focused on families, music, and enjoyment. Currently I teach undergraduate music education students as well as graduate students at Case Western Reserve University (CWRU). Together we talk about how children and adolescents learn music and how we can guide them in their learning. We also tackle larger issues of what kind of music we should be teaching and how to make music education more equitable and open. In addition to teaching at CWRU, I also teach early childhood music classes through a local community music school. In my 20 years of early childhood music teaching, I have had the opportunity to meet many families and hear the stories of their children's musical expressions and development. My husband and I have four children, each of whom is different when it comes to musical participation, interest, and preference.

Wrapping Up the Introduction

This chapter includes themes you will read throughout the book: All humans are musical. Music is important. There are many ways to be musical. Being aware of your own assumptions or biases may help you understand family music-making in new ways. There are many benefits to including music in our daily lives as families.

PART 1

MUSIC IS IMPORTANT

PART 2
MANY WAYS TO BE MUSICAL

PART 3
ALL HUMANS ARE MUSICAL

PART 4
EXPRESSING AGENCY AS
A FAMILY WITH MUSIC

The theme of Part 1 of this book is that music is **important**. In Chapter 1, you'll read about why music is **important** to each child and each family's life. Chapter 2 provides an overview of research about human musicality. In Chapter 3, you'll read about why a family's "musical canon" is **important**. Chapter 4 focuses on the diversity of musical practices across the globe. In Chapter 5, we think about grandparents and extended family members, and how they support family musical experiences. Finally, Chapter 6 is all about your hopes and dreams for your family and music.

CHAPTER 1

FAMILY MUSICKING FRAMEWORK

CHAPTER PREVIEW

- Musicking is a term that refers to every aspect of music-making, including singing, dancing, moving, listening, playing an instrument, creating music, and providing opportunities for music to happen (Christopher Small, *Musicking*, Music/Culture; Middleton, CT: Wesleyan University Press, 1998).
- "Musical parenting" means helping your child develop their musicality.
- "Parenting musically" refers to using music for non-musical goals in family life.
- The ideas come together in the Family Musicking Framework.

Reconsidering the Goals of Music in Family Life

There are four interlocking ideas central to this book: musical parenting, parenting musically, relational musicking, and practical musicking (see below for a definition of the word "musicking"). You'll see a framework later in this chapter that puts all four ideas onto one grid. This grid can help you better visualize the goals of incorporating or using music in your children's lives and in your family life. I will return to these ideas throughout the coming chapters, pointing out examples. But first, let's explain all this jargon! This may seem clunky and overly academic. But the parents I have shared it with have said it helps them to think about their musical interactions with their families in a new way. You can hear me explain these ideas more in Episode 1.5 of the *Parenting Musically* podcast ▶.

A Family Guide to Parenting Musically. Lisa Huisman Koops, Oxford University Press. © Oxford University Press 2024.
DOI: 10.1093/oso/9780197673607.003.0002

What Is Musical Parenting?

When describing families interacting with music, many researchers and teachers have focused on musical parenting.[1] Musical parenting refers to activities families do to help their children develop musically. This could be singing to children, listening to music as a family, or taking children to concerts or music classes. Musical parenting can also include arranging for lessons, supervising practice, and attending your children's recitals and concerts as a supporter. Still other forms of musical parenting include singing together in religious or community settings, having dance parties in the kitchen, and introducing your children to the music most important to your family both at home and in community music settings common to your culture.

Musical parenting is important and valuable. It does not need to be centered on formal or tuition-based programs. Parents, grandparents, caregivers, and family friends are engaged in musical parenting when they bring music into their children's lives. Adults are musically parenting when they encourage their children's musical development and expression. Supporting children's skill and knowledge acquisition in music is musically parenting, too. Interestingly, many of these things can happen on an intuitive level, without the adult realizing it! Some of the participants in the *Parenting Musically* book project commented after several months of interviews that suddenly they were aware of so much music happening in their home. As they continued to reflect on it, participants realized musicking had been happening all along. Taking time to label the activities helped raise their awareness.

What Is Parenting Musically?

There is another important category to consider, and that is parenting musically. Parenting musically refers to ways families use music to accomplish non-musical parenting goals. This could be during routines, like listening to music while cleaning the house or using a song or chant to help your child transition to their car seat. Parenting musically can be useful in times of crisis, such as singing to a child to calm them after a fall or reserving a favorite soundtrack for moments in the car when a fight breaks out. How could music help you get things done a little easier or a little more joyfully? I'm interested in parenting musically because, as a parent, I'm always looking for ways to get things done and strengthen relationships with more joy and less stress.

Using music to make parenting a little easier, less stressful, and more joyful is the key to parenting musically. Some books about music and children focus on the child's development and how music can influence that development. However, I think it is essential to consider how musical involvement and interactions impact the entire family. Psychologist Urie Bronfenbrenner calls this the "ecological systems theory." The ecological systems theory recognizes how the various circles of an individual's life (self, family, close community, wider community) interact and affect one another.[2] The impact on the family system of a child's participation in an early childhood music class, private music lessons, or school music programs could be positive, negative, or mixed. This participation could impact the family's financial, logistical, time, and emotional resources. Paying attention to how musical experiences and opportunities influence individual family members as well as the family as a whole may seem daunting but can be important when considering overall family functioning.

What Is Musicking?

So far, we have thought about the differences between musical parenting and parenting musically. Musical parenting refers to activities families do with the intent of helping their child learn music or acquire musical skills. Parenting musically addresses ways families use music to accomplish non-musical tasks of life or make those moments a little easier. One way to distinguish the two is to remember that the first word in the phrase is the primary focus. With *musical* parenting, the musical development is the emphasis, and parenting is in service of the musical development. For *parenting* musically, parenting goals come first, with music playing the assisting role.[3]

There is another pair of concepts we need to really understand what is happening in various scenarios surrounding families and music. The concepts are based on the work of Christopher Small, who coined the term "musicking" as a way to express that music is not something we hear but something we do. In sharing the idea of "musicking" with families, I have found that they enjoy having a word that is so expansive in answer to "what counts as music?" You can hear more examples in Episode 2.5 of the *Parenting Musically* podcast ▶.

Christopher Small (1927–2011) was a scholar and musician who made a profound impact on several fields, including music education, with his scholarly work on the concept of musicking. Musicking includes everything and everyone involved in a musical event—those who set up the stage, take tickets, conduct, sing, play, and listen. He changed the way many music educators thought about why and how we teach music. His work helped music educators shift from a focus on producing a product to having a meaningful experience.[4]

When it comes to children, the word "musicking" can describe what you observe as

- your infant coos rhythmically to you,
- your toddler delights in exploring the timbres (sound qualities) of various objects and surfaces in the house by banging on them with a wooden spoon,
- your preschooler hums seemingly absentmindedly while puttering in the playroom,
- your kindergartener asks to listen to the same song on repeat in the car,
- your second grader asks his grandfather why none of the music he listens to features female musicians,
- your fourth grader creates an iMovie project on your iPad with video of her LEGO characters and a music soundtrack pulled from iTunes.

Children's musicking can be informal, fleeting, mixed into other activities, and perceptive. Singing, moving, dancing, listening, and creating come naturally to many young children.

> Thinking of your family's musical involvement as *musicking* can help to interpret what you read in the coming pages. Using the idea of musicking can also help you make decisions about musical involvement.

Identifying different purposes of musicking can help us view music in family life more clearly. Some situations call for *practical musicking*, or musicking for a practical purpose. Examples include timing how long to wash one's hands, learning a scale in order to try out for an advanced orchestra, or calming a child. In other cases, families need moments of *relational musicking*. This means musicking focused on building relationships, with less emphasis (or worry) about whether the living room is getting clean or the notes are in tune. Many times, the purpose of the musicking is blended—both practical and relational. Other times, you might realize that shifting an activity from a practical to a blended or relational focus could help make that musicking work better for your family. For instance, piano lessons could be a way for a child to spend time relating to his grandparents through sharing videos of him playing and talking to them about their own experiences acquiring new skills. This represents a blend of relational and practical musicking. Blended goals could provide a more meaningful experience than only acquiring piano-playing skills, a more practical form of musicking.

It is also instructive to note that musicking, and many forms of music education, may be considered "formal" or "informal." Examples of formal music education are participation in teacher-led activities in general music in elementary school and ensembles in middle and high school. Private music lessons are often formal in the sense that there is a clear teacher-student power dynamic and the teacher establishes the learning goals. In formal education, skills and content are often presented sequentially. Dr. Lucy Green is a music education researcher from the UK and one of the early leaders in informal music education.[5] She describes informal music education as marked by student choice, learning by ear, student-driven learning, skill acquisition based on what the child wants or needs to learn rather than a sequence, and the integration of listening, performing, and composing. Informal music education can occur anywhere, including in music classrooms or spaces that seem formal. Formal music education processes can also occur anywhere.

Family Musicking Framework

Is musical parenting the opposite of parenting musically? Not really. If something is practical musicking, can it also be relational musicking? Yes, it seems so. All four concepts of musical parenting, parenting musically, relational musicking, and practical musicking can be understood on a grid, as shown in Figure 1.1. By visualizing them this way you can see how events or actions could be a blend of musically parenting and parenting musically. You could also notice whether a scenario was more practical compared with more relational.

Let's return to the examples that opened the introduction, this time with notes regarding musical parenting, parenting musically, practical musicking, and relational musicking. Note how the caregivers used this framework to navigate situations related to music and parenting. Each story now includes the next steps caregivers took.

Monica can hardly stop smiling as she snuggles her 8-month-old grandson Miles close for the first time. Born during the COVID-19 pandemic, Miles had seen and heard his grandparents during video calls

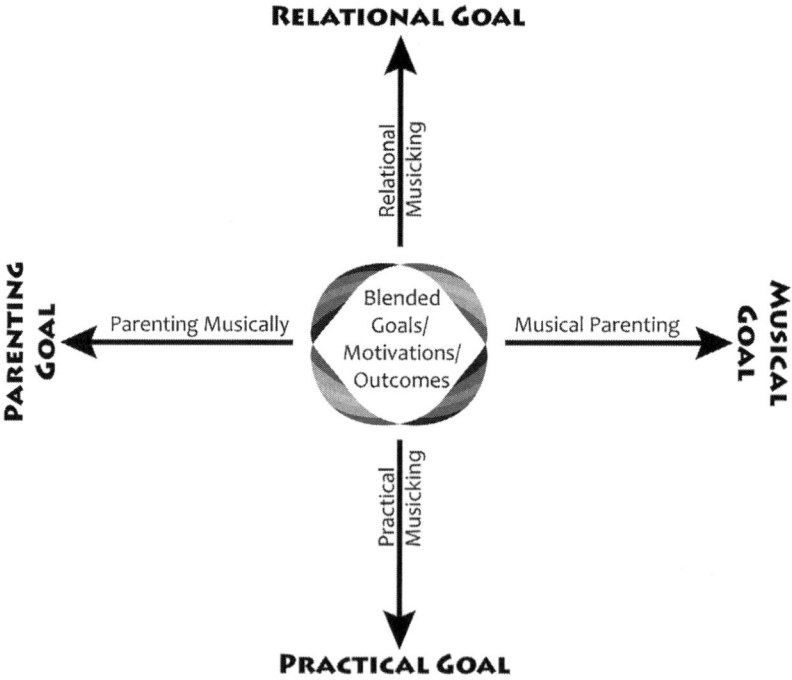

FIGURE 1.1 Family Musicking Framework (Koops, 2020; Used with permission, Oxford University Press)

but is now meeting them in person for the first time. Monica shifts Miles to her lap as she bounces him and sings "For the First Time in Forever" (=relational musicking), one of the favorite songs of the children she supervises in the elementary school lunchroom (=practical musicking). As usual, she makes up new lyrics about seeing Miles for the first time (=relational musicking). She watches him for signs of recognition—does he know her? Does he remember that she sang this song to him via video every week while they were waiting for the COVID-19 vaccine that would allow them to safely be together? (=relational musicking) Monica is delighted to see Miles bounce along and smile at her. "He always turns his head toward you on video calls, Mom," says Monica's daughter. Monica thinks the songs and books they shared over video calls helped establish a long-distance relationship (=parenting musically, relational musicking).

Bree's 2-and-a-half-year-old son, Holden, loves music. Anytime Bree plays music for him, Holden starts to bounce or dance (=musical parenting). Holden was born prematurely, at 29 weeks gestation, and has language and motor developmental delays. He also has difficulty adapting to new social settings. Holden is part of a countywide early intervention program and receives physical, occupational, and speech therapy through that program. Bree wonders how they might incorporate more music into Holden's activities (=parenting musically). Bree asks their social worker about this, and the social worker provides a referral to a music therapy program at a community music school. Bree is excited to meet with the music therapist and find ways to use music to help Holden move toward his developmental milestones (=parenting musically, practical musicking).

LaShanda's 12-year-old nephew, Ethan, has been playing violin since age 4. Ethan began with a Suzuki teacher and has experienced ups and downs along the way. There were some periods where he seemed to enjoy playing and practiced willingly. Other times he cried during practice and wanted to quit. LaShanda has encouraged Ethan to audition for the local symphony youth orchestra, but Ethan says he is not interested. LaShanda is concerned that Ethan might not be living up to his potential with violin (=musical parenting). LaShanda also thinks sticking with the violin is important to Ethan's development of self-efficacy (=parenting musically). As LaShanda listens to Ethan's lesson one week, she worries that she pushed Ethan too hard with the violin. She takes a step back to wonder what all those years of lessons have meant to Ethan and to her (=parenting musically). She takes Ethan out for ice cream to ask more about what Ethan's musical goals are (=relational musicking). Their decision-making process is influenced by Ethan's goals as well as her own background participating in music in school. LaShanda knows that sometimes music lessons are less fun but lead to a goal (=practical musicking). Together they talk through the youth orchestra opportunity.

In each of these scenarios, the family members are using the ideas of musical parenting, parenting musically, relational musicking, and practical musicking to think through the situations. There are elements of motivation, agency (power, control, and authority), family logistics, and goals at play in these scenarios.

ACTIVITY 1   Reflection Questions to Ask Regarding Musical Activities

When considering pursuing a music-related activity or re-evaluating a musical activity, answer the following questions:

- What is my goal as a parent in this situation? Is it a musical goal, a parenting goal, or both? Where does the goal fall on the Family Musicking Framework?
- What is my child's goal or hope in this situation?
- Is there a way to weave together musical goals with parenting goals – to approach the center of the Framework?
- What would it be like to add more relational musicking to a situation that is mainly practical?
- How could we add some practical musicking (either musical skill development or getting something done) to our existing relational musical experience?

In this chapter, we've explored different ways to think about how families use music in their lives. I explained the concepts of musical parenting, parenting musically, relational musicking, and practical musicking. The *Family Musicking Framework* brings the ideas together in a way that could be helpful to families when understanding their current musicking and thinking about future ideas. To close this chapter, let's consider how privilege and research fit in.

Acknowledging Privilege and Resource Availability

While musical involvement does not have to cost money, many times it does. Musical parenting does not need to involve transportation and free time, but some examples do. Many of the books and articles about musical parenting assume a level of privilege. Authors assume that families have extra money, extra time, and extra energy to spend. My hope in this book is to provide a broad range of examples, including those that do not require extra time, money, or energy. Let's think together about ways to make music education and opportunities available in ways that are more just, accessible, and equitable.

Use of Research in this Book

When applicable, I will refer to research studies to support my ideas. If you would like more information, check the footnotes or further reading lists at the end of each chapter. Some of the sources require a subscription to the journal or a library database. They may be available through your local library. You can also contact authors directly by emailing them using the address found on the first page of most manuscripts. Most researchers are thrilled to hear from parents who are interested in their work and may be willing to share more information with you.

I offer a few reading suggestions at the end of each chapter. These may be sources that are central to the ideas of the chapter. Other times, I recommend a book that is from outside of music education or music studies yet contributes to the themes of the chapter.

ACTIVITY 2   Mapping the Family Music Framework

On the blank Family Music Framework in Figure 1.2, try locating current examples from your family or growing up years. As you add examples, consider also including those that you would like to consider for your family, perhaps with a different color. For instance, you could locate "singing our family boo-boo song" as an example of parenting musically with a practical purpose. "Introducing kids to the Beatles" could be musical parenting with a relational purpose.

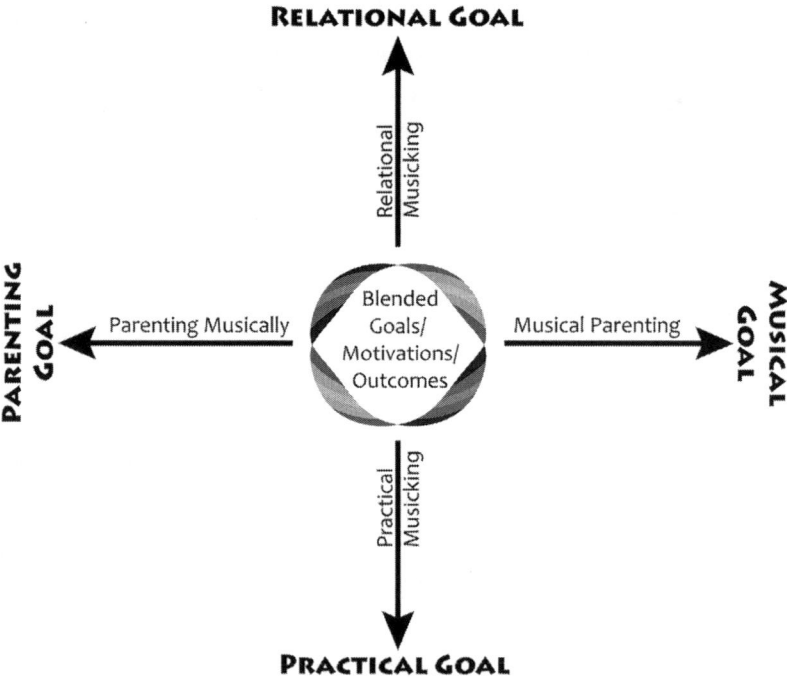

FIGURE 1.2 Family Musicking Framework (Koops, 2020; Used with permission, Oxford University Press)

WRAPPING UP CHAPTER 1

It can be informative to analyze your family's musical interactions. Do you lean toward musical parenting or parenting musically? Do you notice more relational or practical musicking? Becoming aware of these factors can help if you decide you would like to shift any of the priorities or purposes when it comes to your family's musicking.

FOR FURTHER READING

Musicking, by Christopher Small (Wesleyan University Press, 1998): an introduction to Small's ideas about the broadness of music as something humans *do*.

Songs in Their Heads, by Patricia Shehan Campbell (Oxford University Press, 2010): contains rich descriptions of children of many ages and their musical experiences and perceptions.

Parenting Musically, by Lisa Huisman Koops (Oxford University Press, 2020): shares stories from music in daily life for eight Cleveland-area families and themes from home, school, and community musicking.

CHAPTER 2

YOU ARE A MUSICAL FAMILY

> **CHAPTER PREVIEW**
> - All humans are musical, and any family can be a musical family.
> - Music aptitude is a concept that can help you understand why some people learn music more quickly or more easily than others. All humans have music aptitude.
> - There are many ways to do music as a family—and no one right way!

Musical Homes and Musical Families

If someone asked you right now if you are a musical family, what would you say? What defines or determines whether a family is musical or not? Some research participants have told me "Oh, we're not a musical family." Others say something like "I was brought up in a musical home, but my spouse wasn't." In these instances, being a "musical family" or growing up in a "musical home" seemed to be equated with having a special power or advantage. It also seemed these families were defining whether they were musical or not based on the amount of formal musical parenting in the home. But music is something anyone can do. So, any family can be a musical family!

Some families who do not recognize themselves as musical might not have included activities they use to parent musically when considering whether they define themselves as musical. These families might have only considered whether children had formal music lessons or participation in tuition-based early childhood music classes. By recognizing the ways they use music in their daily family life, individuals can realize there is more music happening at home than previously thought.

FIGURE 2.1 An extended family enjoying musicking together. GETTY IMAGES

I imagine there are other families who would like to make music a larger part of their home life yet are not able to, perhaps because of the pressures of work hours, family care, or health concerns. Some individuals may have internalized messages from their teachers, families, or the media that they were "not musical." This was the case with a friend of mine. In elementary school, her teacher told her to stand in the back and not to sing in the school program because she was not able to match pitch. This infuriated me when I heard it and was part of my motivation to become an elementary music teacher. Singing in tune, moving to a beat, listening with understanding, and creating music are skills that can be learned. Music teachers have many activities and sequences that they can use to help a child or adult who is still finding their singing voice, learning to match pitch, or move to a steady beat. No teacher should ever tell a child they are not musical.

All humans are musical, according to ethnomusicologists who have studied the musical activities of people from cultures around the globe. All humans are musical, as teachers like Dr. Shinichi Suzuki[1] and Dr. Patricia

Shehan Campbell[2] have shown us through their teaching methodologies. All humans are musical, you may have noticed yourself, when you see someone who had claimed not to be a singer pick up his grandchild and sing a lullaby. All humans are musical, let's all remember, when we are encountering the topics in this book. This book is not just for families who think music is important, who took lessons as children, or who like to go to concerts. Music is something all humans can do. It can be a part of life both through musical parenting activities and in ways that support parenting musically.

What Is Music Aptitude?

I find the concept of "music aptitude" useful in understanding the universality of human musical participation. Music education researcher Dr. Edwin Gordon spent many years studying the idea of music aptitude. All humans are born with music aptitude, or the potential to learn music. Some humans have a higher music aptitude, which could mean they can advance in piano lessons quickly or without practicing much (my younger brother, for instance). Others might have a lower music aptitude but can still be outstanding musicians and even make music professionally; it just requires longer hours of practice.[3] One of Gordon's students, Dr. Cynthia Crump Taggart, explained music aptitude as a "music learning speed limit."[4] A child can "travel" far musically with a lower or higher speed limit, but the time it takes to accomplish musical goals varies according to the speed limit (or aptitude).

Music aptitude helps explain why some people might think they are not musical. If someone had a lower music aptitude, a teacher might have told them they are "not musical." This is not true, though—the individual just needed longer to work with the material. There are many areas of life that could be described with aptitudes, like various athletic skills or math or reading. Just because a child needs longer to learn certain math skills, we do not say "Well, we're not a mathematical family." We keep finding ways to make math meaningful, try various teaching tools, and stick with it. One role of musical parenting may be to help your child understand that music is something we can learn and that it takes time.

ACTIVITY 3 Encourage Your Child to Be Expressive Musically

As you watch and listen to your young child sing and dance her way through the day, it's obvious that there is music inside! You help support musical development when you encourage your child to be expressive musically, refrain from judgment if your child uses materials in unusual ways to create music, and express enjoyment and excitement for the musical creativity they share with you. Here are some specific examples:

- Give your child special time to make music. Lay out some empty containers and a selection of items like dried beans, rice, or salt to put inside. Let your child practice making new sounds with these "shakers."
- Take your child's lead and make music using just your bodies. Make popping noises with your mouth, click with your tongue, clap your hands, and shuffle your feet in a creative, fun way to make sounds.
- Play echo games with movements as well as sounds, taking turns as leader and follower.
- Invite your child to make up a "mad song" to sing when they are upset.
- Ask your older children to tell you about the music they like to listen to.

Musicking as a Family

There are many ways to engage in music, and likewise there are many ways to be a "musical family." Here are a few:

- listening to music together,
- singing along to soundtracks in the car,
- having dance parties,
- going to outdoor concerts,
- teaching yourself guitar chords using online tutorials, or
- participating in group music-making at religious events or sporting events.

The most surprisingly adamant "let's all sing" moment I've had in recent years was on a Disney Cruise in 2019. It was Pirate Night and the host carefully, sequentially taught the crowd the high and low voice parts of a sea chanty and cajoled us all into singing it out. While I would not describe it as transcendent or particularly beautiful singing, I was struck by how it brought a group of strangers together. I saw people laughing and making eye contact with people across the deck as well as within their own families. I wonder what it would be like if more people in our society in general expected everyone to be musical and participate in musical experiences, the way the Disney cast members expected it of those on the cruise?

There is no prerequisite to being a musical family. You can start today. You don't need to be able to read music, your children don't have to take private lessons, you don't have to like a certain type of music. Let's all introduce our children to the music we love to listen to, let's all grab on to opportunities to weave music into our lives, let's all dance, and let's all sing. We are all musical families.

ACTIVITY 4   Family Music Bucket List

My friend's family makes a bucket list each summer of activities and events they want to do. This is helpful because it causes them to look ahead to the events coming up in the community. It provides a chance for the children to say which museums, parks, or playgrounds they want to be sure to visit. This family gathers the brochures from the library, county park system, and outdoor concert listings as inspiration. They also include at-home items like games, picnics, and movies.

For this activity, make a Family Music Bucket list. Start with ideas to learn or do at home. Add outdoor concerts held in community spaces or shopping areas. Check listings for cultural fairs or events coming up. Social media sites specific to your community that list family-friendly activities are another good place to look. Find out what your children are interested in. Post the list in a prominent location. Enjoy the activities and use the list as a record of your family musical adventures!

WRAPPING UP CHAPTER 2

In this chapter, we explored the starting point that all humans are musical, even though some messages in our culture can suggest the opposite. The concept of music aptitude can help us understand that learning certain types or elements of music might be easier or harder for individuals. Yet all humans have the potential to learn music and to do music. There are many ways to include music in family life, both those that fit into parenting musically and those that are expressions of musical parenting.

FOR FURTHER READING

Children's Home Musical Experiences Across the World, edited by Beatriz Ilari and Susan Young (Indiana University Press, 2016): a compelling portrayal of the musical lives of 7-year-olds in 12 different countries across the globe.

The Ways Children Learn Music: An Introduction and Practical Guide to Music Learning Theory, by Eric Bluestine (GIA Publications, 2000): Chapter 5 of Bluestine's book contains further explanation of Gordon's idea of music aptitude.

CHAPTER 3

CELEBRATING YOUR FAMILY'S MUSICAL CANON

> **CHAPTER PREVIEW**
> - Many families have a group of songs and musical pieces that are important to them.
> - We can refer to this as your family's "musical canon."
> - Having a set of songs common to your family can help create closer emotional ties, provide emotional "anchors" later in life, and contribute to routine and structure.
> - Family musical canons shift over time. Returning to a playlist or album from an earlier time can be a fun way to reminisce.

What Is a Family Musical Canon?

Have you heard people talk about "canon" in relation to a book or movie series? For instance, part of the Star Wars canon is Darth Vader telling Luke Skywalker he is his father. Canon is a slang term used within fanfiction to refer to an original body of work (books, movies, etc.). "Canon" is also used in music. In classical music studies, scholars use the term canon to refer to the musical works that have been incorporated into study over time. Certain composers and specific works have been included in the Western European music canon, while others have been excluded.

Consider your own musical canon or your family's music canon, perhaps as it is or as you would like it to be. Who are the artists, and what are the musical pieces and genres that form the core of the music you value most? How did they come to be included? Did you ever have a certain piece or artist that was part of your canon for a while that you outgrew or came to dislike? If you were going to look back on your family's music canon in thirty years, what would you like to remember?

Over the last several generations our personal music canons have migrated from physical objects (records, cassette tapes, CDs) to electronic files. Playlists provide a fascinating way to capture our musical canons at specific times of life. Having a "Kids' Car Playlist" with music that both you and your children enjoy can be a way to build routines, continuity, and security into daily life. You might remember a specific road trip as the one in which the family sang the *Mary Poppins* Broadway soundtrack all the way from the suburbs of Cleveland, Ohio, to Hilton Head, South Carolina. Or the holiday party when your teenager made a playlist with her grandparents' favorite music from their own teen years.

Your family's musical canon extends beyond music listening. Do you sing a song for birthdays? Sing lullabies? Participate in cheers or chants at sporting events? Sing at worship services? All of these add to the depth of your family musical canon.

ACTIVITY 5   Discover a Relative or Friend's Musical Canon

You can learn a lot about someone by hearing the music they like to listen to. Choose a family member or friend and ask them the questions below. If your child is old enough, invite them to be the interviewer. A video of the interview could be fun to look back on!

- What is your favorite music to listen to?
- Do you listen to different music at different times? How do you choose? (Follow-up questions: based on activity? Mood? Who you're with?)
- What music did you listen to when you were a teenager?
- Do you have any favorite childhood memories of listening to music?
- What songs did your family sing when you were growing up, such as Happy Birthday or lullabies? Did you sing in the car on road trips?

In interviewing Dr. Kenitha Roberts for the *Parenting Musically* podcast, I heard about the family canon of music that she introduced to her daughter,

Reyna. Now a country music star, Reyna was born two months prematurely. Kenitha turned to music to help Reyna overcome the developmental delays associated with premature birth, and in the process, intentionally introduced her to a wide range of genres. Early exposure to this wide range may have helped Reyna to find her voice within country music. Hear more in Episode 3 of the *Parenting Musically* podcast ▶. Kenitha's use of music provides an example of musical parenting through listening, as she kept finding more genres of music to introduce her young daughter to. Helping Reyna through music is also an example of parenting musically, as Kenitha and Reyna addressed specific non-music developmental goals through their musical activities.

ACTIVITY 6 Reminisce with Your Child About Musical Moments of Your Childhood

Children love to hear stories. Stories help kids feel connected to the larger circles of their lives, like extended family or community. Think back to stories from your early years that include part of your family's musical canon. Do you remember listening to a certain artist or album with specific family members or friends? What were you doing—washing the car, riding somewhere, baking, cleaning? Or did a grown-up sing a specific song while washing the dishes or putting kids to sleep?

Tell your child your music listening story. If possible, find a recording of the piece to share or sing the song from the story. You could even recreate the story.

Family Musical Canon and the Long Game

Parenting young kids can seem like it is all about the present moment. Feeding, clothing, daily care, and guiding can be all-consuming. But take a moment to think about the "long game."[1] What seeds do you want to plant now that will grow and bear fruit later?

One such idea is that of teaching and modeling coping skills or emotional resilience. There are many types of coping skills you can begin using with children that they will continue as adults—both healthy and unhealthy. Many of these coping skills children will simply pick up from watching you.

Here's where music comes in. When kids see you use music for emotional expression, they learn that music can help with life's up and downs. For example, if you have a frustrating day of work and come home bearing that frustration, you could say "Ugh, I'm so frustrated! I'm gonna put on my angry music playlist for a while!" Saying this out loud will help children understand that life can be frustrating and that listening to music is a way to work through that frustration.

ACTIVITY 7 Identify Music for Specific Emotions

Do you currently have specific music you or your children use when experiencing various emotions? Create playlists for specific emotions, such as "Calm Down Playlist," "I'm Sad Playlist," and "I'm So Excited Songs!" Talk with your child about how in some cases, when you are sad or angry, music that feels sad or angry to you can help you feel those emotions and then move on. Other times, you might want happier music to help draw you out from the sadness or anger. Talk through scenarios while everyone is calm, and then start trying the playlist when the occasion is right. Researchers Dr. Eun Cho and Dr. Beatriz Ilari found in a study with mothers and young children that using playlists strategically helped in the tasks of parenting and led to improved mood or less distress on the part of children.[2]

The music you listen to together as a family can later become your child's calming playlist or happy playlist or arrrrrggh music. Listening to music as a teen or adult that one listened to during childhood can add an additional layer of emotional support. Research on musical memories supports the idea that listening to music brings back emotions and sensory memories[3].

One of my research participants from a study on music with tweens several years ago spoke persuasively about this idea as a hope for her children, saying,

> They're going to return back to the songs [we listened to as a family]. . . . If they have a relationship with music that takes

them back to a time and place or an emotion that's satisfying, those are good anchors to have in life. If they remember later our favorite songs that we would totally get silly and dance to in the kitchen, and then later as an adult going through a hard time they'll download those songs. (p. 416)[4]

By listening to music as a family now, you are having an important experience in the moment. You are also providing "good anchors in life" that can help your child with emotional expression and resilience in years to come.

WRAPPING UP CHAPTER 3

Music listening may seem as unintentional or unimportant as elevator music at times. Yet, bringing intention to what your family listens to, as well as sings or plays, gives you the opportunity to create shared memories, meaning, and experiences. An individual or family's "musical canon" is also a great way to get to know others better.

FOR FURTHER READING

Music Is My Life, by Myles Tanzer and Ali Mac (Quarto Publishing, 2020): spotlights 80 artists categorized into suggested listening for 12 situations ("Music to celebrate life with," "Music to shout about it," "Music to focus with"). The authors share a wide variety of genres, and each page contains an artist bio, highlights of specific songs, and suggested listening.

Psychology of Music: A Very Short Introduction, by Elizabeth Hellmuth Margulis (Oxford University Press, 2019): summarizes key topics in the study of the psychology of music, including music and language, rhythm, and memory.

Why You Love Music: From Mozart to Metallica, the Emotional Power of Beautiful Sounds, by John Powell (Little, Brown, 2016): seeks to explain why music affects us the way it does, including why music is important to humans throughout the lifespan.

CHAPTER 4

DISCOVERING NEW MUSIC AS A FAMILY

CHAPTER PREVIEW

- In Chapter 3 you learned about the value of having a family musical canon. Chapter 4 gives suggestions for ways to discover new music to add to this canon.
- When seeking new music, consider making connections to your community.
- Technology provides a way to make connections to music beyond your community.
- Music listening can be the gateway to learning to sing or play music that is new to you.

Discovering and Expanding Your Family's Musical Preferences

Have you noticed that there are some artists, groups, or albums that your whole family enjoys, and others that are limited to certain members of the family? Maybe everyone except one of the children enjoys a certain soundtrack. Or the kids love to listen to Kids Bop, but as parents, you can't stand it. There is also the issue of individuals' love of mastering material, including books, shows, movies, and music, by listening to it over and over. However, sometimes other family members do not want to hear the material repeatedly.

As you read this chapter, keep in mind the idea of "musical preference." Musical preference, or taste, refers to what an individual finds appealing. Each member of your family may have their own musical preference, and these preferences may change over time. You can find some music that everyone in the family enjoys.

ACTIVITY 8 Become a Researcher of Musical Preferences

Discovering your own family members' musical preferences is not always straightforward. If you share new music when your children are tired or hungry, they may appear not to like it. But your kids might just be tired and hungry! Some kids enjoy hearing something new any time, while others prefer to encounter new sounds within a specific environment or time. As an elementary general music teacher, I realized there are few one-size-fits-all strategies or approaches. Discovering musical preferences and bridging to new listening is definitely not a one-approach-always-works situation. However, discovering these musical preferences can provide a point from which to explore. For instance, if your family loves the soundtrack to *Encanto* you could read about the musical influences on that soundtrack. You could then seek out Latin-pop and Colombian music. Pay attention to the music in the shows and movies your family enjoys. Then explore the musical influences of those soundtracks.

Research Connection: Global Music and Kids

In her book *Music, Education, and Multiculturalism*, Dr. Terese M. Volk summarizes reasons for teachers to include multicultural music in the music classroom.[1] These reasons can apply to families including a broad range of listening for their children, too. Here are a few of the justifications Volk summarizes, based on many researchers' work:

- **New sounds.** Listening to many genres of music can open children's ears to new sounds. Like new tastes, if children experience new sounds early or frequently, they may be more accepting of the sounds when they hear them later.
- **Global connections.** Listening to music from cultures around the globe is a way to connect children with the people from those cultures worldwide. Listening to music from many cultures can help children become global citizens—more aware and more caring about our global community.

Diversity of musicians. Connecting with musicians from many places, either in person or virtually, helps children encounter the vastness of musical expression. Seeing people make music different from the music they call their own helps children appreciate the many ways that humans express themselves musically.

ACTIVITY 9   Finding New Music

Some parents I've talked to assume their children should listen to "kids' music." There are many wonderful children's artists who can be fun to listen to. But let's compare this to food. We don't usually limit our kids to eating "kids' food." Just as many families seek to introduce their children to a wide range of foods, it can be beneficial to introduce your children to a wide range of music. Children may be more open to listening to new styles of music in early childhood than they are during adolescence.[2] Listening to many different genres of music can help to uncover music that your child connects with.

Streaming music services, both free and for a subscription cost, provide an easy way to discover new music. You could designate one family member each week to plan a listening calendar or choose playlists. Using a service that provides recommendations based on your prior listening could be helpful in finding new things. But that could also be limiting. Check for features on your streaming service that allow you to discover new music. Ask your friends, in person or on social media, for suggestions of new music for family listening. You might find that one friend is continually searching through music and finding great new artists.

Another approach could be "New Music Tuesday"—on Tuesdays (or whichever day), a family member chooses a new artist or genre for the family to listen to during breakfast. This could also work by the month. On the first of the month, take some time to discover someone new. Spend the month listening to this artist's music at various points, such as play time, meals, dance parties, and car trips. As your kids grow older, help them to find and introduce new artists or genres to the family. This provides children with a sense of agency (power, control, and authority). Kids love to be the one to teach their family something new!

An extension of these ideas is to create playlists for holidays or family trips. One dad I know creates playlists of artists from certain states. While the family drives from Ohio to Missouri, he plays the playlist that corresponds to the state they are driving through. Another dad said he made playlists for specific holidays in certain years for their extended family—New Year's 2020 or 4th of July 2023. Having a soundtrack for specific family events can deepen the memories from the event. Tweens and teens can take charge of creating these playlists as well.

ACTIVITY 10   Start with a Live Music Event

Another way to get to know new music as a family is to find a live music event in your area. A few ideas: a cultural festival, museum exhibit, or outdoor concert. Sometimes you might just happen upon something, enjoy taking it in, and then go home to learn more about the music and culture. In other cases, you can look ahead at a cultural events calendar or outdoor music series. Pick an event as a family that interests you. Then spend the time leading up to the event learning a little about the music. For young children, look for an event where it's okay to move around and talk.

For example, there is an outdoor concert series near our community that features a range of musicians and genres, such as jazz, funk, and classic rock. A family could choose one of the groups on the schedule and get to know their music on YouTube and music streaming services prior to the concert. At the concert, family members will be excited to hear their favorites from the band.

ACTIVITY 11   Attend Free Concerts in Your Area

A fun, free way to expand your family's music listening experience is to attend concerts by schools, community organizations, and universities in your area. Typically, individual recitals and concerts at these schools are free and open to the public. This is a convenient way to try a steel pan ensemble, a capella groups, or a solo tuba recital! Search the music department web pages of institutions in your area. My university students love seeing community members at their concerts.

ACTIVITY 12 Music and Dinner Around the World

During a spring break week when their family could not travel due to the COVID-19 pandemic, my friends Leslie and Keith gathered their three kids and used the "Roll the Dice" feature on Google Earth to generate random locations.[3] Each family member received a location and planned a meal inspired by food from that region. They worked together to create the meals. The family listened to music from the region while planning, preparing, and eating the meal. An alternate version is to look for new music to listen to paired with takeout food inspired by a certain geographic region. You could also make it a once-a-month activity.

ACTIVITY 13 Making Meaningful Music Connections

The musical world is seemingly limitless. Thanks to streaming audio and video services, we have access to music from many locations as well as recordings of music composed in past time periods. When guiding your children to discover new music, consider starting with an existing interest or connection.

Here are a few ideas to get you started:

- Your child is studying a specific topic or culture in school. Extend the project at home by learning about music from the culture.
- You reconnect with a high school friend who is now living abroad. Ask your friend for some examples of the music that is popular in their neighborhood.

- Your family is obsessed with a specific videogame. Research the composer of the videogame music and look for other music by this composer.

ACTIVITY 14   Go to a Music-Related Museum or Landmark

Look around for music-related museums or music landmarks in your area or in locations you travel to. Search Google or Pinterest for "music museum" or "music landmark." These outings can be fun as well as provide a springboard for larger discussions with your children. Mandy Smith, director of education at the Rock & Roll Hall of Fame, suggested that caregivers plan a route through a museum or experience that will fit their children's energy in Episode 9 of the *Parenting Musically* podcast[4] ▶. At the Rock Hall, Mandy suggested, start in the interactive exhibit called The Garage, where children can see, touch, and play musical instruments, before heading through the other exhibits, then returning to The Garage. An example of a music landmark is Louis Armstrong Park in New Orleans, Louisiana. A visit to this park could be the beginning of learning about Louis Armstrong and his contributions, or you could plan a family trip after months or years of listening to Armstrong's music together.

WRAPPING UP CHAPTER 4

This chapter included many ideas for discovering new music or encountering music together as a family. Each family member will have their own musical preferences, but you can also develop a family musical preference. Try some of the ideas from this chapter on finding new music and think of your own as well. Keep in mind that some of these ideas will work better for your family than others. There are also some ideas that can work for your children in a few years, but not now. Even choosing just one strategy could aid in expanding family listening.

FOR FURTHER READING

Around the World in 80 Musical Instruments, by Nancy Dickmann and Sue Downing (Welbeck Editions, 2022): illustrated guide to 80 musical instruments drawn from cultures worldwide.

Music and How It Works: A Complete Guide for Kids, by Charlie Morland (Penguin Random House, 2020): overview of music history, musical genres, and some insight on music psychology.

Mama Lisa's World: International Music & Culture, by Lisa Yannucci (https://www.mamalisa.com/): includes collections of children's songs and games from cultures around the world.

CHAPTER 5

CHERISHING YOUR ADDITIONAL ADULTS IN FAMILY MUSICKING

CHAPTER PREVIEW

- Grandparents, aunts, uncles, extended family, and additional caring adults can play an important part in children's musical lives.
- These individuals may be living close by or farther away.
- Extended family and friends can provide a unique relationship for your child.
- "Mutuality" is a concept that reminds us that having the opportunity to encourage or share with children has benefit for adults.
- If you do not currently have additional support like this, think about ways to connect with neighbors or community members.

Be Present for the Ordinary Moments

I hope I never forget the sight of my grandparents sitting on the paisley mint green couch in our living room. They lived about a 15-minute drive away in Michigan during the spring and summer; in winter months they were many hours away, in Florida. But when they were in town, we saw them often. They came for every birthday and babysat if our parents had evening meetings. But Grandpa and Grandma also just stopped by and watched us do our homework, swim laps in the pool, or practice piano.

This interest in our ordinary lives struck me as a young teenager. It becomes more profound as I grow older. My grandparents made no demands on us, there were no expectations for us to entertain them or play games. We did those things other times. But on the ordinary days, Grandma and Grandpa gave us their presence and interest while we did our children's work of learning and building skills.

The fact that they were willing to sit and listen to scales and fumbling attempts to learn new pieces made me more confident when it came to performing. I looked for my grandparents in the audience at choir concerts and piano recitals throughout childhood and college, as well as the performances of my general music students when I was teaching after college. My grandparents, like many grandparents, smiled no matter what. They expressed their appreciation and noticed how we had improved. They never commented negatively or critiqued, because they did not see that as their job. Our grandparents were our cheerleaders!

This experience of my grandparents as supportive listeners played an important role in my confidence as a musician. Think about your own childhood cheerleaders. Who were they? How did their presence encourage you? If you did not have supportive adults in your life, can you identify the areas in which you would have liked support? Throughout this chapter we will consider ways we can find supporters for our children.

As you consider the extra adults currently in your family's life, think about how interactions with your children impact them. The idea of "mutuality" suggests that adults, particularly older adults, can benefit from their relationships with young people.[1] The adults can offer children material resources and unconditional audience support. The children provide a reason to stay active and a connection to the adults' own musical interests. The word "mutuality" reminds us that there is mutual "give and take" to the relationship, as well as benefits for all sides.

Throughout this chapter, consider that many of the suggestions can apply both to in-person and long-distance interactions. Grandparents can sing to their grandchildren on video calls from the earliest days. As children grow older, grandparents and extra adults can respond to the children's musicking. One of my friends, a preschool teacher, told me that she regularly sings with her 3-year-old grandson during video calls. Recently he sang a song for her and his parents explained, "Mom, we have no idea what this song is, but he keeps singing it." Grandma immediately recognized it as "Here We are Together," a welcome song she sings with her preschool students as well. Grandmother and grandson laughed and sang it together, and it was a special moment of relational musicking for my friend because she was able to connect with her grandson through a shared musical experience.

A Note to the Grandparents, Extended Family, and Friends

Maybe you are a grandparent, aunt, uncle, sibling, cousin, or important additional adult reading this. What are some ways you can be a part of a child's musical life? First, you can be a musical role model. Let the children in your life see you enjoying music and using it in various ways. Talk to them about concerts you have attended or would like to attend, what your favorite music is, and what you would still like to discover musically. Sharing these experiences or favorites are a way for the children in your life to know you better. If you have always wanted to learn a new instrument or join an ensemble, letting the children around you see that process can be a powerful example to the children of lifelong learning.

Second, consider providing musical opportunities. A friend shared that her father-in-law shows his 3-year-old granddaughter songs and videos that he saves on his phone that he thinks she will enjoy. Sitting together and watching is a relational musicking opportunity. For others, providing music opportunities could include paying for musical toys, instruments, classes, or lessons. This could also mean providing logistical support for these activities, such as driving or taking care of other children during the event. Musical opportunities could be bringing children along to free community music events or outdoor concerts. Another way to provide musical opportunities is to seek out free events in the community, like library story times or library programs with a music emphasis.

Third, you can be a cheerleader and supportive audience. Kids need adults to pay attention to them and listen to what they are saying—or singing or playing! This can occur either in person or long-distance. If you are long-distance, you could interact using video calling, audio calling, or through responding to videos. Along with offering your presence, try using

FIGURE 5.1 Grandfather guiding his grandson in learning to play the guitar. GETTY IMAGES

"noticing" comments. Rather than "You're such a good singer" or "You're so smart," try specific comments. "I heard you play so many notes on the piano! I saw you use both hands!" or "That song you sang reminded me of the ocean. The notes went back and forth like the waves." These descriptive comments, rather than evaluative comments, can help children build a growth mindset.[2] Growth mindset refers to the belief that working hard at something (music, math, spelling, etc.) is the way to get better at it. This is in comparison to fixed mindset, which is when someone believes they are just naturally good or bad at something no matter how much effort they put into it.

Supporting children's musical endeavors can help children's musical self-efficacy as well as overall self-efficacy and expression. Self-efficacy refers to an individual's belief in their ability to learn and do things that may be challenging at first.[3] Providing unconditional positive regard is an important part of this process. I spoke with an emerging singer-songwriter, songstress jo, and her mom, Nicole Ochenduski, about the importance of family support to jo's budding career. In Episode 10 of the *Parenting*

Musically podcast[4] ▶, jo described the no-strings-attached support she has received from her family and how much confidence that has given her. It meant even more, jo said, knowing that her parents and grandparents weren't on board with every artistic choice or style addition:

> So my advice would be to let kids harness their creativity in everything they do, even if it's something you personally do not agree or align with, because . . . having that support system from the base is going to provide them with nothing but a love and passion for what they do.

ACTIVITY 15 For Grandparents, Extended Family, and Friends

This activity is for the grandparents, extended family members, or friends who are reading this section. While listening to the children in your life make music, or even ahead of time, make a list of "noticing" comments. This is a way of showing your attention and providing positive responses. These comments can be in response to children's informal musicking as well as on more formal occasions. Here are some examples:

- "It's great to hear you hum songs to yourself while you're drawing!"
- "That's so fun—you changed the words and made your very own song!"
- "You look so happy when you're drumming and clapping to different songs!"
- "I just love watching you play. Your fingers move so fast!"
- "I love seeing you sing up on stage with your whole choir. All of your voices come together so beautifully."
- "I can't believe you created that beat yourself. I always wanted to learn to do something like that. Could you create one for my ringtone?"

Note that on some occasions children may prefer not to be listened to. Perhaps they are making music that is personal to them or they prefer to have an audience at a different part of the learning cycle. Be sure to respect children's wishes for feedback, supportive silence, or privacy.

ACTIVITY 16 Map Your Family's Musical Web

If you are a parent, think about the individuals around you who can serve as an additional adult in your family's musical life. It's okay to ask for many types of help as a parent, and this is one of them! Brainstorm a list of ways you would like to interact with grandparents, extended family members, or community elders, with mutuality in mind. Do you know someone who plays the guitar or harmonica who would enjoy teaching your child, and benefit from the interaction? Do you have a neighbor who would sit on their porch and listen to your children play their instruments occasionally? If you do not currently have such relationships, would you be interested in cultivating them? Consider a nearby house of worship or retirement community as a way to connect with adults nearby.

ACTIVITY 17 Thank Your Extra Adults

Choose a day as a family to express thanks to the extra adults in your family's musical life. Include the adults who supported and encouraged you as a child as well as those currently encouraging your family. Write a note or text to let these special people know how much their presence means.

WRAPPING UP CHAPTER 5

In this chapter we considered the importance of additional adults in children's musical lives. Some readers may be those extra adults, looking for ways to provide enrichment or joy through music to the children in their lives. Remember the idea of "mutuality" and think about how these interactions could be meaningful for you as well as for the children. To parents, remember to reach out to a variety of extra adults. You may realize this is already happening with friends and neighbors. Be sure to thank them for their encouragement and support!

FOR FURTHER READING

My Family Plays Music, by Judy Cox and Elbrite Brown (Holiday House Publishing, 2003): introduces the child-narrator's family members by the genre of music and instrument they play. This is an example of a child's web of important adults.

Growth Mindset, by Carol Dweck (Random House, 2006): explains the author's research and theory of growth versus fixed mindset, with applications for family members and teachers.

Y is for Yet: A Growth Mindset Alphabet, by Shannon Anderson and Jake Souva (Free Spirit Publishing, 2020): gives examples and explanations of growth mindset for children ages 4–9.

CHAPTER 6

WHAT ARE YOUR FAMILY'S MUSICAL HOPES AND DREAMS?

> **CHAPTER PREVIEW**
> - Specifying your musical hopes and dreams for your family is an important part of understanding the role of music in your family's life.
> - Your hopes and dreams can be different from those of your partner. Your children's may be different still.
> - Musical hopes and dreams can be interconnected with hopes and dreams for your children in other developmental areas.
> - A mismatch between a family's hope and dreams and those of a music teacher could create misunderstanding. Seek to communicate your hopes and dreams to the music teachers your family works with.

Identifying Your Family's Musical Hopes and Dreams

I love hearing people's musical hopes and dreams. One friend shared that she has always wanted to be able to sit down at a piano at a party and play the "Peanuts" theme song. A family member hoped to learn bass recorder so he could play duets with his grandson on trombone. Personally, I wanted to learn to play the harp since I was 5. A few years ago, the time was right and I found a harp teacher and started lessons.

Sometimes these hopes and dreams are individual, and other times they relate to our aspirations for our families. I imagine how fun it would be to sit around a campfire with my family, roasting marshmallows and singing camp songs. What do you imagine for your family? Do you hope to sing along to soundtracks in the car? See your children start a garage band with their friends? Play their musical instruments at their grandparents' wedding anniversary open house?

Hopes and dreams can start as a spark of an idea or a desire and grow to a more certain idea. This seed of a hope or dream can be something you notice another family experiencing. Some hopes and dreams could fall into the category of musical parenting, focused on musical goals. Others may be more aligned with parenting musically, centered on extramusical (areas other than music) goals.

> As a parent or extended family member, what are your hopes and dreams for the children in your life? What do you most hope for them right now, at their current age? What are your dreams for them as they grow?
>
> Now think about music. When you look at your child, what would you love for them to be able to do with music right now? And what are your hopes as they grow older? How do these musical hopes and dreams fit in with the bigger picture of their general development?
>
> What are your hopes and dreams for your whole family when it comes to music? How would you like music to be a part of the routines, rituals, and relationships of your daily family life?

There could be a strong connection between the general hopes and dreams you have for your children and the musical hopes and dreams. One of the families I worked closely with for my book *Parenting Musically*, the Petersons, dreamed of their children acquiring musical skills that would serve them in their present school situations, in the future for college, and throughout their lives. The Petersons viewed these musical skills as linked to life skills as well. Mrs. Peterson commented, "Yeah and I mean if you think of music, you can play an instrument or do something musical until you're ninety-five, you know what I mean? But you can't play football until you're ninety, it's one of those things" (*Parenting Musically,* p. 159). In the Petersons' extended families there was a strong tradition of family and community music-making throughout the lifespan. Learning to play instruments was a way for the children to participate in relational musicking with extended family.

These dreams were not just tied to musical development, though. The Petersons also shared at length their desire for their children to develop self-efficacy. They viewed learning to play stringed instruments as an important pathway to their children's development of self-efficacy. The Petersons believed this self-efficacy then influenced other areas of their children's development and would serve as a core strength as they grew up.

Specifying musical hopes and dreams can help you make decisions and establish priorities. It could also help you decide what to put on a child's birthday or holiday wish-list, such as music-related experiences or items. Becoming aware of hopes and dreams might lead you to set aside 15 minutes a week to find new music to listen to. Articulating hopes and dreams can also help when talking with other adults in your child's life about music involvement in order to align expectations or understand others' points of view. This can be whether to participate in a library music and movement class; Suzuki violin lessons; beginning band, choir, or orchestra; or extra-curricular opportunities during high school. At each of these decision points, return to your musical hopes and dreams for your child, along with the hopes and dreams of additional important adults. This discussion could also occur when you are facing a developmental hurdle with a child related to social-emotional development or school. You could consider whether musical experiences in the home, at school, or in the community might be a part of addressing the hurdle together. In addition to clarifying the hopes and dreams, consider which ones may fall into the musical parenting realm, which are more related to parenting musically, and which are blended.

Observe what your child is drawn to. Would they love to be able to play the Star Wars theme song on the piano from memory? Be part of a garage band? Play an instrument in the marching band? Sing in an all-state choir? Sing in an a capella group? Brainstorm the steps it would take to begin to move toward these hopes and dreams. You could ask your child directly about their hopes and dreams, but be aware of whether your child is saying what they think you want to hear.

Another perspective is to think about how your children can get ideas for their musical hopes and dreams. Do they have the chance to see other children engaged in music-making? Attending a marching band show at the local high school, hearing live music at a farmer's market, and watching videos of people making music in many corners of the globe are ways to spark interest. My friend's son loved to watch the drummers at outdoor concerts starting from his toddler years. When he was 3, a drummer gave him his drumsticks at the end of the concert. The little boy set up elaborate drum sets of pots and pans, a musical act as well as one of creative engineering. He composed his own drum music, proudly using the drumsticks he had received from the drummer.

When There Are Different Hopes and Dreams

Here is an important thing to keep in mind: Sometimes the music teachers in your life might have their own hopes and dreams—their own agenda. This might not align with your hopes and dreams. The mismatch could be because the teacher doesn't know your goals, or possibly because the teacher is trying to make certain things happen. For instance, a professional musician friend of mine started her daughter in violin lessons. Her daughter's teacher assumed that my friend, as a professional musician, put a priority on her daughter reaching a high level of achievement. This is an example of musical parenting. But my friend was more interested in her daughter having a joyful experience and avoiding a perfectionistic approach, even if she was not playing at what the teacher considered "the highest level." For their family, the parenting musically goal of enjoyment without pressure to be perfect was more important. The mismatch in expectations was something the parent and teacher needed to address. Parents and caregivers need to be advocates for their children in private music lesson settings and teach their children to be self-advocates as they grow older. This is a skill that can transfer to many settings.

A difference in goals between teachers and families can also happen in school music programs. A band teacher might assume that a 7th-grade bassoonist's dearest wish is to be in the top high school band in a few years. But the child might not learn well when pressured or pushed and prefer to play in the non-auditioned band for a few years. This is another instance when holding both the ideas of musical parenting and parenting musically together is important. You, the parent or caregiver, are the one who sees the whole picture, not just the music lessons aspect. Work together with the teacher and your child to clarify goals.

Building Relationships to Nurture Hopes and Dreams

As parents and family members, build relationships with the music teachers in the school music programs in your area. Begin by expressing your support for the teacher and their program. Ask what ways you can support the program. If the teacher is open to ideas, consider advocating and offering your support in the following areas:

Number of performances and location of performances. Would you like to see the choir perform in locations in the community sometimes instead of only on stage? Would you be willing to help chaperone a music class or ensemble performing at a nursing home or other community location?

Competition. This can be a difficult topic, but it is one that is important to discuss with school music teachers. It is possible that teachers are pushing for music competitions because their administrators require it or they think the community expects it. If you would like to see a program with more emphasis on creativity, for example, you could start a conversation about reducing the level of competition.

Access to instruments. Does the school currently have a way to provide instruments for all students? If not, could you work with a family group or non-profits such as the school Parent Teacher Organization (PTO) to find a way to increase accessibility through a used instrument donation drive or scholarships for rentals?

Vernacular music offerings. If your school district currently has mainly "traditional" groups of band, choir, and orchestra, would you like to see an expansion into steel drum, song-writing class, music technology, or guitar? This is another area where a parent group could partner with music educators for change.

Remember that music teachers face many pressures. Be patient in building supportive relationships. Offer to put together a group of parents and family members to work on any initiatives. This involvement could also be an expression of parenting musically. Let's say increasing musical access and equity are values you hold as a family. By working together with teachers and other families to build these elements in your community and school programs, you may be teaching your children social justice involvement and community organizing techniques through the development of the music program.

A final point is to think about building your musical network to help your family as you work toward hopes and dreams. You explored this web of extra adults in Chapter 5. Grandparents, extended family members, neighbors, and friends may serve as musical role models and inspiration to your children. These individuals may also be able to provide lessons or lend instruments. Sometimes they give gifts of money for classes and lessons. Fellow parents may help you find opportunities for your child, alert you to scholarships, and help with the important task of carpooling to extra-curricular opportunities.

ACTIVITY 18   Musical Hopes and Dreams Inventory

Use the following guide to consider a more specific list of your musical hopes and dreams for your child.

Hopes and Dreams for Children's Musical Engagement

KEY QUESTIONS

- What do we hope our child will know and be able to do with music?
- Why do we want our child to participate in music, either a specific activity or music generally?
- What do we hope our child will take with them when they leave our home as a young adult as far as musical inclinations, skills, or practices?

WHAT ARE YOUR FAMILY'S MUSICAL HOPES AND DREAMS?

- Mark any statements that express your hopes and dreams for music and your child. If you have multiple children, this may differ between children. Complete once for each child, using their initials to keep track.
- Return to the statements you checked and circle those that are most important to you.
- Some prompts are open-ended and could refer to any type of musicking (formal or informal; singing, playing, listening, creating, etc). Others are specific.
- When you have finished, go back and look at the items you checked. How can you as a family go about meeting the hopes and dreams you checked? What resources are available (family, neighborhood, broader community, school, online resources)?
- What are your child's hopes and dreams for music?
- Consider bringing this page along when talking with a private music instructor or school music teacher about your child's participation.

I want my child to participate in music so they can . . .

_____ Experience joy through musicking
_____ Connect with community through musicking (adults/children)
_____ Connect with self
_____ Connect with immediate family
_____ Connect with extended family
_____ Connect with peers
_____ Connect with the divine
_____ Participate in worship activities using music
_____ Participate in community music experiences (e.g., dance at weddings)
_____ Participate in school music

I want my child to participate in music in order to . . .

_____ Support executive functioning (organizing, planning ahead, meeting goals, time management, etc.) through musicking
_____ Support self-actualization (achieving goals, rising to one's potential)
_____ Strengthen extramusical (areas other than music) learning[1]
_____ Strengthen emotional intelligence

_____ Strengthen empathy
_____ Strengthen social-emotional awareness
_____ Have a strategy to expression emotions for tough times as a child
_____ Have a strategy to expression emotions for tough times as an adult
_____ Learn songs they will remember and draw on as an adult
_____ Receive music therapy[2]: music serving as a therapeutic tool for physical development
_____ Receive music therapy: music serving as a therapeutic tool for emotional development
_____ Receive music therapy: music serving as a therapeutic tool for social development
_____ Get a college scholarship

I hope my child will be able to . . .
_____ Sing confidently alone
_____ Sing confidently in a group
_____ Sing and not worry about how they sound
_____ Sing in a specific style/genre: _____ (Why that style/genre?)
_____ Play an instrument, any instrument
_____ Play a specific instrument or instrument from specific genre: _____ (Why that instrument/genre?)
_____ Read music notation
_____ Play by ear
_____ Improvise
_____ Compose
_____ Describe or analyze music they listen to
_____ Talk about music with peers
_____ Talk about music with family
_____ Go to live music events (What style/genre? Why?)

In their musicking, my dreams for my child are to . . .
_____ Enjoy the experience now; not be concerned about the long term
_____ Build skills they will be able to use in the long term
_____ Experience a challenge—e.g., other areas (school) come easily; I want them to learn to tackle something difficult and stick with it

_____ Experience success—e.g., other areas (school) can be difficult; I want music to be their place to relax and shine
_____ Experience *flow*—"this is what I was made to do"
_____ Experience mastery—steady progress; being able to do something they couldn't do a few weeks ago (playing new songs)

One of my favorite ways our family currently incorporates music in daily life is . . .

_____

_____

_____

_____

_____

I picture our family interacting with music in this way . . .

_____

_____

_____

_____

_____

Questions this exercise brought up . . .

_____

_____

_____

_____

_____

WRAPPING UP CHAPTER 6

In this chapter you considered the musical hopes and dreams you have for your family. Completing the checklist is one way to think more deeply about these hopes and dreams. Talking to the children in your life is another important step. Musical hopes and dreams can be connected to parenting hopes and dreams more generally, a facet of parenting musically. Now that you are thinking more about musical hopes and dreams, you might start noticing some new ideas or opportunities coming to your family.

FOR FURTHER READING

Gift from the Sea, by Anne Morrow Lindbergh (Pantheon Books, 2003): I find reading and re-reading this classic centering when focusing on the "big picture" of navigating family life.

Slow Family Living: 75 Ways to Slow Down, Connect, and Create More Joy, by Bernadette Noll (Penguin Publishing Group, 2013): Reading some of the ideas in this book have helped me to think differently about how to go about pursuing the hopes and dreams we have for our children.

PART 1
MUSIC IS IMPORTANT

PART 2

MANY WAYS TO BE MUSICAL

PART 3
ALL HUMANS ARE MUSICAL

PART 4
EXPRESSING AGENCY AS
A FAMILY WITH MUSIC

The focus for Part 2 is the many ways that humans are musical. Part 2 contains five chapters, one each for the activities of singing, listening, playing instruments, moving, and creating. In each chapter, I will ask you to think about these activities in different ways. Keep watching for any assumptions or stereotypes that you may carry. If they are not serving you, leave them at the door. Throughout these chapters you will see that there are many ways for families to express their musicianship. There is no one right or necessary way.

CHAPTER 7

SING WITH YOUR KIDS

> **CHAPTER PREVIEW**
> - Your voice is important to your children.
> - Adults can improve their singing voice, intonation, and confidence.
> - Children's initial singing is higher than many adults sing.
> - Males and females go through a voice change around the time of puberty.
> - Use caution when considering private vocal lessons for children before high school.
> - There are many ways to support children's vocal development and vocal expression.

"Those Who Wish to Sing, Always Find a Song" ~Swedish Proverb

"You have a beautiful voice, Ms. Lisa. I wish I had a better voice," said a grandmother in my music and movement class recently. "I'm glad my granddaughter can hear you sing," she continued. "That's better than if she hears me."

I have heard comments like these frequently. However, I was quick to reassure this grandma that her voice is important to her granddaughter, more important than mine. No matter the vocal quality or intonation: your children need to hear your voice!

Our voices are so personal. Maybe you are not comfortable singing in front of a large crowd—or even a small crowd. A music teacher may have told you at some point that you should mouth the words rather than sing during a concert. If this happened to you, I am so sorry. That teacher should never had said that. The teacher should instead have worked with you to help you find your voice or find your in-tune singing. Unfortunately, this can be a common experience, as researchers have documented.[1] Push back if you hear someone referring to an individual as unmusical or "tone-deaf." Music and singing are things we can learn!

> Do you consider yourself to be a singer? If not, how would starting to embrace that identity of singer change how you interact with your children musically? Anyone can be a singer. You are a singer!

Benefits of Singing

The voice is an instrument that is always with us. Critical early attachment between parent and child occurs in part through vocalizations, also known as communicative musicality.[2] See more in Chapter 13 about communicative musicality and why it is important for your young child. Parents can strategically and sensitively use their voices to sing to children to calm, soothe, entertain, guide, and connect in various moments. All of these are important ways to strengthen the parent-child relationship. Be sure to match your child's needs and mood to the form of singing interaction.[3]

Singing can help you get things done with your kids, too! Clean-up songs, tooth-brushing songs, process songs—the learned songs as well as the tunes you make up on the spot can help you get through the activities of the day. Singing can be a fun way to pass time with your kids if you're stuck in line or traffic. Singing activities can also be an enjoyable addition to infant and toddler routines—see Chapters 13 and 14.

No matter your personal feelings about your own voice, sing to the children in your life. It is a unique and personal gift that only you can give to them. Children of all ages benefit from hearing the singing voices of their parents and caregivers. There are good reasons that lullabies are found in all cultures.[4] Lullabies serve to soothe children as well as connect them with their grown-ups. Singing also helps grownups to be more relaxed.[5]

FIGURE 7.1 Mother and daughter singing into hairbrush "microphones." GETTY IMAGES

Can Adults Improve Their Singing Voices and Confidence?

Another grandmother I know described herself as an uncertain singer before she had grandchildren. She participated in early childhood music classes with her grandchildren, and the classes included activities that were designed to help children hear the tonic pitch and become in-tune singers. Over the course of several years, this grandmother noticed that she had become more confident singing with others and that her sense of pitch had improved.

If you classify yourself as a "non-singer" or "unconfident singer," it's never too late to improve. The best way to get better at singing is to sing! Sing to your children in your life, sing to your pets, sing in the car, sing in the shower. If time allows, join a community choir or choir at a house of worship. Participating in the warm-ups and singing with others can help you to gain confidence and improve intonation. It might also be helpful to cup your hand around your ear while singing with others to better hear your voice as it relates to others. You can find online resources by searching Google or YouTube for "singing in tune for beginners" or "finding your voice for beginners." You'll find a variety of resources, and as an adult you can select those you deem of higher quality and with agreeable presenters. There are also apps and software programs that help with learning to sing in tune. As discussed below, I do not recommend the use of online materials for children's vocal lessons.

Find music you love to sing along to and sing it often! If you have young children, find a lullaby album you enjoy that fits your voice, like Christina Perri's "Songs for Carmella: Lullabies & Sing-Alongs" or Ziggy Marley's "Family Time." As your children get older, look for albums and songs you all enjoy singing along with. This is a way to weave music into daily life while building your singing skills.

Children's Initial Singing Range and Your Comfortable Singing Range

Adults' speaking voice range varies, but in general is lower than children's speaking voices. Adults' singing voice ranges are also often lower than children's. When singing to your children, I encourage you to sing in the range that is most comfortable to you. If you are still finding your confidence as a singer and your range is only a few notes, that is just fine. Look for recorded music that is in a comfortable range for you to sing along with as a way of increasing your confidence, as well as enjoying singing. However, when you are singing *with* your children (not just *to* them) and want them to match pitch, see the suggestions below.

Vocal teachers and researchers have found that it is easier for children ages 6 and younger to sing along to a song using the notes between and including D and A above middle C compared to higher or lower pitches ⏵. This is called "initial singing range."[6] For reference, Taylor Swift sings "Jump Then Fall" in the key of D, mostly using the notes between D and A. Children's singing voice range expands throughout elementary school.

When talking to an infant, most adults naturally use a higher, sing-song voice called "parentese." But this sometimes changes when it comes

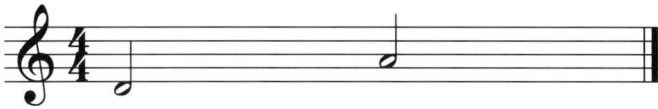

FIGURE 7.2 Music notation for D to A above middle C

to singing with toddlers and older children. However, it is important for adults to keep using their higher range so children are able to sing along at pitch. If possible, those with lower voices can sing in a light, high tone at the upper end of their range. Another option is to have your child begin singing a song, and then you join in at the range your child chooses.[7]

ACTIVITY 19   Experiment with Range

Try discovering your child's preferred range for singing. This will vary by child and based on their age. Record your child singing while alone, such as while playing independently or swinging. Then use a piano or app to find the notes your child was using. You can use a piano app or tuner app (search your app source for "piano keyboard" or "tuner" to find a free app) to check the pitch. What is your child's preferred range?

Next, sing a song with your child that is in your comfortable range, probably below middle C. Does your child sing along? Does the pitch seem accurate?

Finally, try singing in the range you hear your child use. What do you notice—does your child sing out more? Is the singing more tuneful? Remember, even if you feel a little silly singing in this higher range, it's worth it if it helps your child connect with you and sing with you.

Singing through the Adolescent Voice Change

While most of this book focuses on children birth to age 12, the next section of this chapter provides a small preview into the teen years. You're probably familiar with the sequence of events with the male voice change around the time of puberty. Less frequently discussed, but very important, is the topic of female voice change. Dr. Bridget Sweet's book *Thinking Outside the Voice Box: Adolescent Voice Change in Music Education* provides excellent background and information to understand all adolescents' voice changes.[8] She makes the important point that adolescents need to know what is happening during their voice change: hormones cause their larynx to grow, resulting in lower voices for all genders compared to their childhood voice (the male voice change results in a greater difference than the female).

There are musical parenting angles as well as parenting musically considerations when it comes to voice changes for all adolescents. From a musical parenting standpoint, encourage your child to keep singing throughout the months or years of the voice change. Let it be a topic of curiosity and normalcy rather than embarrassment. For instance, one 13-year-old I was teaching expressed frustration that she sounded different singing her choir part than she did the previous month. I explained to her about the female voice change, and she seemed to appreciate giving a label to what was happening. Six months later she returned to that choir part, sang it, and commented, "Did you hear that? The breathiness is gone, I think I've gotten through my voice change."

When it comes to parenting musically, your goal during your child's voice change can be to help them continue to express themselves even if they feel self-conscious about the changes in their spoken or sung expression. During vocal changes, individuals sometimes have a narrow range (just a few notes) that they are comfortable and confident singing. You can look together for music that has a narrow range to sing along to. You could also experiment with singing an alto or tenor line to favorite songs, as harmony lines can be positioned on several notes close together, thus in a small range.

Voice changes may hold particular significance for families of children who are gender expansive or transgender individuals. For an excellent resource on working with gender expansive and trans young musicians, including during vocal changes, please see *Honoring Trans and Gender Expansive Students in Music Education* by Dr. Matthew L. Garrett and Dr. Joshua Palkki (New York: Oxford University Press, 2021).

ACTIVITY 20 Blast from the Past: Listen to Your Voice on Home Movies

If you have access to videos or audio recordings from your growing-up years, take some time with your child to listen to your voice during those years. How did you sound when you were a young child? Do your expressions or inflections sound like your child now? Continue with vocal examples from several different eras. Listen together for how your voice sounded during and after your vocal change. Your child might enjoy going back to listen to their younger voice as well!

ACTIVITY 21 Create an "Audio Photo Album"

Abner Ramirez and Amanda Sudano, the husband-and-wife folk duo JOHNNYSWIM, shared one of their musical parenting practices: regularly recording their children singing. In Episode 13 of the Parenting Musically podcast, Abner described it: "So we have all these [recordings], and I love it because it becomes almost like an audio photo album of memories, because you hear those little voices"[9] ▶. Chances are you might already have lots of sweet little videos floating around of your children singing. Here are two suggestions for organizing an Audio Photo Album:

1. Set a reminder to record your child periodically, however often you would like. This could be monthly or every three or six months. I like to set reminders in an online calendar.
2. Send and/or store the recordings using a digital keepsake account (for example, child1.keepsakes@gmail.com). Read more about creating a digital keepsake account in Chapter 13. Using this email address and possibly an online storage space such as Google Drive could be a convenient way to create your audio photo album.

Should My Child Take Vocal Lessons?

When our children show an interest in learning to play the piano or guitar, one reaction can be to find a private lessons teacher to teach them. If your child wants to learn to sing, you might have a similar response. However, many teachers and researchers recommend proceeding with caution when considering individual formal vocal lessons for children.[10] The voice is an instrument, and if a child overuses their voice or is asked to sing in a way that is not healthy, long-term vocal damage can occur.

One of the most common scenarios would be that a teacher is used to working with older voices and pushes a child to sing too high, too low, or with too much power. It can be okay for a while but eventually it may result in a vocal injury such as vocal nodes. Vocal nodes are like blisters on the vocal cords. If a person has vocal nodes, they often require vocal rest (no singing or talking) for weeks or months and may require voice therapy.[11]

Many music educators recommend that children interested in developing their voices enroll in a children's chorus. This provides age-appropriate vocal training and experiences. Search YouTube for examples of children's choirs in your area to get an idea of the types of music the ensembles typically sing. You and your children may also enjoy exploring performances by well-known children's choirs from other geographical regions as well as international groups.

Another suggestion for children interested in developing vocal skills is to take lessons on another instrument, such as piano or guitar. This would provide some fundamental music knowledge as well as skill on an accompaniment instrument. If your child wants to be a singer-songwriter, being able to play the piano or guitar is a plus.

Keep in mind that the piano or guitar lessons could be formal or informal, in-person or online lessons. There are also apps and YouTube tutorials that can help someone learn piano or guitar. I would not recommend using vocal tutorials on YouTube because of the importance of protecting young voices. If you are ready to find a voice teacher for your tween or teen, ask a trusted choral teacher or chorus director for a recommendation.

Many Ways to Support Children's Voices

Just as there are many ways to be musical, and many ways to parent musically, there are many ways to support children's voices. Taking private vocal lessons is not the only way to help your child develop their voice. As discussed in this chapter, taking private lessons is probably not the right way until at least late middle school or high school. Here are a few ways you can help support your child's vocal development:

- Encourage vocal exploration at all ages—for toddlers, vocal exploration could be making animal sounds. For older children, vocal exploration could take place with a karaoke mic. See chapters 14–16 for more ideas on sung musical play with children at various ages.
- Show interest and appreciation in their singing.
- Find picture books at the library based on songs (ask the librarian or search for "Children's Songs—Texts" in the library catalog), and sing along with them.
- Sing out loud yourself, and model a healthy attitude toward your own voice.
- Avoid giving feedback that could be perceived as negative.

ACTIVITY 22　Explore Acoustical Spaces

Whenever my family walks or bikes through a tunnel, my children yell "Echo! Echo!" They recognize the change of acoustics and are interested to hear how it alters the sound of their voices. For this activity, go on an exploration to find different acoustical spaces. Choose a song together and sing it in different spaces—the bathroom, a closet, the garage with no cars parked in it, the car, inside a tube slide at the playground, an empty stairwell at an office building or parking garage. Wonder together about why the sound changes in the different spaces. You can use an acoustical space as part of routines as well. I overheard a grandparent at the library say to their preschooler, "Okay, it's time to go. Let's go listen to the echo in the stairway!"

WRAPPING UP CHAPTER 7

While some messages from the media or society may have led you to believe that you can't sing or your voice is not acceptable, this is not true. Each person's voice is important, particularly to the children in your life. If you do not currently feel comfortable singing, there are ways to help build your confidence and skill. When the children in our lives see and hear us singing, it shows them how we can use singing to soothe distress, to pass the time in the car, to make a wearisome task more enjoyable, and to draw closer together in relationships.

FOR FURTHER READING

Thinking Outside the Voice Box: Adolescent Voice Change in Music Education, by Bridget Sweet (Oxford University Press, 2019): provides holistic guidance for music educators and families in supporting adolescents during the vocal change years.

Adolescents on Music: Why Music Matters to Young People in Our Lives, by Elizabeth Cassidy Parker (Oxford University Press, 2020): dives deeply into what music-making means to adolescents via interviews with dozens of young musicians.

Honoring Trans and Gender-Expansive Students in Music Education, by Matthew L. Garrett and Josh Palkki (Oxford University Press, 2021): includes interviews with dozens of trans and gender-expansive persons as well as teachers and family members with music-related applications.

TIPS: The Child Voice, edited by Maria Runfola and Joanne Rutkowski (Rowman & Littlefield, 2010): provides information and activity ideas for supporting children's vocal development from early childhood through adolescence.

CHAPTER 8

MUSIC LISTENING TOGETHER

CHAPTER PREVIEW

- Listening is a form of musicking.
- Creating joint music listening opportunities with your family holds multiple benefits.
- Broadening your family's listening—new genres, new artists, new ways to listen—is a way to expand musicking for all ages.
- Talking to family and friends about music listening is a form of relational musicking.

Listening IS Musicking!

You can read in Chapter 1 about the idea of musicking,[1] an all-encompassing verb for music-making that includes all forms of musical participation. Listening might be the best kept secret of family musicking that I've come across. Many of the families who participated in research studies over the years told me "not much music is happening at our house," and yet their music listening practices were expansive and intentional.[2] Music listening played an important role in their musical parenting and the activities involved in it. Listening together provided an opportunity to introduce children to genres, musicians, and specific albums or songs that were important to the family. Music listening evoked emotional connections to both past memories and current experiences. Participants also described the importance of control when it came to listening. For instance, at times, siblings had to negotiate for who would get to choose what to listen to in the car. Additionally, an element of parenting musically occurred when parents spoke to their children about themes that arose in music listening, such as colonialism in *The King and I* and social privilege in *Hamilton*. The parents had the opportunity to discuss their family's moral and socio-political views in the context of these examples.

> Some children, especially tweens and teens, may feel their musical tastes are very personal and private. They may be open to sharing their music listening with family members but choose not to talk with peers about it. Or perhaps they will talk with friends about music but not connect with family.

Music listening can be a great way to connect across generations, as well. Our kids think it's fascinating to hear about the audio technology we had access to when we were kids. "Now tell me again," they like to tease, "What is a cassette tape?" They love hearing the music that their grandparents enjoyed when they were teenagers. Making playlists for specific events or with certain themes is a meaningful conversation starter or family activity. Affiliating with musical genres can be a way both to differentiate from one's family members or to connect with one's family members—sometimes even simultaneously.

Many of us, adults and children alike, engage in repeated listening. Repeated listening can be a way to learn material deeply or experience an emotional state. Listening to a portion of a song or a whole song repeatedly can play an important role in self-regulation for neurodivergent individuals.[3] Erin Hopkins, a music educator and researcher specializing in music education with neurodivergent individuals, encourages parents to "think about the song's content and emotion to understand why their child might be choosing that song in particular to repeat, especially for children who struggle to use spoken language. Are they listening because it's fun and makes them feel good, or is it related in some way to something going on in their life that they're trying to process or communicate?"[4] Bringing this understanding to the situation of repeated listening is an example of parenting musically. Be patient when family members choose to engage in repeated listening. Use physical distance or headphones for other family members if aural space is needed.

Benefits of Joint Music Listening

Music listening technology makes it easy for each family member to listen to their own music with headphones. There may be advantages to individual music listening if your kids are listening to a song on loop and you've had enough, or you have older kids whose music is not age-appropriate for the littles. However, I would recommend that families consider the benefits of joint music listening.

First, joint music listening gives a shared experience in the moment for the listeners, providing an opportunity for relational musicking. Research with families as well as peer groups from four countries (Kenya, the Philippines, New Zealand, and Germany) indicated that joint music listening led to increased social cohesion, or strength of relationships.[5] This joint musical experience could also include dancing or singing along. Your kids might ask what words or phrases mean and provide the chance for verbal interaction. You could discuss how the music makes you feel or what it makes you think of. Family members could also comment on instruments or voices they hear, discuss whether they like the music or not and why, or draw comparisons to other music. Episode 12 of the *Parenting Musically* podcast ▶ showed that you can also go deep on topics brought up in the music. This is a parenting musically tactic described by Risa Goehrke, director of Brand and Content Strategy at the Rock & Roll Hall of Fame, and John Goehrke, director of Fan Engagement and On-Stage Experience at the Rock Hall. They pointed out that while kids perceive music as entertainment, it can be a starting point for discussions as well as a way to connect to learning at school or as a family.[6] Joint listening provides a rich basis for family discussions and parenting musically.

Second, listening together helps create a common set of references in the family. "I'm in dire need of assistance" is a line delivered by the actor portraying George Washington in the piece "Right Hand Man" in the musical *Hamilton*. A research participant noted that she would perform this line when she was overwhelmed and needed her children to understand and give her a minute. I can think of many such song lyrics that are meaningful to my family of origin and a second set familiar to my own children now. I've noticed my youngest, age 7, is proud when he delivers the right musical quotation for a certain situation.

Third, listening to music together builds shared memories that you can draw on in the future. It can be hard to think beyond the next year or two (or month!)—but try for a moment to imagine your family 10 or 20 years from now. The shared experiences, including music, books, food, rituals, and trips taken during childhood can help create a family closeness in the future. Building shared memories through music listening applies to extended families and friends as well. This is an example of parenting musically through music listening, creating a strong fabric of shared memories.

The Magical Space of the Family Vehicle

The car can be a unique musicking space for families. Based on observations of my own children interacting musically while strapped into five-point car seat harnesses, I did a research study with families called "Songs from the Car Seat."[7] Families kept journals and took videos about in-car music-making. I found that family vehicle musicking was marked by opportunities for parent-child reflection, sibling interactions due to proximity within boundaries, and a decreased number of distractions compared to the environment at home. Families described instances of musical parenting, such as introducing their children to new artists. Examples of parenting musically included using music to calm fussy children and pass the time.

Singer-songwriter Rodney Crowell famously wrote the song "I Walk the Line (Revisited)" reflecting on the first time he heard the song "I Walk the Line" by Johnny Cash, while riding in the car with his father and grandfather. Hearing Johnny Cash's song as a 5-year-old, Rodney said, was a turning point for him musically. Crowell was married to Johnny Cash's daughter Rosanne from 1979 to 1992 and they raised a family together, including daughter Chelsea Crowell.

Chelsea described her own music listening in the car experience for Episode 12 of the *Parenting Musically* podcast ▶:

> And I think I would have been about 4 or 5 years old, and we were in Hawaii, and I was in the back of a jeep. But I remember the opening drums to "Cathy's Clown" coming through the radio, and this is very [similar] to my dad's story about hearing "I Walk the Line" for the first time, because it was like these speakers all of a sudden just were coming out of the ethos, out of the center of the earth, and I heard this drumbeat, and

I was like. you know, what in the world. and then I hear their harmonizing. . . . It was such a wildly profound experience of hearing that for the first time.

Both Chelsea and Rodney remembered pivotal music-listening experiences that occurred while they were out riding in a car with family members. Chelsea jokingly closed her story by advising parents to play music for their kids when out driving around town. That's excellent advice!

What is it about the family vehicle that makes it a space for music listening? The sound of the music is different because of the acoustical space of the car and the sense of being together "inside the bubble of sound" with family and friends.[8] There are less distractions there than at home. Depending on where you are going, there might be fewer siblings present (perhaps you are taking one child to a medical appointment) or extra friends along (carpooling to soccer). The parent is physically occupied and separated from the child by the front seat/back seat, yet hopefully emotionally and socially present. This provides an opportunity to listen together and talk together about what you are hearing. For young children that could be "Did you hear that drum beat?" or "It's your favorite song!" For older children, the conversations can go deeper.

ACTIVITY 23   Keep a Listening Journal

The families I have interviewed have sometimes expressed surprise by how much music their children listen to. It's usually more than they had realized! For this activity, pay attention to the music your family listens to for a week—write down where you are, what the music is, and who chose it. This awareness can lead to a desire to seek out different music, or a sense of satisfaction with the amount and types of music your children are hearing, or some other insight. You might realize that one child is dominating the music choices in the car, and together set up a schedule for who gets to choose the music. You could also note that there are more opportunities to use music listening for the purposes of parenting musically, such as providing a timeline for getting ready in the morning or helping the family wind down before bed.

Sample Listening Journal

Day/time	Where are you?	What are you listening to?	Who chose it?
Example: Tuesday morning, 8:45 am	Example: In the car, driving to preschool	Example: *Encanto* soundtrack	Example: Julia

Reflection questions after keeping a listening log:

- Are there parts of the day you could add music listening to?
- Are you as a parent having the opportunity to choose some of the music? If not, would you like to?
- Would you like to make any adjustments to how your family decides what to listen to?
- Would you like to make any adjustments to your children's access to playing music on their own (via Smart devices or other technology?)?
- Would you like to make any adjustments to the amount of variety of music listened to?

The listening journal can be kept in a simple notebook or on a device. If your family enjoys keeping a listening journal, there are several published journals available—search a bookstore for "music listening journal."

ACTIVITY 24 Where and When Does This Music Come From?

Music exists within cultural contexts. Exploring where the music we enjoy comes from gives a deeper appreciation. Who composed it? Who performed it? What genres influenced them? When was the music created? Why was it created—was this music for a specific occasion? Dr. Jason Hanley, vice president of Education and Visitor Engagement at the Rock & Roll Hall of Fame, helps families explore these questions in his book, *We Rock: A Fun Family Guide for Exploring Rock Music History* (Hobart, NY: Quarry Books, 2015). Dr. Hanley presents 52 "music labs," each focusing on a rock musician or group. He includes historical, social, and cultural context and playlists as well as suggested activities and guided listening information.

You could adapt the ideas from these labs and apply them to additional genres of music.[9] Hear Jason share examples from his book as well as explain its foundational principles in Episode 7 of the *Parenting Musically* podcast ▶.

ACTIVITY 25 Interview Grandparents and Elders About Music Listening

Set your kids up with a video or audio recorder to interview grandparents or neighbors with questions about their experiences listening to music growing up. Here are some sample questions:

- How did you listen to music when you were my age? Were there records? Cassette tapes? CDs? Did you listen to the radio? Were there music concerts on TV?
- Do you remember ever wanting a certain album? What was it? Did you ever get it?
- Do you have any special memories of listening to music with other people? Tell me all about it!
- Did you ever go to a music concert? What was it like? Who was the performer?

WRAPPING UP CHAPTER 8

In my research with families, I found that music listening was in some cases the most well-developed and extensive musicking activity in which the family engaged, often across multiple generations. Recognizing this helped the families to see they were incorporating music in their family's life through listening. Joint music listening holds important benefits, so be sure to create opportunities for family members to listen together, not just on their own headphones. Talking to grandparents or elders about the music they listen to is an opportunity for relational musicking.

FOR FURTHER READING

We Rock: A Fun Family Guide for Exploring Rock Music History, by Jason Hanley (Quarry Books, 2015): provides a guide with 52 activities to help families focus on the historical, social, and cultural context of rock musicians and groups.

Websites from institutions like the Rock & Roll Hall of Fame (https://www.rockhall.com/rock-hall-edu), Musical Instrument Museum (https://www.mim.org/educator-resources/), Carnegie Hall (https://kids.carnegiehall.org/) and the Auckland (New Zealand) Philharmonic Orchestra (https://www.apo.co.nz/community-education/families/apo-whoa/). In some cases, these materials were designed for use during the COVID-19 pandemic lockdowns and have remained useful resources going forward.

Cheaper by the Dozen, by Frank B. Gilbreth Jr. and Ernestine Gilbreth Carey (Thomas Y. Crowell Co, 1948): a fun chapter book about a family with 12 children growing up in the early 20th century. Read or listen to the audiobook as a family, noticing the ways the Gilbreths listened to music and responded to music together, in small groups, and individually.

CHAPTER 9

FOUND SOUNDS AND RHYTHM BANDS

> **CHAPTER PREVIEW**
> - Playing instruments includes much more than piano, guitar, drums, and band and orchestra instruments. Young children can play simple percussion instruments as well as homemade instruments.
> - Playing instruments together at home or the playground is a fun activity.
> - Instrument time can also be a way to motivate, such as when built into a tidying chore.
> - Set boundaries around how instruments are handled and when it is okay to play.

Thinking Broadly About Instrument Playing

In my music classroom at Woodbridge Elementary School in Zeeland, Michigan, "playing instruments" did not often include playing the types of instruments many adults think of when they hear the term. Although I played the piano and guitar for my students, as well as my flute for them on occasion, my students did not usually play the piano, guitar, or any band or orchestra instruments. We did play rhythm sticks, tone bells, xylophones, shakers, drums, and all types of other small percussion instruments. The third and fourth graders played that most beloved of elementary instruments: the recorder. The recorder gets a bad rap from many people, but I loved teaching it because it allowed the kids to have a way to play melodies on their own. Keep reading for my top tips on at-home recorder practice. In elementary music we also did activities with "found sounds," further described below.

As shown in the paragraph above, there are many possibilities for instrument playing that exist outside of the "traditional" instruments of piano, guitar, flute, violin, trumpet, and all of the other band and orchestra instruments. The goal of this chapter is to provide suggestions for activities at home and in the community with rhythm instruments and found sounds. You can turn to chapters 20–22 to read more about how to encourage the children in your life to practice, play, and thrive within more formal instrumental instruction.

In this chapter, I focus on four categories of instruments: body percussion, rhythm instruments, found sounds, and recorders. Keep in mind that one of the best ways to inspire children to play instruments, both those discussed in this chapter and other instruments, is to play them yourself! Just as we encourage all parents and caregivers to sing to and with their children, everyone can play instruments for or with children. From harmonica to claves to ukulele to kazoo, show the children in your life that musical instruments are available and enjoyable to play.

Benefits of Playing Instruments

Playing instruments is fun! It is a way to have a satisfying musical experience, either on one's own or as part of a larger group. The diversity of sounds instruments make—including instruments that very young children can play—add to the enjoyment and learning that come with instruments. Instruments can inspire children's musical creativity—and adults' creativity as well.

It's important for children to see that we do not have to play at a professional level to have a satisfying or enjoyable musical experience. Showing them this, and also saying it, helps children to recognize their own musicking with instruments as important and valuable right now. Sometimes children might think that what they are doing is just preparation for later when they can play more notes or "better." However, helping everyone see and value the musical experience in the moment is a way to honor children's musicking. You can help children recognize the multi-layered value of musicking now as well as building skills for future musical involvement.

Body Percussion

"Body percussion" refers to sounds made by the human body like clapping, stomping, swishing hands, snapping, and tapping or slapping legs or arms. Have you noticed how musicians use these sounds as part of their musical performances? Body percussion is used in musicking by many cultures across the globe. It holds an important place in African American music history. When enslaved people were denied drums and other instruments by plantation owners because of the communication and organizational power of drumming, the people of African descent created new ways of expressing their musical traditions. These new ways included the hambone, juba dance, tap dance, step dance, and beat-boxing.[1] Check for YouTube videos with examples of these forms of musicking.

Rhythm Instruments

Growing up, I loved to visit my Aunt Gracia's house. In her piano bench she had a plastic bag marked "rhythm band." There was a triangle, tambourine, maracas, and little cymbals. I loved to organize my brothers and younger cousin and parade with the instruments through the house. It was a simple set of instruments, not the highest quality, yet it inspired me to create a musical procession and practice musical leadership.

Having simple instruments like this, or homemade instruments as described below, can open a world of possibilities for family musicking. You can build your instrument collection easily by visiting garage sales or watching for neighborhood giveaways. When sourcing instruments, be sure to check for choking hazards if your children are under 5.

Think about where in your living space you would like to store the instruments. You could decide to have them in a location where children can help themselves whenever they would like to make music. For instance, you might keep a basket in the living room with shakers, a hand drum, and panpipes. You could also decide it is best to keep the instruments put away until specific times. My sister-in-law, who lived in Johannesburg at the time, gave us a vuvuzela (loud plastic monotone horn) when South Africa hosted the world cup in 2010. We have kept the vuvuzela on a high shelf except for a very few occasions.

ACTIVITY 26   Create a Soundtrack for a Picture Book

Choose a picture book that features more than one genre of music, such as *My Family Plays Music*, written by Judy Cox and illustrated by Elbrite Brown (Holiday House, 2018). In *My Family Plays Music*, a child describes each family member and the genre of music they play, then demonstrates various classroom instruments she likes to play along with each family member. Information is included on all the genres featured in the book. Find recordings of each genre covered in the book and listen to them while you read the book. Dance to the music and play along with your own rhythm instrument collection.

One way of categorizing rhythm instruments comes from the Orff-Schulwerk approach for teaching children music. In this method, teachers and students classify instruments as woods, metals, skins, and shakers/scrapers.[2] Woods are instruments like wood blocks, rhythm sticks, and xylophones with wooden bars. Metals can be triangles, finger cymbals, and jingle bells. Skins refers to drumskins stretched to make a drum sound, which includes drums and tambourine heads. Shakers and scrapers are instruments that make sound by shaking or scraping, like maracas or guiro, a percussion instrument from Puerto Rico. Tambourines are both metals (jingles) and skin (the drum part if it is covered). Knowing these categories, you can ask your family members to each select from a different one so the sound is not overwhelmingly jingly or only drums. This can also help with keeping the overall volume level lower.

Xylophones (wooden bars), metallophones (metal bars), or glockenspiels (small metal bars) can be great instruments for kids. The size of the bars provides a visual representation of pitch—bigger bars are lower, smaller bars are higher. If a child plays from low to high or high to low, they will hear a scale. Children can make up their own melodies on a barred instrument, play two notes in a pattern as an accompaniment (C and G, for example), or play known melodies by ear. There are affordable toy xylophones available from many retailers. The instruments used in general music class have a much more beautiful tone but are also expensive. You could watch for "used Orff instruments" on social media buy-sell sites. Or keep your eyes open—your house of worship or community organization may have a set of the instruments and allow your child to play them with supervision.

I have seen teachers ask preschoolers to handle rhythm sticks as valuable instruments. The teacher shows the children how to hold the sticks and asks the children to gently put the sticks away when they are finished. Setting expectations around simple musical instruments in your home could be a way to set the stage for caring for more complex and expensive instruments later. This care also shows that we value the musicking that comes from simple instruments.

On the flip side of that, it can be interesting for children to experiment with different ways of playing instruments. One teacher I observed invited the children to use their xylophone mallets in a lesson to play anything and anywhere in the music classroom except where they usually did (on the xylophones). The children used their mallets to explore the timbres (type of sound) of instrument cupboards, wooden chairs, and cinder block walls. They held the mallets with the handle facing out and used it to scrape along the radiator, using a technique like playing the guiro. The children also clicked their mallets together and tapped them on their shoes to create new sounds. This creativity and thinking beyond what is traditional has long been a hallmark in musical composition and performance.

If you search YouTube for "Jimmy Fallon classroom instruments," you can find an array of videos featuring comedian Jimmy Fallon, the band The Roots, and guest musicians. You'll see the band playing classroom instruments like xylophones, drums, shakers, kazoos, and drums. During the COVID-19 lockdown, when the studio was shut down, these segments featured "at-home instruments." These are a great example of the next topic, "found sounds."

Found Sounds

Ethnomusicologist Dr. John Blacking (1928–1990) defined music as "humanly organized sound."[3] It follows, then, that voices or standard musical instruments are not the only ways to make music. As described in the body percussion section, we can make music with our hands and feet (clapping, snapping, stomping, swishing). Humans also use a variety of objects, both from nature and those that were made by people, to create music. A pots and pans drum set is a classic example of making music with found sounds. The musical group Stomp is popular for their musicking with found sounds like trash cans, sticks, water, brooms, and paper ripping (search YouTube for examples).

Found sounds are anything your child finds, in your house, car, or outside, that can make sounds. You may have noticed—and possibly experienced irritation by—the way children so naturally make noise with anything at hand! What is the difference between noise and music? Following Blacking's definition, to be classified as music, the child would be intentionally organizing the shaking, scraping, drumming, or tapping sounds in some way. What can sound like noise to you could be music to your child. Children's exploration of how to make sounds, which sounds they like, and how sounds fit together are also a form of musicking.

One way to encourage found sound musical exploration within limits is to set times or places when you ask for your child to be still. My kids love to explore the sounds of fork against plate and glass while sitting at the table when I am getting the last few dishes set for dinner, but that is a stressful time for me. A comment like "Let's practice that later in the back room" is a way to set the boundary without squashing the natural creativity. Another possible response is "If you'd like to play percussion right now, you may play this bowl drum with a spatula."

Providing children with positive attention is a way to help foster a positive relationship and build their self-efficacy.[4] This positive attention to musicking is also important when children are practicing instruments—read more on this in Chapter 21. One way to show this attention is through taking photos or videos of children's musicking. I have noticed with children in my research studies, as well as my own kids, that when I pull out my phone to video something they often straighten up and become more intent in it. It's as though my children see my interest and willingness to video as a sign that they are doing something special. But sometimes the exact opposite happens, and they stop what they are doing if I get a camera out. Notice which forms of attention your child prefers. Be sensitive to your child's preferences of whether or not to be recorded. It could help to say that you would like to share the recording with a relative or that you are keeping a digital memory book. Think carefully before sharing photos or videos on social media.

Another way to encourage children to make music with found sounds is by doing it with them. You could go for a walk outside and look for a stick, then listen for what kinds of rhythmic sounds you can make with the stick and other materials—a tree, long grass, scratching it in the dirt. Ask your child to listen to the sounds of nature that they find to be musical and have children name them, such as animal calls, wind, and rain. Let your child record these sounds on your phone. Later you can listen to them together or use them in compositions (see Chapter 11 for composition software and app suggestions). Search "soundscape recordings" online to hear soundscapes that others have collected from specific areas of the globe. Or you could have a scavenger hunt in the house to find some objects that make a fun sound, then play the found sounds during a family dance party. This could also be combined with a tidying activity, described below.

ACTIVITY 27   Found Sound Instrument Tidying Game

Tidying the house can be a struggle. Once I gave everyone oven mitts and tongs and pretended the stuff to be tidied was space garbage we had to put away but couldn't touch. It was fun but took a long time. Here's one that you could do more regularly:

Let's say there are books, toys, clothes, school papers, and random objects scattered around the kitchen, dining room, and living room. Gather your family and explain the game. Describe found sound instruments and give a few examples among the detritus to be tidied. "Find something that's yours. Think, could this be my found sound instrument? If not, put it away. If yes, put it here on the table. You can only have one item on the table. When everyone has put away five (or whatever number your family can manage) items, we'll play our found sound instruments. *Choose a found sound instrument today, then put everything else away!*" When everyone is ready, play the instruments together, perhaps while marching around or while dancing with recorded music playing. This can also be repeated with the "found sound music" as a break, then tidying five more items for several rounds of tidying. If it goes well and you repeat the game another day, you can just call *"Choose a found sound instrument today, then put everything else away!"* as the reminder.

ACTIVITY 28 Multi-Generational Jam Session

Gather some rhythm band instruments or found sounds for a multi-generational jam session. The adults or older children could play the rhythm band instruments with the younger children, or if the adults and older children play other instruments, give that a try. One year our neighborhood had the annual holiday cookie exchange and carol singing at our house. I played the piano, a few neighbors played their guitars, and two 6th-graders played along on their clarinets for the holiday songs they knew. I set out a basket of jingle bells, tambourines, and maracas. My youngest son was about 18 months old at the time, and I remember the expression of delight on his face as he meandered around the crowd, shaking his jingle bell and smiling at everyone.

A multi-generational jam session can be much less formal than that—simply putting a favorite tune on the Bluetooth speaker or audio system at a volume loud enough to hear it while also playing those instruments or found sounds and singing or dancing along. If you or your children are sensitive to noise, keep the volume of the recording lower and let everyone know they need to play softly enough to hear the recording. This can be especially important with larger groups.

ACTIVITY 29 Conducting

Conducting is a way for children to show agency, or power, control, and authority. If the child is conducting, they control whether the adults are playing, and how fast or loud. There are many areas of life in which children do not have control. Conducting games or activities provide an opportunity for a child to experience agency.

A variation on the jam session activity above is to invite your child to be the conductor. They could point to various people or instrument groups to show when to come in. For instance, if you are playing along to a recording and two people have shakers and two have tambourines, the conductor could point to indicate when the shakers play, when the tambourines play, when both play, and when both are silent. Teach your children this by modeling it once or twice.

The conductor could also indicate whether to play loud or soft based on the size of their hand gestures. If you are playing instruments without an external recording, the conductor could also indicate speed by speeding up or slowing down with their hand movements. If you would like to teach your children the standard conducting patterns, search YouTube for "basic conducting gestures."

Recorders, and Other Noisy Things, in the Home

The recorder is the butt of many an internet joke and meme these days. However, I ask you to keep an open mind when it comes to recorders. Certainly, there are pros and cons. The pros: Recorders are wonderful instruments. They have a history dating back to the Middle Ages, and yet you can purchase one for $5 from local stores. I have seen children as young as 2 or 3 learn to play several notes on the recorder, particularly if the back thumb (B) hole is taped over (medical or painter's tape works well). Learning to play the recorder can provide children with the opportunity to play an instrument by ear, to learn to play from notation, or both.

The con: The sound of a child practicing the recorder can be disruptive to family life and to parent mental functioning. If your child is learning recorder at school and practicing at home, or if your child is learning on their own at home, here are a few suggested rules:

- Only play while seated
- Never play in the car
- Carefully cover the finger holes—remember "no leaks, no squeaks"

An important music teacher tip is to ask your child to play "in chin position." This means the child places the curve of the mouthpiece on their chin and fingers the melody while thinking the notes in their head ("audiating"). Chin position practice is an important mode for home practice.

Additional ideas:

- Practice in a bathroom with the vent fan on to provide a sound barrier. Bonus: your child can look in the mirror to see their fingers and check that they are covering the finger holes!
- Play along to soundtracks from YouTube, either those specifically designed for recorder or more generic drum tracks. Search "Beginner recorder play along" to find resources. Better yet, have your child or a sibling create a backing track.
- Use the phrase "Remember: warm, slow air" to remind your child how to properly blow into the recorder. Thinking about warm rather than cool air, and slow rather than fast, helps reduce the number of squeaks and shrillness.
- Get an extra recorder and let your child teach you what they are learning. Be sure your recorders are the same brand, because it's easier to stay in tune that way.
- Invite your child to practice outside—be mindful of time of day and how close you are to neighbors.

While it can be challenging to have a new recorder player in the house, I encourage you to find a way to make it positive for your child and workable for you. The recorder may end up on the top of the fridge (i.e., "in timeout") occasionally, but the recorder can be an important part of a child's musical journey. Some of these suggestions can also apply to other noisy toys or items your children bring home.

ACTIVITY 30 Instruments at Playgrounds

More and more playgrounds are installing outdoor instruments such as drums and xylophones. If you see outdoor instruments, spend some time exploring them with your child. Talk together about how the instruments sound and take turns trying different ways to play them. For instance, slide a mallet across a xylophone, then play individual bars. Try tapping the edge of a drum and then play in the middle. How are the sounds different? Provide time for your child to play the instruments solo. Ask for a turn to play solo yourself. If your child is interested, suggest playing together.

If there are not outdoor instruments at the playgrounds you currently visit, consider asking friends in the area if they know of any playgrounds that do have them. Meanwhile, have fun exploring new playgrounds when possible in search of some of the instruments! At playgrounds without instruments, you can discover found sounds and make your own instruments. You could also be in touch with your local school or community organization that maintains the playgrounds you visit most often to ask if they would consider adding outdoor instruments.

WRAPPING UP CHAPTER 9

In this chapter, I described several categories of instruments you can use at home that fall outside of the piano, guitar, and band and orchestra instruments. These categories included body percussion, rhythm instruments, found sounds, and recorders. Playing instruments together as a family is a way to add delight to family musicking. It also provides a way for children or adults to participate in a sing-along if they do not know the song. It is important for children to see adults playing instruments.

FOR FURTHER READING

Rubber-Band Banjos and a Java Jive Bass: Projects and Activities on the Science of Music and Sound, by Alex Sabbeth (Jossey-Bass, 1997): combines the science of sound and craft ideas to create instruments. This provides a link between found sounds and acoustical principles.

Music Is in Everything, written by Ziggy Marley and illustrated by Ag Jatkowska (Akashic Books, 2022): a picture book that accompanies Ziggy's song by the same name that highlights the music that is in our environment.

CHAPTER 10

DANCE PARTIES THROUGH THE DECADES

> **CHAPTER PREVIEW**
> - Dancing is a form of musicking.
> - Dancing includes creative movement as well as patterned movements.
> - Dancing together as a family holds benefits that vary as children get older.
> - Likewise, families often find their dancing interactions shift as children get older.

Dancing IS Musicking!

Music and dance are intertwined in many cultures across the globe and in previous eras as well as today. Much of the music of today is created to be danced to. While we don't expect to see people dancing to classical music at a concert today in places like Carnegie Hall, throughout most of human history, music and dance occurred side by side. From religious observance to court dances to informal entertainment, most music was created to be moved to.[1]

For many children and adults, dancing may be their primary or preferred mode of musicking. Some people might think of this as "expressing the music through dance," but that puts dance into a subservient role. Remember, music and dance are interwoven. In some cultures, there is a single word for music and dance.[2] We sing, we play instruments, we listen, we create, we dance. Christopher Small included dancing in his definition of musicking.[3]

In this book, I am using the word dance to refer to all forms of movement to music. This could include the more formal movement that occurs at a public event like a wedding or bar mitzvah dance, as well as informal dancing in a family's kitchen or living room. Dancing also includes creative movement, described more below. I encourage you to think of all types of movement that are related to music or musical elements as dance. Just as all humans are musical, all humans can dance. If you are someone who says or thinks "I don't dance" or "I can't dance," then just try some of the ideas in the chapter and tell yourself you are moving to the music.

> Are you comfortable moving to music? If not, what are some ways you could become more comfortable? Is there a role model in your life who could help?

Benefits of Dancing

Dancing is a way that a child can show you their response to music. Through dance, a whole family can participate together in musicking, including community musical experiences. Dancing provides visual and spatial information for musickers as well as auditory input.[4] Moving together to a beat can lead to positive social behavior like helpfulness in both adults and children.[5] Also, dancing is enjoyable!

Creative Movement and Laban Effort Elements

Acting out a picture book is a way to get started with creative movement. *Dance Like a Flamingo*, by Moira Butterfield and Claudia Boldt (London: Welbeck Editions, 2020), includes information about a range of animals and suggestions about how to dance like those animals. Books like these provide a nice amount of suggestion to get you started without being overly technical. Props that move with you, like ribbon bracelets or scarves, can add enjoyment.

Another way to focus on specific movement elements is through using the Laban effort elements.[6] Rudolf van Laban (1879–1958) was an

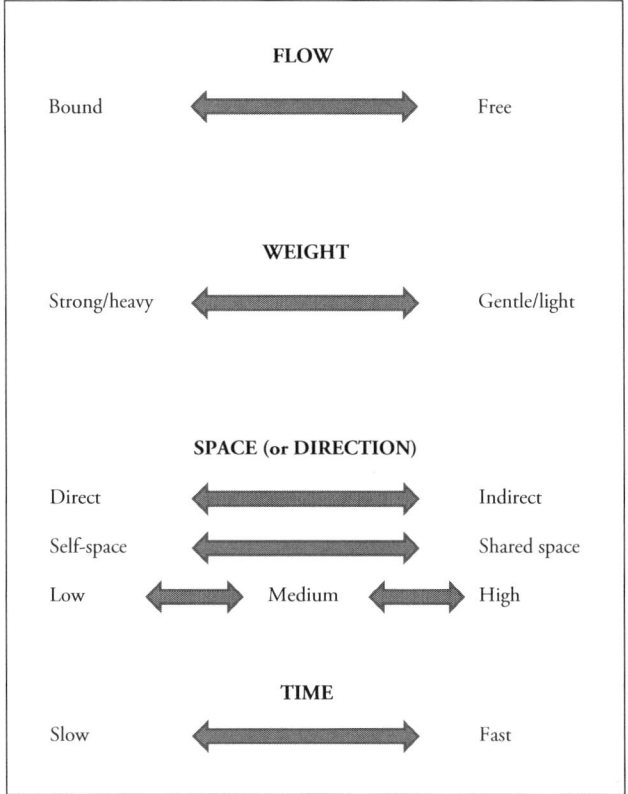

FIGURE 10.1 Laban Effort Elements

Austro-Hungarian dancer and choreographer who analyzed professional dancers' movements as well as developed a notation system for dance. The Laban Effort Elements stem from his analysis of dancers' movements. He noted that any dance movement could be understood as a manifestation of the four effort elements: flow, weight, space, and time.

Considering these four Laban elements provides a helpful structure within which to explore movement with your child. Each element can be thought of as a continuum. You can explore one element at a time or try two at a time. Note, the various elements do not have to align as they do in Figure 10.1. That is, bound movement is not always combined with strong/heavy or slow, etc.

ACTIVITY 31 Laban Movement Activities

The next six paragraphs give some examples of moving with varying elements of flow, weight, space (high/medium/low; self-space/shared space; direct/indirect), and time. Pick one or two from each category and write them on a note card. Explore the elements one at a time. Experiment with using the ideas for parenting musically purposes—to ease a transition to or from the car seat, or to give structure to cleaning up blocks.

You can explore flow with your child by moving with "continuous fluid movement,"[7] or flowing, circular movements. Try flowing (moving in continuous circular motions) focusing on your arms, your knees, your shoulders, and your feet. Keep your hips unlocked in order to move with flow. Pretending to paint the floor or stir soup are ways to feel continuous fluid movement. You can do these movements with or without singing or playing recorded music. Explore the range of bound movement to free movement by pretending to move through various substances. If you're moving through honey or Jell-O, that is an example of bound movement. Moving through feathers or bubbles is an example of free movement. Children are typically ready for this imaginary play around age 2.

Activities to explore the element of weight are best done first with a real prop and then using the imagination. You could load a backpack with books (not too heavy!) and take turns moving with it around a room, then switch to a backpack with a stuffed animal. Exaggerate your movements so your child sees the difference. Switching to an imaginary game, you could pretend the floor is covered with eggshells and you want to move around the house without breaking any (light movement). Then say, "Let's break them all!" and stomp around with strong weight.

There are multiple ways to explore the element of space. Try playing "move and freeze" (move when you hear the recorded music, freeze when the music is paused). During each pause name a space to move in: high space, medium space, low space in relation to your body height. You can also add more specifics: low space in front of you or high space behind you.

Self space/shared space is another way to explore space. This can be a strategic concept to teach from a parenting musically standpoint. "Stay in self space" requires children to be aware of their space and those around them. I remind my kids to stay in self space during meals. Learning to move (and live!) in shared space is also important. You can have fun trying to move while sharing space only at the elbows, the knees, etc. When thinking about shared space you can also talk about moving together—not too fast or too slow. For example, if you hold hands and spin in a circle, you need to move at the same speed so one person isn't pulled along uncomfortably.

Direct and indirect is a little more complicated but can provide another fun movement game in the house. Sometimes dancers or musicians move directly from one place to another (or from one note to another, like a scale). Other times they move indirectly—in music, this is when the music winds up and down and back and forth and around. We can try this in space by moving directly (from the chair to the fridge in a straight line) and indirectly (from the chair, meandering to the window, stopping by the living room, then the garbage can, before arriving at the fridge). Play a game where you take turns assigning each other how to move, directly or indirectly. You could add some tidying in—"Please take this sock indirectly to your laundry hamper!"

The final Laban element is time, or fast and slow. Dance and freeze games provide an opportunity to practice fast and slow. Choose music with different tempi (speeds) so you and your child can try moving at various speeds. You could also vary movements from quickly to slowly or vice versa. Having the chance to talk about speed and practice it concretely can also help if there are times when you need your child to quicken or slow their pace. If you are trying to get out the door, you could say "Let's set our speeds together: get your shoes on quickly!" Or if everyone is moving too quickly and bumping into each other or making a mess, say "Whoa, whoa. No hurry. Let's slooooow it down."

Living Room Dance Parties

Dancing comes naturally to many children, from the early bouncing to music on through creative movement in preschool and beyond. Many of the families I have worked with for research studies have shared that they have regular dance parties in the kitchen, living room, and outside with young children. These dance parties can serve as an opportunity for the children and adults to do something together that may take the form of mutuality (providing varied benefits for multiple generations), as discussed in Chapter 5.

ACTIVITY 32 Mirroring During Dance Party

During your next dance party, try mirroring your child's movements. Join in their movement ideas, first doing exactly what they do, then extending the ideas a little bit. For instance, if your child is spinning, then you spin alongside at first. Then extend the idea by holding out your hand and spinning together. If you child is interested, trade roles, and ask your child to be your mirror. Use this as an opportunity to introduce different dance moves or creative movement elements. You could also try focusing on one of the Laban effort elements while playing the mirroring game.

FIGURE 10.2 Mother and child mirroring one another while dancing. GETTY IMAGES

Dancing Together as Kids Get Older

Depending on your child's temperament and whether there are younger children in the family, dance parties can continue for many years. However, there might come a day when a spontaneous move-and-freeze kitchen dance party is no longer a common occurrence in life. Here are some ideas for dancing with children in elementary school and beyond.

- **Prepare for social dancing.** If you are planning to attend a family event with dancing like a bar or bat mitzvah or wedding, teach your children some of the dances they will encounter. Use YouTube for tutorials.
- **Tech-directed dancing.** Video games like "Dance Dance Revolution" or "Just Dance" can be a fun way to dance as a family. The games provide additional structure for the activity, teaching dance moves and dictating the order and timing.
- **Ask your child to teach you dances learned from social media.** Even if your kids do not directly access YouTube or TikTok, they may have learned dances from friends or at school from these sources. Have fun being the learner while your child gets to teach you some new dances.
- **Learn from a loved one.** Ask a friend or family member to teach your family a folk dance or a dance from their childhood.

ACTIVITY 33 Learn a Dance from an Elder

Asking a grandparent, aunt or uncle, or neighbor to teach your family a dance from their culture or childhood can be a pathway to relational musicking. It can also be a fun way for children to view their family members and elders in a different context. For example, if your children primarily view their grandparents as caregivers and soccer cheerleaders, it can be eye-opening to see their grandparents dancing and teaching the younger family members something from the elders' youth. After learning the dance and dancing together, you could look for a video or photo of the dance either in home movies and photos, online, or at the library. Children could also research the origins of the dance and learn how it may have changed through the years.

Ways to Learn Dancing

In addition to asking an elder to teach your family a new dance, there are many other ways to learn dancing. You could enroll in a ballroom dancing class through a community recreation program or an adult beginner dance class at a local dance studio. Watch for street festivals or community celebrations that include dance instruction. Some events feature a lesson for beginners prior to the start of the event. Dancing can be specific to the community—line dancing, contra dancing, salsa, swing. YouTube and TikTok are also great ways to learn dances—find the artists and channels that fit your family.

A research participant I worked with for a study called "Mama's Turn" decided to take piano lessons, in part for herself but in part because she knew it would have a positive impact on her young children.[8] Could the same be true for you and dance? Would taking some dance classes or lessons be enjoyable for you as well as help your children learn to express themselves joyfully through movement?

ACTIVITY 34   Create a Family Dance

Choose a piece of music you love and create movements to part or all of the piece. This could include some sections where everyone does the same movements, other sections where each family member improvises their own dance, and yet other sections with shared space movements, such as parents lifting and spinning children. A variation of this activity is to create a complicated "secret handshake" among family members or siblings.

WRAPPING UP CHAPTER 10

Dancing is an important way to be musical as a family. Dancing can be both a joyful and expressive way to interact with family members. Some dances have strong cultural or historical links, which can deepen relational musicking. Learning a dance from family members or friends is a form of relational musicking.

FOR FURTHER READING

Giraffes Can't Dance, written by Giles Andreae and illustrated by Guy Parker-Rees (Orchard Books, 1999): In this story, the main character encounters prejudice about who can dance and what counts as dance. He perseveres to value and express himself through dancing.

Dance Like a Flamingo, written by Moira Butterfield and illustrated by Claudia Boldt (Welbeck Editions, 2020): This book includes lyrical text with facts about various animals followed by specific suggestions of how to dance like that animal.

Brain-Compatible Dance Education, by Anne Green Gilbert (National Dance Association, 2006): A manual for teaching dance concepts, skills, and choreography to early childhood through adults.

CHAPTER 11

CREATING MUSIC, CREATING MEMORIES

> **CHAPTER PREVIEW**
> - Children are naturally creative with music.
> - As grown-ups, we can help foster that creativity throughout childhood.
> - Engaging in musical creativity can have benefits including musical growth, self-expression, and self-actualization.
> - When adults model musical creativity, either on their own or as part of a family activity, children learn both content and process.

Creativity Comes Naturally . . . But How to Help It Stay?

Children are naturally creative in many ways, including musically. Researchers have documented the little songs children sing in their cribs, while playing, and throughout their days.[1] Researchers and teachers have also asked, When does this musical creativity stop, and why? Some researchers think it is linked to formal schooling, as children learn to value re-creating other music.[2] Children are also told to be quiet in their classrooms so they do not distract or disturb others. There may also be a social component as children become more aware of what others think of them and their creativity. This diminishment in musical creativity has been noted in other areas of expression, such as the visual arts and poetry.[3]

I have noticed a resurgence of musical creativity on the part of individuals during their early years as parents or grandparents. Many of the parents I interviewed for various studies spoke about making up songs to help their children get to sleep, as a special song to sing when the child is mildly injured, or for steps of the bedtime routine. The songs may also create a long-lasting emotional connection. When my oldest was a few months old, my husband and I were finishing graduate school and preparing to move to start my university position. My mom created a little lullaby ▶.

This lullaby, which she sang while rocking her granddaughter in her own grandmother's antique rocking chair, proved to be calming to baby and grandmother alike—and to me as well during a time of major life transitions. My mom went on to sing the lullaby to her other 11 grandchildren, substituting their names.

FIGURE 11.1 Grandma Bonnie's Lullaby by Bonnie Huisman

Parents also may become creative at adapting the words of a known tune to help calm a child, make a child laugh, or get through a routine. These are prime examples of parenting musically—using music to get the job done! This also provides a model for your child. Soon you will hear them making up new words to a known song.

Musical play, as described throughout this book, is a way to encourage continued musical creativity. A specific approach to facilitating musical play is through providing "loose parts." In her book *Inspiring Musical Play in Elementary General Music Through Loose Parts,* Dr. Vanessa L. Bond explains the use of loose parts in various music play settings. Loose parts are materials provided for individuals to explore, tinker with, build, and manipulate. For musical creativity, loose parts could include the found sound items discussed in Chapter 16, Activity 60. Loose parts could also be open-ended toys or household objects. Children can explore the sound possibilities of loose parts, use them as characters in a mini-opera, or create a diorama of loose parts, followed by transforming the visual to creative movement, as a few examples. Family members encourage or enhance musical play by honoring child agency (power, control, and authority), allowing the child to direct the play.[4]

> What can we do to keep the musical creativity alive? How can we encourage that creative impulse that leads children to "sing little songs" as they continue into middle childhood and adolescence? And what would be the benefit of encouraging musical creativity, if we found a way to do it?

Benefits of Musical Creativity

We have a body of research that points to benefits of creativity: improved physical and mental health, enhanced enjoyment, and increased life satisfaction.[5] Within the field of music, researchers who have studied the benefits of song-writing and music composition have noted that these activities facilitate self-expression, can provide space to address difficult or intense emotional experiences, and may lead to enjoyment and satisfaction in accomplishing a challenge.[6] Musical creativity can be one of the tools in a family toolbox as a means for

- Promoting the positives of life (for example, creating a song about things we are grateful for),
- Helping kids cope with the downsides (creating and playing musical pieces that help to express grief, frustration, anger, or boredom),
- Cultivating healthy relationships with self, siblings, peers, and adults throughout adolescence,
- And creating music for music's sake!

Justin Andrews, grandson of the legendary Otis Redding, is director of Special Projects and Outreach at the Otis Redding Foundation. He oversees the student activities and summer camp, Otis Music Camp. In Episode 8 of the *Parenting Musically* podcast, Justin confirmed the long-lasting impact of providing teens with instruction, tools, and space to express themselves creatively through music: "When kids get to have the opportunity to create on their own, and create whatever they want without any limitations, it gives out a much better product. And the kids have more and more self-confidence as they go forward in their life and school and their career." ▶

ACTIVITY 35   Hand Orchestra Thunderstorm

The hand orchestra thunderstorm is a favorite activity in the general music class, and it can transfer nicely to family life—even during an actual thunderstorm, with the power out! Start by exploring what sounds you can make with your hands that can fit with a thunderstorm (snap, clap, pat legs, thump table). Assign each sound a letter or symbol and draw a musical map on a piece of paper.

Take turns as a family deciding what sound comes next, whether it is soft, medium, loud, super loud, etc., and whether it stays the same volume or changes (volume is shown by moving up and down on the paper). After you have created it together, take turns being the "conductor" by following along on the map

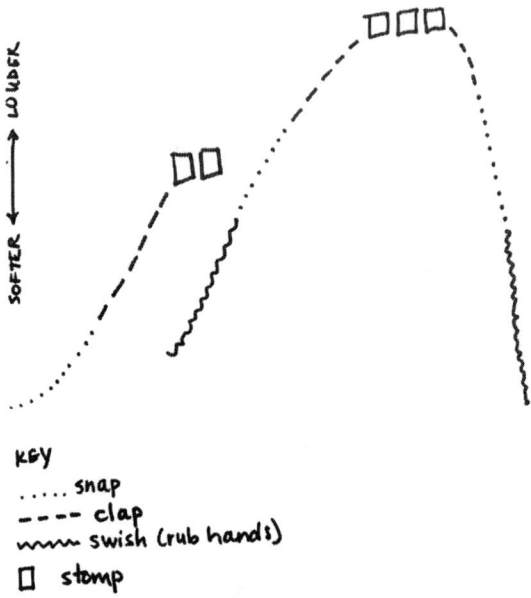

FIGURE 11.2 Example of "Hand Thunderstorm" notation

while the family performs the thunderstorm. The conductor can decide how fast to go, or even whether to start at the end and perform it backward. If you are focusing on certain musical skills or content in your musical parenting, such as musical symbols for dynamics, try weaving it into the activity.

ACTIVITY 36   ABA Composition

One early composition lesson I taught my general music students was to compose a piece in "ABA" form. This means you create one section, then an alternating section, followed by repeating the first section. An example of this is any song with a chorus, a verse, then a return to the chorus. You could create an ABA composition with playground instruments like this:

- "Let's make a song! What should it be about?" *-Get ideas from your child*
- "Super, dinosaurs. What kind of dinosaurs should the first part be about? . . . Velociraptor, great! What would the velociraptor music

sound like?" -*Explore together, then settle into something you can recall later*
- "What's another kind of dinosaur, one that's really different from a velociraptor? . . . T Rex, okay!"—*Repeat exploration and decision*
- "What if we play the Velociraptor music, then T-Rex, then Velociraptor again?"—*You can also make up a story together for what is happening that would create this situation in dinosaur world*
- "Let's play the whole thing! Do you want us to make a video of it?"

As you can see, this has much more structure than a typical afternoon at the playground. When my kids were preschoolers, I found it helpful to have these types of formulas to help guide our playground time. I wanted to stay engaged with my children but found some structure necessary. As you play with the ideas you will find your own approaches and structures.

ACTIVITY 37   Rhythm Round

Maybe because I used to teach elementary music and maybe because I have four kids of my own, I admit to doing the "teacher clap" to get my family's attention sometimes—the "long long short short long" clap that they echo to show they are listening. Here's a game you can play starting with that idea but then heading almost anywhere.

The leader claps, stomps, chants, or otherwise creates a four-beat pattern (like "long long short short long"). Everyone else repeats the pattern, but meanwhile the leader is demonstrating the next four-beat pattern—so everyone has to stay on their toes! This can continue until someone else wants to be the leader. It is the type of activity you could learn as a family at home, and then turn to in situations of waiting, such as waiting in line at an outdoor restaurant.

Creating these four beat patterns might not seem like "musical creativity" compared to writing a song or a piece of instrumental music. However, playing with the building blocks of music is an important step along the way to improvisation and composition.

Producing Music

My friend's teenage son grew up playing the violin, singing at home, and hearing his parents engage in community music. He still plays the violin but now his primary musical interest is in "producing music." This term here refers to using technology, including recording technology and software, to create, manipulate, and record music, sometimes using pre-existing sources. My friend's son has a laptop, small digital keyboard, MIDI controller, and two-channel audio interface for incorporating electric guitar and electric violin. Using the Garage Band software on a Mac iPad and laptop, he learned to make beats, compose, and incorporate electric instruments by watching YouTube tutorials, experimenting, and learning from his dad.

Some schools include music production as a music class or career tech elective. Dr. David Thompson, founding instructor of Career Tech Music Production at GlenOak High School in Plain Township, Ohio, noted that the equipment needs for music production have streamlined in the last 20 years. Now teens can produce their own music starting with just a smart phone or tablet and apps like Garage Band, Soundtrap, and BandLab. As their interest and expertise grow, they can add a plug-in keyboard or microphone.[7]

ACTIVITY 38 Create Loops

Loops are repeated musical fragments, usually quite short. They are extensively used in hip-hop music as well as in other musical genres. Loops can have multiple tracks, creating a layered sound. Working with loops together as a family can be a fun activity that you do using an app on your phone while waiting to pick someone up at school or while traveling in the car. It is also something you can do asynchronously and even long-distance—grandparents could contribute a track to the loop, adding relational musicking to the mix. Once you have your loop, you could use it as a ringtone or as part of a larger project. Search for "app for making music loops" to find online resources, many of which are free, or check the apps below:

- Chrome Music Lab (https://musiclab.chromeexperiments.com/)—includes many fun musical play activities; try "Rhythm" or "Melody Maker" for creating loops
- Garage Band (free download for iOS)—search for a tutorial on how to use loops
- BandLab (free download for Android or iOS)—includes a collaboration option
- Scratch Music Projects —Dr. Andrew R. Brown and Dr. S. Alex Ruthmann's book *Scratch Music Projects* (Oxford University Press, 2020)[8] includes project descriptions with an accompanying website with examples. Use the child-friendly computer programming language Scratch to create music

ACTIVITY 39   Song-Writing

Depending on your children's ages, writing a song can be something you do as a joint project or more of a side-by-side activity as they grow older, with your child writing one song and you writing a separate one. There are many apps and programs that can help—do an Internet search for "song writing" or "song writing apps" and check for lists of apps with reviews. Online notation software like flat.io or Noteflight may be useful if you would like to have music notation for your composition.

If you are writing a song with a younger child, listen for a little melody they sing while playing. With their permission, take that melody as an idea and expand it—repeat it at the same pitch or up or down a little; sing the melody backward, slower, or faster. Sing one phrase, then wait for your child to fill in the next musical idea. Try not to let your grown-up ears dictate how and where the music will go. It is common for younger children to create songs with shifting beat patterns and start in one key and end in another.

Middle- and high-school children might prefer to write their own songs, but they could be encouraged to see you as a grown-up also creating a song. You could start by taking a known chord progression (Google "Singer-Songwriter Chord Progression" for examples and tutorials). Improvise a tune, gradually settle into the notes you like, and add lyrics. If you play an instrument, try playing and singing your composition.

Remember to consider the value of musical creativity. You or your child may never share your musical composition outside of your family, although you might. For many of us, the expressive and creative act is more valuable than the product. If you are a perfectionist or have a harsh inner critic, keep reminding yourself and your child that the creative musical journey itself holds growth and joy. And if you end up singing your songs at your child's life events and celebrations, that's wonderful, too.

The Importance of Modeling

Being a model in musicking for your child is important for each of the activity categories in this section of the book: singing, listening, playing instruments, dancing, and creating. Providing a model of musical creativity is especially important because, in many cases, children may not have "everyday" models of musical creativity. They can perceive music to be something that someone else creates, like Billie Eilish or the Beatles or Bach. However, you can show the children in your life that everyone can be musically creative by doing it yourself.

Music educator Dr. Edwin E. Gordon pointed out that children can learn music in the same way they learn language: by listening, then speaking (or singing), followed by reading, then writing.[9] When speaking/singing, children put words together into their own phrases and sentences. We would never limit our children to saying sentences that had already been created.[10] Likewise, why would we ask them to only play the piano songs from their piano book or to only sing known songs?

ACTIVITY 40   Creating Digital Gifts for Family Members

I recently saw a friend post on our neighborhood page, "Does anyone know a service that could help me make a video with a soundtrack for my parents' 50th anniversary using a set of photos and home movies?" Several people commented with local business recommendations, but the comment that caught my eye was, "Literally any teenager with a phone can do this." I have seen elementary aged children play with apps like iMovie to combine video clips and photos and add soundtracks. The soundtracks could be pre-recorded music or music of their own creation.

For this activity, think together as a family about a digital project that would make a thoughtful gift for a family member. This could mean collecting and digitizing photos or home movies, soliciting recorded tributes from friends and family members for a milestone birthday or anniversary, or producing and filming a short skit. Teenagers can then use iMovie or similar apps to combine, splice, and arrange the materials, as well as add music.

Choosing music can bring a relational musicking element to the project. Do we know what Grandpa's favorite bands were when he was growing up? What music does Grandma associate with her young adulthood? The finished product can be shared directly from the app in which it was created or published to an unlisted YouTube link. Additional ideas for digital gifts are composing and recording a song, recording a cover song, and creating a special playlist for a loved one. You could also complete this activity as a gift to yourselves to remember a special summer vacation or a "day in the life of our family."

WRAPPING UP CHAPTER 11

In this chapter, I encouraged families to think about musical creativity as something children naturally do. Sometimes children lose or hide this creative impulse, especially if they are told to keep silent or to only play what is on the music page. Retaining or regaining musical creativity can bring musical and expressive benefits. Provide a creative musical model for your child by making up little songs for family routines, experimenting with music technology together, or creating with found sounds.

FOR FURTHER READING

Pretend Play in Childhood: Foundation of Adult Creativity, by Sandra Russ (American Psychological Association, 2013): explores the links between play and creativity.

Music Learning Today: Digital Pedagogy for Creating, Performing, and Responding to Music (2nd ed,), by William I. Bauer (Oxford University Press, 2020): provides many examples of how to use music technology to create music. This is written for teachers and could be valuable for families as well.

PART 1
MUSIC IS IMPORTANT

PART 2
MANY WAYS TO BE MUSICAL

PART 3
ALL HUMANS ARE MUSICAL

PART 4
EXPRESSING AGENCY AS
A FAMILY WITH MUSIC

Part 3 is intended to be read on a need-to-know basis, with you as reader dipping into chapters based on the age of the children in your life. Each chapter focuses on a specific age group and includes an overview of musical development for that age group, key information related to development, and several activity suggestions. The information helps contribute to the aim of increasing family members' agency in interacting with structures that govern children's musical activities (school and community settings). Much of this content is connected to the chapters in other sections of the book. Check out the "Children are Musical!" chart in the appendix at the end of the book for more information on milestones and suggested activities for each age group.

Evaluating Research

Before we jump into the "ages and stages," I'd like to share a brief guide on how to evaluate authors' use of research. You have probably heard reference to research studies that show music affects the brain. Not every research study that is published contains results that are generalizable (apply to a wide part of the population). Some published research studies are pilot studies. These are important to the overall development of the topic but are not intended to be shared widely starting with "Research tells us . . ."

When reading an article or social media post that refers to research, watch for how the author includes the specifics of the research study. Does the author write something like "In a study with 74 participants . . ." or "The results did include some conflicting information, however"? Those phrases suggest a deeper understanding on the part of the reporter. A shallower reporting can look like this: "Studies show music helps kids _____" with no explanation of the study method or results.

It is common for researchers to do studies that result in findings that contradict their own earlier studies or disagree with findings of researchers who have done similar studies. This is not a bad thing. It shows that we are learning and gaining a better understanding. Often the researcher will write about why those differences may have occurred—maybe the first study was done with one age group and the second with another.

Students in research classes learn the concept "correlation does not imply causation." This means that if a researcher finds a correlation (relationship) between two factors, it does not mean that one causes the other. Often there is a third factor at play. For example, research that seems to show that band students have higher SAT scores is correlational. We do not know that it was the music that helped with the SAT scores. It could be that the band students happen to also have caregivers who read out loud to them more as children, and that influenced the SAT scores as well as the decision to be in band. If you read something that claims music participation impacts other areas of development, check to be sure it is not a correlational study. There are other research study designs that seek to establish causal relationships through experiments with multiple groups and different treatment conditions.

Remember that researchers approach the topic of music and childhood development from many angles and disciplines: music perception, music education, music therapy, psychology, pediatrics, and education, to name a few. Watch for why authors are using research. Are they using research to sell you a product (musical toy) or a learning program? Ask extra questions in these situations.

When it comes to research, be a skeptic. Don't take my word for it when I share research studies in the coming chapters. Google the researcher and find out more about them. If you have access to the article, read the abstract. But more important, be a researcher yourself.

There are many interesting research studies related to children and music. For instance, several researchers found that fussy children calmed down more when their mothers sang upbeat play songs than when they sang lullabies.[1] This experiment occurred in a laboratory. Try it with your child—if they bump their head, does a lively song help calm them more than a soothing lullaby? Does it depend on whether your child was content or fussy before the injury occurred? Does one thing work for you but something different work for your partner? Test out the research results you read.

CHAPTER 12

MUSIC BEFORE BIRTH

> **CHAPTER PREVIEW**
> - The most important aspect of music in the prenatal period is how parents use music for their own relaxation and enjoyment.
> - Fetuses can hear beginning at 27–29 weeks gestation, and babies recognize the music and sounds they heard in utero for several months after birth.
> - Activities such as creating playlists and connecting with role models are ways to prepare for parenting musically.

Overview of Musical Development in Utero

A fetus can hear sounds coming from outside the womb starting at 27 to 29 weeks gestation. Researchers have explored whether fetuses respond to music in the womb through movement, with some researchers noting a link between fetal movement and music.[1] You might notice that your baby responds to specific types of music or sounds. I remember my third child dancing exuberantly in the womb when we went to a jazz club a few weeks before he was born. There is no research that these exposures have any lasting effects, but they may be interesting for you to notice.

Music can play an important role during pregnancy on parents' health. Research is clear that listening to music can help reduce stress. Focus any attention to music during pregnancy on using music for yourself—for stress reduction, relaxation, and enjoyment.

Will Your Baby Be Smarter if You Play Classical Music Before They Are Born?

One of the participants in my research study for the book *Parenting Musically* told me she felt guilty that she hadn't played classical music while she was pregnant with her children. "I know that probably would have helped," she said. I was glad to share the news that there is no research evidence that playing classical music for unborn children has a lasting impact on their development or learning.

Researchers have found that newborns seem to recognize the voices, music, and sounds they heard before birth. But there is no indication that one style or genre is better than another. My advice is to listen to the music you enjoy while you are expecting. Sing lullabies and other songs to your child before birth.

Some of the research done on music and the brain in the past has since been disproven or debunked. This includes the Mozart Effect, or the theory that listening to classical music will help children to do better at math or spatial awareness activities. There is, however, a growing body of substantiated research that indicates musical experiences and musical training affect the brain. This body of research is discussed in Chapter 17. However, these studies do not currently include fetuses.

ACTIVITY 41   Your Music Playlist

If you do not already have your own music playlist, make one, or ask someone to make a playlist for you. You can decide what would be most useful or have multiple lists. Here are some ideas:

- Songs you love that you want to listen to for fun,
- Upbeat songs to help you have the energy to care for your child in the middle of the night,
- Songs you find comforting to help keep you calm when your baby is crying,
- Heroic songs to remind you that you are doing hard things and getting them done,

- Songs that help you get back to sleep in the middle of the night after being up with your baby.

We live near a high school and one day I heard the marching band playing a John Williams medley (*Star Wars, Jurassic Park*, etc.) as I took out the garbage. It was a lovely moment of affirmation for me to hear the heroic music playing as I completed the heroic tasks of family care that morning.

ACTIVITY 42   Look for Role Models

As expectant parents or as soon-to-be aunts, uncles, or friends of a new baby, you have probably already noticed some caregivers who interact with their children the way you would like to interact with your coming baby. Take some time to identify role models—they could be parents at the park, work friends, or neighbors. Don't stare, but observe some of the ways they relate to their child. Do they have certain phrases they use? Ways of talking to their child?

You can find role models who are childcare teachers, librarians, and folks who are not parents as well. Watch for people who treat children the way you want to treat your child. Write down the phrases you hear them use or the ways you see them interact. Once I was at the church nursery and I saw a mom telling her preschooler it was time to go, but he didn't want to leave. "Let's be ninjas and go find your brother!" she whispered. She took her son's hand, and they snuck off together. I remembered and reflected on that moment and sought to imitate her playful and engaged approach.

How do your role models interact musically with the children in their lives? Do you notice adults singing to the babies they are holding? Dancing with toddlers at the grocery store? Introducing their preschoolers to new music each week while driving to school?

Community and family elders can be wonderful role models when it comes to parenting musically. Ask your relatives what songs they remember from childhood or what ways they incorporated music into their family life. Make recordings of songs relatives sing that you can play for your baby. Ask elders how they used music to get through the day with young children.

Shortcuts for Busy Expectant Parents

My mom jokes that before my younger brother was born, she did every chore and project around the house she could think of because she assumed she would not have time to do so again for years. If you are feeling that way about projects, ignore this paragraph. If you happen to have a little time or energy for reading, check out chapters 5, 13, and 18 of this book. In chapter 5 you'll consider the role grandparents and extra adults play in your child's musical life. This is a good time to think of the ways to connect with these important people. Chapter 13 provides an overview of musical development in the first year, along with musical activities for you and your baby. In chapter 18, you can read about participating in an early childhood music class. If that's something that appeals to you, you could look around at classes or even visit one you are interested in if that is permitted.

WRAPPING UP CHAPTER 12

This is the shortest chapter in Part 3, in part because there is no need to add anything to your to-do list as an expectant parent. The activity suggestions provide a few ideas of things you could do if you have extra time leading up to your child's birth. Most important, take good care of yourself.

FOR FURTHER READING

Baby 411, by Ari Brown and Denise Fields (Windsor Peak Press, 2022): This is not a music-related book, but this is the book I wished I had read a month or two before my first child was born.

CHAPTER 13

CONNECTING WITH YOUR INFANT THROUGH MUSIC (BIRTH TO 12 MONTHS)

CHAPTER PREVIEW

- During infancy, babies are capable of musical responses.
- It is vital that parents and caregivers sing with their babies during this time period.
- Back-and-forth musical exchanges, as informal as cooing, build connections between caregivers and babies, and also facilitate early verbal experience and development.
- Music can help make many of the tasks of infant care easier and more fun for children and adults.
- Practice incorporating music into routines when you are calm so you can easily use music when you are stressed.

Overview of Musical Development, Birth to 12 Months

> What are you noticing about your baby and music? Does your baby like to hear you sing certain songs? Make sounds while you are singing? Bounce to music?

Take a look at the "Children Are Musical!" chart in the appendix for an overview of milestones and suggested activities for newborns through

12-month-olds. The first recommendation is to sing to your baby! Sing lullabies, play-songs, and anything you enjoy. Lullaby singing and communicating with your infant using a high, sing-song voice is universal across cultures with good reason.[1] These interactions can soothe a crying child, aid in child-parent attachment, decrease parent stress, provide an enjoyable interaction, and contribute to your child's brain development.

Babies can make many vocal sounds when they are born. Many of these sounds can be classified as singing. Babies can respond to adults or children singing to them by cooing or "aaaaahing" in the spaces between lines of a song. All of this serves an essential bonding function with parents, as described in the section below on "Communicative Musicality."

I enjoyed noticing when my children were able to make new sounds as they progressed through the first 12 months and beyond. When you sing or babble with your baby, think about using a wide range of sounds and syllables—ba, pa, ka, da, ma, choo, zing, fee, etc. Try a new sound and then watch for how your child responds. Sometimes you could sing a song using a repeated syllable rather than the lyrics. This can make it easier for your child to sing along or respond to the song ▶.

In the first few months, babies are especially soothed by voices and sounds they heard while in utero. It might surprise you to notice that a barking dog or sibling practicing violin does not wake your baby in the first few months. This also holds for music the baby heard while in utero. People may laugh about playing rap for a newborn, but anything the baby heard can be soothing in the first few months. There is not conclusive research about when this effect goes away. You can monitor your child and notice whether the things that were soothing early on continue to be.

Before your child can move on their own, move with them! Move while holding your child in your arms or while wearing them in a baby carrier. Dance to music while holding your child. Try various movements while soothing a crying child—does your child prefer gentle bouncing? Spinning? Slow rocking?

When your baby is around two to four months, try wrist rattles or sock rattles. Put on some music, dance in view of your child, and see if they respond with their own arm or foot movement. Around this time your child might bounce to music while you hold them upright on your lap, their feet resting on your legs. Another way your child can dance is while strapped in the car seat—you might notice arms and legs moving along with music!

In addition to rattles, you could try enclosed jingle bells, large shakers, and drums as your child moves through the first year. Remember to assess any potential toy or instrument to prevent introducing a choking hazard. Some instruments are designed especially for children. As a parent, be cautious even if it is clearly intended for children. I always hid the soft foam drum mallets because my children liked to chew on them and could have ripped some foam off.

If possible, play a wide range of music for your infant during the first 12 months. Music researchers Dr. Sandra D. Trehub and Dr. Franziska Degé described infants as "musical connoisseurs."[2] They noted that infants are highly interested in music, can discern slight differences in pitches and rhythms, and can remember music. In Episode 11 of the *Parenting Musically* podcast, singer-songwriter Chelsea Crowell and her father Rodney Crowell, also a singer-songwriter, described their excitement and interest in discovering what kind of music Chelsea's newborn daughter responded to: "It is also about curiosity. . . . 'Oh, are you gonna like this Everly Brothers song?' And then, [watching] the look on her face, is she dancing along? You're going through all this music that you love and seeing what she loves." ⏵. This conversation on the podcast provides an account of the joy family members can experience while sharing music with an infant.[3]

Communicative Musicality

There is a sub-field within the research of infant development called "communicative musicality." This term refers to a theory that intuitive parent-child communication from the earliest moments is musical in nature.[4] This communication could take the form of "motherese" or "parentese," referring to the way people speak in a higher and slower voice to young children. (Some also do this with small pets—"What a good doggie!!!") Infant-directed speech is found in cultures across the globe.[5] Researchers think this intuitive inclination to speak to babies with a higher voice and slower rhythm helps babies to learn language. Communicative musicality also includes echoing sounds (musical babble) between baby and caregiver.

It's valuable to know about the idea of communicative musicality because it reinforces the importance of singing to and with your newborn, as well as cooing and babbling. Make eye contact and sing. Sing anything! Sing songs from your own childhood, songs you make up, and your favorite songs from current artists. Sing, and sometimes pause. At first, your child will probably just listen, maybe with their mouth open, and gaze. But soon your child will coo and sing back in those pauses. This back-and-forth is called "serve and return" (think of a tennis ball).[6] It is a building block of social development.

Music and Your Child's Brain

Researchers are excited to find out how musical experiences affect a child's brain development. If this is an area that interests you, check out *The Music Advantage* (Dr. Anita Collins, Allen & Unwin, 2020) and *The Child as Musician* (Dr. Gary McPherson, editor, Oxford University Press, 2016). Both books are full of carefully documented research studies to provide context on the work that has been done and the work researchers are continuing.

Research studies with babies as young as two days old, as well as with older infants, suggest that music exposure and engagement positively impacts children's language learning. Studies have focused both on the melodic nature of music and the rhythmic components, with positive results in both categories. Another study found that singing to infants is common across demographic groups, but that parents sing less as their children grow older.[7] It is beneficial to keep singing to your children and with your children as they grow.

An additional group of recent research studies focuses on the social effects of musicking with infants. Researchers have found that infants assign social meaning to music[8] and learn early socialization skills through music.[9] In one study, 14-month-olds who moved to the beat with adults were more helpful in a research response task.[10] Researchers have also documented that children learn musical knowledge and skills through exposure to music—of course![11]

While there is a large body of research on music and the brain, there is still much to be understood. For instance, a recent study proposed a model for understanding the connections between how the brain processes rhythm in speech and music.[12] The authors noted that researchers are aware of the connections but have not yet determined the mechanism for the connections.

ACTIVITY 43 Set Up a Digital Keepsake Account

I spent hours choosing a baby book for our first child. I went so far as to make a chart comparing the features of the seven baby books I was considering. So far, I've filled out about half of it, and even less for the subsequent children. While we were in the hospital for the birth of my youngest child, my then nine-year-old wrote in his baby book, so that's a start.

Clearly, I'm not doing great with filling out the baby books, although I have high hopes of finishing them all, along with decades of photo albums, when I retire. I have all the data! Photos, videos, school papers sorted by child, sweet pictures they drew, pages filled with stars the day they learned to draw stars. I've even kept journals for each child sporadically with notes about what's new, what they're excited about, and milestones.

Although I haven't kept up with the baby books the way I imagined, one thing I started that I'm very happy about is that I set up an email address for each child with the word or idea keepsake in it (e.g. child1.keepsakes@gmail.com). I send photos and videos to these "keepsake" accounts for my kids any time there's something especially cute or memorable. Sometimes it's just a quick email with a funny thing they said. It's never too late to set this up. You can always go back through your videos and send the files to the account.

A digital keepsake account is a flexible way to store musical memories of your child through the years. From cooing as an infant to bopping as a toddler, through little songs they make up, and on into older childhood, having these musical moments organized will provide a meaningful set of memories. For longer videos of musicking, you could upload those to an unlisted YouTube link paired with the email account or use media storage platforms like Google photos. See Activity 21, "Create an 'Audio Photo Album'" in Chapter 7, for additional suggestions.

Music in Routines with Infants

There are many repetitive tasks when caring for an infant, and music can make these tasks easier, more pleasant, or more enjoyable.

Music for soothing. When your baby is crying, try soothing them with music. This could be you singing, humming, or rapping. You could also try various types of recorded music. Remember, in the first few months, babies tend to be soothed by music and voices they heard while in utero.

Music for feeding. Some babies enjoy hearing sung music while they are feeding (nursing or bottle feeding), but others may be distracted by it, especially as they grow older. When your baby is ready to try solid foods, playing recorded music can be a way to set an enjoyable atmosphere.

Music for diapering. You will be spending a lot of time with your child at the diaper table over the next few years. Build up a repertoire of songs and chants (rhythmic speech) to engage your child. If your baby is tired or fussy, they may not want to have their diaper changed. Having a few of their favorite songs in mind can help in a tense situation. Making up songs or chants about the steps of diapering and dressing can bring a little silliness to the tasks. Having a diapering and dressing routine that includes music can also be useful when outside the home. Even though your baby is in a different location, hearing the same song could provide comfort.

Music for bathing. Bath time is also a great time for singing! You can learn some bath time songs by looking through books at the library or looking online. Changing words to known tunes is also a fun source for bath time songs. For instance, using the song "If You're Happy and You Know It," change the words "clap your hands" to "wash your tummy" or "scrub your toes." Naming parts of the body is a way to introduce those words to your baby from an early age.

Music for traveling. Traveling with an infant can be stressful for everyone. If you are traveling in the car, keep a playlist of the songs that are most enjoyable and those that are most soothing for your infant. Vary the music based on your baby's mood. Sing out loud to your child. While having musical babble conversations together, leave room for your child to respond.

Music for playing. Sometimes all of the care activities of a baby, especially if you have older children, are all-consuming. Yet it is wonderful to take the time to play with your baby! Listen to various music with your baby and keep track of their responses to different styles and genres. Try the hide and seek and "a-choo" games described in the following activities. Play

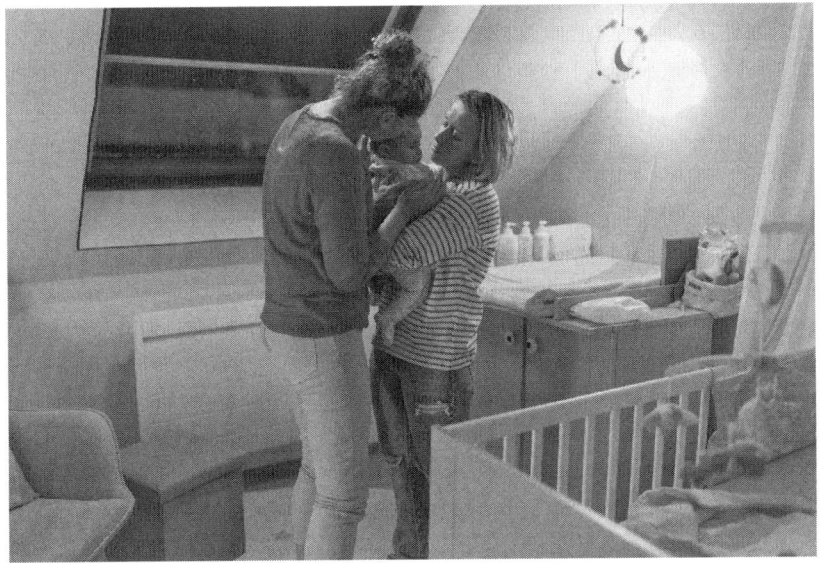

FIGURE 13.1 Mothers calming their infant during the night. GETTY IMAGES

move and freeze games while holding your infant, moving in various ways. Have a living room dance party.

ACTIVITY 44 ⏵ "Where's _____?"

Using chiffon scarves, bandanas, or lightweight cloth napkins, cover a part of your head and your infant's head. Be sure not to cover their mouth or nose. Sway side to side while singing a song. At the end, sing "Where's _____" (your child's name).[13] Pause, take a surprised breath, and sweep the scarf off your child's head. Sing "There's _____!" When we do this in class, we sing the "Where's" on the fifth note of the scale (dominant) and the name on the first note of the scale (tonic or home tone). Repeat this with your own name. As your child gets older, lean over so they can pull the scarf off your head. This music game can be played via video calls with loved ones who are far away. It can be adapted in many ways, including during diaper changes, baths, and in the high chair.

ACTIVITY 45 ▶ "Ah-choo!"

Balance a small beanbag or small stuffed animal on your head. Move smoothly so the item does not fall off while you sing a favorite song. At the end of the song, pause, then sing "Ah-choo!" In class we do this on the fifth and first scale degree as explained in Activity 44. Extend the "Ahhhhhhhh" longer, pause, and then sing the "choo." With younger infants, they may just watch you. As they get older, hold the beanbag on their head as you move with them, followed by the Ah-choo. As your infant is able to sit independently, try putting the beanbag on their head. At some point your child will be able to time the Ah-choo themselves by deciding when to drop the beanbag and will delight in controlling your voice to respond! You will see a sparkle in your child's eye as they make you hold the "Ahhhhhhhh" longer and longer, then finally tip the beanbag off their head for the "choo." Soon your child will be able to join in with singing the Ah-choo.

Please note, the scarves and beanbags are not toys for your infant and should not be used by your child unattended. Instead, they are props to guide some of the ways you can do music activities with your little one.

Music to Care for Yourself as a New Parent or Caregiver

Most new parents I've talked with agree that having and caring for a new baby can be wonderful but can also be exhausting, isolating, and anxiety-provoking. You can use music to care for yourself as the parent or caregiver to a new child—and any time in your parenting or caring journey! Taking care of yourself makes you a better parent.

You may already have playlists of music you love and music you use in various situations. Listening to music can help regulate emotions and connect interpersonally with those with whom you share listening.[14] This emotional regulation can include feeling an emotion more deeply, redirecting to a different emotion, redirecting away from worries.[15] Listening to music can also help increase your energy if you are tired or help you wind down if it is time to rest.[16] As you are up at night to feed your child, consider listening to music rather than a podcast, audio book, or TV, at least part of the time. Listening to music offers potential benefits to you not found in other media listed, as well as to your infant "musical connoisseur."[17]

If your baby is crying and you find yourself getting tense, try singing. Sing anything! Hum low in your range or sing out a tune or rap. Make up new words if you like. Your singing is a natural way to connect with your baby and to soothe them. Importantly, it is also a good way to help you as the parent or caregiver to relax and de-stress.

Traveling with an infant, both around town and for longer trips, can also be stressful. This is another important time to listen to music, both to calm your child and to calm yourself. Choose music that you like. It's important for infants to hear a wide range of styles and genres, so let the time in the car be with music that is most relaxing or enjoyable to you as the parent. Also try singing for your child unaccompanied. I remember when my daughter was crying in the back seat and I was driving, hearing me sing comforted her more than hearing recorded music. It also helped me to stay calm and feel like I was offering something directly to her, even when I couldn't reach back to her.

Music and Relationships with Infants

Communicative musicality highlights the relational role of back-and-forth vocalizations between parents or caregivers and infants. Additional forms of musicking are a good way for additional individuals to interact with your baby. If someone is rocking your child, ask if they would sing one of their favorite songs to your baby. If there are young children nearby, like siblings or cousins, you could ask them to dance for your baby while you are holding your infant. We were with an infant recently who was completely captivated by watching my daughter Julia tap dance! As your infant gets older, you could invite children to play alongside your infant with musical toys or props. Older siblings and cousins could play their instruments for an infant. This can be a moment of pride for the older child.

Music can also help connect your infant with relatives and friends who live farther away. Ask grandparents to record themselves singing lullabies and play songs to your baby that you can put on a playlist. Have them sing these same songs to your infant during video calls to build relational connections. Try the "Where's _____?" game (described earlier in this chapter) via video call. Ask your loved ones to get books from the library that can be sung, such as "What a Wonderful World" (illustrated by Ashley Bryan) or "I Love You Too" by Ziggy Marley. Have a long-distance dance party via video call.

Perhaps you will take your infant along to worship services or community events with music. Watch for how your child is reacting. If they show signs of distress, move farther away from the music source or wait for a different opportunity. If they show signs of interest, watch for an "audiation stare."[18] When infants are absorbing new information or music, they often stare at the source with an open mouth, as though they will take in the sounds and sights through their mouth as well as eyes and ears. This is developmentally appropriate and a wonderful sign that your infant is absorbed in learning.

Musical Toys

There are many toys, swings, bouncers, activity centers, mobiles, and more for infants that feature built-in music! If possible, read reviews of the sound quality online or listen to the music before you buy a musical toy. Choose something that will not annoy you. Listen to how "real" the music sounds (rather than tinny or like a toy from two decades ago) and how much variety of music is included with the toy. If the toy or object gives you the choice of choosing the music yourself or recording your own voice singing to your child, all the better. Also remember you have the option to not put batteries in the toy or object if you like it generally but don't like the music. Low-tech toys like rattles, shakers, and drums are ideal for infant play and exploration.

WRAPPING UP CHAPTER 13

Your baby's first 12 months are a time of unparalleled growth and development in every domain. This is a time of great growth for you as a parent or caregiver as well. Infants have remarkable music perception and response abilities, far beyond what many people would guess. Music is a vital part of an infant's life both for the musical learning and the other benefits. Use music as a tool during any part of your day and night with your infant. Remember that music is important for the adults, too, particularly in helping you relax or stay connected to your own musical enjoyment.

FOR FURTHER READING

The Musical Child, by Joan Koenig (Houghton Mifflin Harcourt, 2021): The author draws on her work at a musical preschool in Paris to share overview and activities for children age birth to 6. The book includes links to supplemental audio recordings and explanations of the activities.

Mom Brain: Proven Strategies to Fight the Anxiety, Guilt, and Overwhelming Emotions of Motherhood—and Relax into Your New Self, by Ilyse Dobrow DiMarco (Guilford Press, 2021): This book is not about music, but it may be a useful resource as you transition into the role of parent.

Roots and Branches: A Legacy of Multicultural Music for Children, by Patricia Shehan Campbell, Ellen McCullough-Brabson, and Judith Cook Tucker (World Music Press, 1994): This book and CD set include 38 songs and singing games. Each is recorded by a member of the culture from which the song comes, and the authors share childhood pictures and stories from the artists as well.

CHAPTER 14

MUSICKING THROUGH THE DAY WITH TODDLERS (AGES 12 TO 36 MONTHS)

CHAPTER PREVIEW

- Rapid growth and development are hallmarks of the toddler years.
- Listen for the "little songs" your toddler sings.
- Enjoy playing with your toddler using music.
- Connecting with your toddler through music can help your toddler form a secure attachment, which is essential to healthy growth and flourishing.
- Be aware of the ways you can use music to help your child develop and express themselves musically (musical parenting), as well as how you can use music to accomplish non-musical tasks (parenting musically).

What delights your toddler when it comes to music? What delights you about interacting with your toddler and music?

Overview of Musical Development, 12 to 36 Months

The toddler years are full of fun and chaos! During these months children often learn to talk and sing; walk, run, and dance; exert their wills; and learn to be in communities. Check out the "Children Are Musical!" chart in the Appendix at the end of the book for an overview of musical development during the toddler years.

When it comes to singing, toddlers usually speak and sing in a range higher than adults speak. When you sing with your child, try to use this higher range (see Chapter 7 for more information on this range). Sing many different types of songs *with* your child, as well as singing songs *to* your child. Ask family members to share favorite songs as well. Many children's songs from the United States have a similar "sound" (major tonality and duple meter). But it is important for children to hear a wide range of sounds, not just similar-sounding children's songs all the time.

This variety is important in your toddler's music listening as well as their singing. Pay attention to your child's responses to music. One family I worked with for my book, *Parenting Musically*, kept playlists for their children. Starting when the children were old enough to express opinions—during the toddler years—the Murphys allowed their children to be the judges of what went on the playlists. Mom and Dad introduced new music and played it in the car on the way to daycare, checking to see if their kids would ask to hear that music again or how they responded when the music came back on. In this way, their children had input building their playlists.

ACTIVITY 46 Build a Playlist with Your Child

You probably have many of your own playlists already, and maybe you have created playlists for your child as well. For this activity, be intentional in building the playlist with your toddler. Pay close attention to how your toddler responds to various music. Try some new selections, but let your child's response guide you on whether to add the piece to the list.

Your toddler's ability to move and their range of movements will increase exponentially during the toddler years. They will be able to bounce, rock, and wave with music. You'll also see them learn to jump! It is delightful to watch the face of a toddler who achieves lift-off in a jump after many attempts when their feet do not leave the ground. Toddlers can spin, stomp, tiptoe, fly (zoom around with arms extended), and do many other types of movements. As a parent or caregiver, have fun exploring these movements with your child. This could occur during playtime. Pretend to be different sizes of dinosaurs. How do the movements differ? Try pretending to move through different types of substances (swimming, moving through mud, moving on Mars, etc.). Using specific movement can also be a fun way to motivate a toddler to complete a transition. For instance, "Let's see how many jumps it takes us to get over to our shoes!" or "Do you want to tiptoe or stomp from the door to the van?" Creative, intentional movement is a form of musicking. Enjoy moving without music as well as when music is added.

Do not judge or evaluate your toddler's musicking. Most toddlers do not sing in tune or keep a steady beat. During the toddler years, enjoy your child's musical expressions. There is no benefit in pushing your child to be able to play a steady beat or sing in tune. Children move through the steps toward singing in tune and moving to a steady beat naturally as they explore musical ideas and engage in musical play.[1]

There are many musical instruments toddlers enjoy playing. They can drum bowls, pots and pans, and real drums with hands or mallets. Toddlers can shake maracas and homemade shakers. With supervision, toddlers enjoy playing rhythm sticks (or wooden dowels or other sticks). Toddlers love to explore instruments like ukuleles and guitars. Ukuleles are less expensive than guitars and are a good size for toddlers. You can find tutorials on YouTube for learning chords yourself, then seat your child in your lap while you create the chords with your left hand and your child strums the ukulele. Playing the ukulele may be a prompt for your child to sing "little songs," as described below. If you have access to a xylophone, this is another great instrument for toddlers. Ask your child to play by bouncing their mallets on the xylophone bars, then by sliding the mallets across the bars.

Children love playing pianos and keyboards! Teach your toddler to ask before playing the piano or keyboard if you're are at someone's home. Allow free exploration time so your child can find the low and high notes and discover loud and soft. Hold your child on your lap and say "Let your hands go for a ride on my hands!" With their little hands on your hands, play a song or just try the different ranges yourself.

The toddler years are also an ideal time to encounter instruments close-up and learn a little about how they make sound. If you have a relative, neighbor, or baby-sitter who plays an instrument, ask them to play a little bit for your toddler. Some of my favorite moments teaching early childhood music classes came when my university students visited and played their instruments for the toddlers. Watch for the look of wonder and delight on your toddler's face when they get to see and hear an instrument up close.

ACTIVITY 47   Listen for "Little Songs"

Toddlers engage in spontaneous song throughout their days. Listen for these little songs your child sings. Often, you can hear the little songs while your child is playing independently or riding in the car. You might also hear your child singing in their crib while falling asleep for a nap or at bedtime. Dr. Meryl Sole, a music educator and researcher, studied the vocalizations of children in their cribs between being put down for bed and when they fell asleep. She found that children used this time and sang their little songs to experiment, self-soothe, reflect on their day, and explore ideas.[2]

In order to make up their own spontaneous songs, your child needs to have moments of quiet or silence. Be sure that you do not always have music playing or the television on when your child is awake. Silence can provide an opportunity to process the world and create their own response.

Singing to and with your child will also provide inspiration for their little songs. As they grow older, you may hear fragments of known songs woven into your child's spontaneous songs. Balance repetition and novelty in your singing and music listening with your child. Repetition provides the opportunity to master a song. Novelty gives different musical ideas and opportunities to find new musical favorites.

Now that you are listening for little songs, you'll probably hear them more often. You could enjoy keeping an electronic diary of the spontaneous songs. If possible, audio or video record your child singing a little song and store it with a tag or send it to your child's keepsake email account (see Chapter 13). You and your child will enjoy watching and listening to the little songs in years to come. Some children, however, stop singing when a phone or camera comes out. If that is the case, just enjoy their songs in the moment.

Pay attention to when your child sings their little songs. Is it bedtime? In the car? While playing with trains? As your child grows older, show how you value their spontaneous songs to encourage them to keep singing. Provide the creative conditions they prefer to prolong their expression using spontaneous songs. For many children, these songs begin to disappear around age 7.[3] This doesn't need to happen, though—children can continue to sing their little songs while playing LEGO when they are older children, for example. Nurturing this creativity can lead to a foundation for musical improvisation and composition as children grow.

Connections Between Music and Language

Early childhood music researcher and educator Dr. Edwin Gordon described a useful concept in understanding children's musical development: musical babble. He wrote that musical babble is similar to the language babble that children produce as they are learning to speak.[4] Musical babble is pitched sounds (sung) or rhythmic sounds (chanted or spoken) a child makes as they are exploring their voice and playing with musical ideas. Children often try to echo short sounds they hear from caregivers, at first without accuracy, and later with greater accuracy. We say short words to children, such as "Da-da-da-da-da! Can you say da-da?" We can do that musically by singing or chanting short patterns on syllables like ba or pa, with combinations of long and short sounds ⓘ.

You can provide your child with an opportunity to experience musical babble by modeling musical babble. But you will probably notice that your child engages in musical babble regardless of any prompts! That is because this is a natural part of the language learning process. Children's earliest utterances have musical qualities, such as pitch and rhythm. As your child progresses through the musical babble and begins speaking clearly, you can encourage them to continue to play with sounds and rhythms. This could help their musical development as well as their language development.

Some children in this age group are referred for speech therapy if they are not meeting developmental speech milestones. In addition to resources from your pediatrician or speech therapist, you could consider music therapy. Music therapists are credentialed professionals who work with individuals using music to accomplish non-musical goals. Music therapists have found that musical activities can be used to help children with developmental delays or disabilities meet non-musical goals.[5] In episode 4 of the *Parenting Musically* podcast, GRAMMY-winner Kailani Pèa's mother, Pua, spoke about how she used music to help Kailani overcome his childhood speech impediment.[6] You can hear more of my conversation with Pua Pèa, along with a response from music therapist Claire Morison, in Episode 4 of the *Parenting Musically* Podcast ▶. If you are concerned about your child's verbal development, talk to your pediatrician. Ask about music therapy services in your area.

Put Down Your Phone

And now I have a request, and this is the one guilt-trip in this book. For most of this book, I have tried to remind the readers that you don't need to do it all and not to feel guilty if you don't do this or that. However, put away your phone and take off your headphones when you are with your children. I am talking to myself as much as you here. It is tempting and so much more fun to go through the day with your phone and headphones. You can do laundry and dishes and tidy, take walks, play at the playground, all while staying connected, listening to an audiobook or podcast or talking on the phone. But this disrupts the communicative musicality you develop with your infant, as explained in Chapter 13. It interferes with secure attachment, described in this chapter. In a sobering article entitled "The Dangers of Distracted Parenting" in *The Atlantic,* early childhood educator and author Erika Christakis pronounced today's parenting as the "worst possible model of parenting—we are always present physically, thereby blocking kids' autonomy, yet only fitfully present emotionally."[7] View your phone and wireless headphones as tools that have very good uses but limit your screen time and headphone time when you are around your children. Keep your eyes, ears, and heart open so you can engage with your children responsively.

ACTIVITY 48 ▶ Yoo-hoo!

Here's a fun way to model vocal exploration for your child. When you hear them awaken from a nap and cry or call for you, instead of saying or shouting, "I'm coming!," try sing-songing "Yoo-hoo, [child's name,], I'm coming!" Use a sing-song voice for all of this. When your child becomes familiar with the game, just sing "Yoo-hoo!" on various notes or hold the words out for different lengths of time. Your child might start singing "Yoo-hoo" back to you as you make your way to where they are.

You can also try a "yoo-hoo" while playing hide and seek with your toddler. Hide and seek is a fun game to play with your very young child. When they need a hint as to your hiding place, call out "Yoo-hoo!"

As kids grow older, I've found it helpful to have little games that my children respond to so I know where they are in the house. If I call "Yoo-hoo, Joshua, where are you?," I can get an "In my room!" or "In the basement!" sung back in answer.

Music in Routines with Toddlers

You can continue to use music in routines with toddlers as described in the section on routines with infants. Some new routines that may occur during the toddler years are self-dressing, toileting routines, tidying, and separating from people or objects.

Self-Dressing. Independence is a hallmark of the toddler experience. "Do it myself!" is a frequent refrain of toddlers. Encouraging your toddler to dress themselves encourages independence. Music can help! If a child is resistant or hesitant about getting themselves dressed, try singing new words to the "Hokey Pokey" to encourage your child to get dressed: "You put your first arm in, don't take your first arm out, you put your first arm in, and you shake it all about!"

Learning to independently put on boots, coats, mittens, and more is a long process. Mrs. Kim Tate, an early childhood music teacher and preschool teacher, wrote "Shoes Off," a song for her students so they knew which order to put on their outdoor gear when transitioning from the preschool classroom to outdoor time ▶.[8]

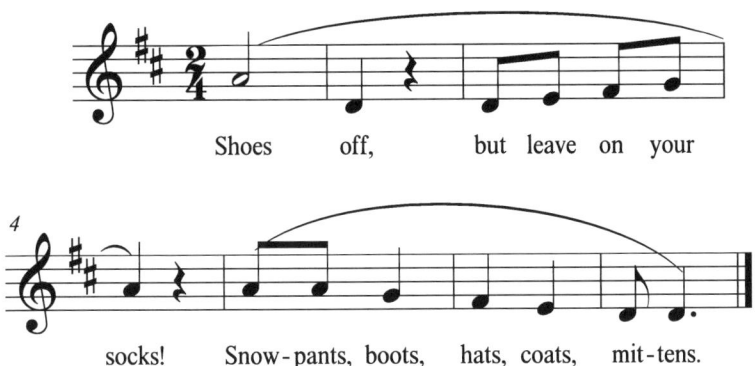

FIGURE 14.1 Shoes Off by Kimberly Tate

You can also try playing recorded music while your child gets dressed. If the goal is independence, eventually it's better if you are not hovering and instructing which item to put on. Having a song playing can help the child stay focused and enjoy the process. You could even have a playlist you use when you help your toddler get dressed, then continue to play the songs when they are dressing themselves.

Toileting Routines. Toilet training can be stressful. One way to incorporate music is to provide a relaxing ambiance for both you and your child. You could create a playlist that includes songs reminding you as the parent to keep things in perspective and that everything is going to be okay (it really will). Toilet training is easier if you can keep your sense of humor, so consider adding some funny songs as well.

There are many little tunes and songs that others have created to help children with the steps of toileting. Search "potty training songs" in YouTube and you will find songs from favorite TV shows and characters. I've heard from many research families that they make up their own potty training songs, and these songs can be the best loved in the end.

Tidying. Toddlers can ransack a room like no one else. You will want to have many ideas in your toolbelt when it comes to tidying. One such tool is a clean-up song. Many people are familiar with the clean-up song from the children's TV show *Barney*. Personally, I get very tired of this song and try to find alternatives, one of which is described below.

ACTIVITY 49 ▸ "Hokey Poky What a Mess" Clean-Up Chant

An alternative tidying chant is "Hokey Poky, What a Mess," a clean-up chant my husband, Jed, wrote for our Music & Movement class when our oldest daughter was a toddler. He spent a lot of time tidying with her and noticed three parts to the cleaning-up process: gathering toys, filling a container, and looking around for what else needed to be tidied. The chant goes like this:

> *Hokey Poky, what a mess! What are we ever gonna do? Hm . . . aha!*
>
> *Gather gather gather, gather gather. Gather gather gather, gather gather.*
>
> *Fill . . . look . . .* (repeat as many times as necessary).

Another idea is to play a recorded song during clean-up time. You can start with a short song for a younger toddler, possibly two minutes. Work up to three or four minutes for an older toddler. The song provides a pleasant soundscape and a sense that the tidying is time-limited.

Separating from people, places, or objects. It can be hard for a toddler to say goodbye to a person, such as a parent at daycare drop-off or a visitor to your home. Leaving places like playgrounds can also be difficult. It can be hard for toddlers to let go of objects, like when it's time to put away a toy. Another challenging situation is when toddlers get their hands on something that is not for them, like a breakable object.

Having a common "goodbye" song may ease the transitions in all of these scenarios. Using it consistently can also help a toddler recognize that transitions are a common part of daily life. We transition toward and away from people, places, and objects within the safety of knowing that Grandma, the playground, and the toy are saying goodbye for now but will be there again soon.

MUSICKING THROUGH THE DAY WITH TODDLERS

ACTIVITY 50 ▶ Goodbye Song

You could make your own goodbye song by writing new words to a known tune. For example, try singing these words to the tune of "Frere Jacques" ("Are You Sleeping?"):

Goodbye _____, goodbye _____. (insert name of person, place, or object – Grandma, playground, magnet blocks . . .)

See you soon! See you soon!

I had so much fun. I had so much fun.

See you soon! See you soon!

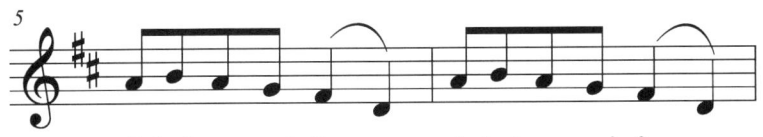

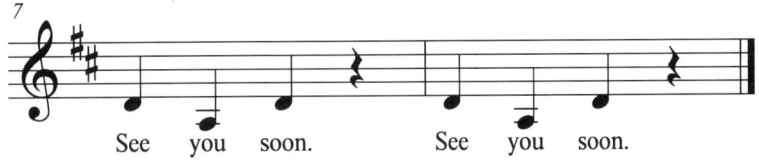

FIGURE 14.2 Goodbye Song tune: Frère Jacques. Folk song lyrics adapted by L. Koops

Choose a tune that your family enjoys and try writing a goodbye song. Be sure to include the idea that you will be back or that we'll have another chance soon.

ACTIVITY 51   "Shake It Off" Boo-Boo Response

As toddlers get up and moving, slight injuries become a daily occurrence. Choose a fun, up-beat song to use when comforting a crying toddler. Researchers Dr. Laura Cirelli and Dr. Sandra Trehub found that babies in distress were more consoled with familiar songs than unfamiliar songs or talking.[9] Dr. Cirelli described the method for this research study in Episode 11 of the *Parenting Musically* podcast ▶.

I used to sing a peppy version of "This Little Light of Mine" to my children when they had minor bumps or falls. In addition to comforting my child and helping me stay calm to evaluate the injury, the song provided a helpful time-based measurement. Usually, my child stopped crying within one or two verses. If it took more than that, it was a signal to me that my child needed something more (ice, a phone call to the pediatrician's nurse on call, etc.).

Music and Relationships with Toddlers

Using music during routines with toddlers is one way to help them form secure attachments. During the toddler years, and throughout childhood, children need secure attachments with the adults who love and care for them. In Episode 3 of the *Parenting Musically* podcast, Dr. Kenitha Roberts, mother of country music star Reyna Roberts, described the ways she used music in parenting Reyna ▶. She incorporated music into parenting to help Reyna address developmental delays associated with Reyna's premature birth. Mother and daughter also connected through listening to a wide range of music in the car and at home for dance parties and karaoke. Responding to Kenitha's and Reyna's story, psychologist and author Dr. Lisa Damour noted their example of secure attachment. Damour explained the importance of attachment as "parents' ability to invest in the child, meet the child where they are, and really try to understand the world as the child would see it. And then try to accommodate that and help growth happen in that framework."[10]

Music can aid in developing these secure attachments. Activities like the back-and-forth exchanges of musical babble described in the last chapter, moving together to music, and singing during daily routines can all contribute to attachment. For children or families who have special physical or emotional needs, music therapy can further help to form these healthy attachments.[11] Music therapists are credentialed professionals who study music, psychology, physiology, and the therapeutic use of music with children and adults. In their work, music therapists support clients in accomplishing individual goals using music. Music therapists work with all ages in a wide range of settings: hospitals, schools, community music schools, and outreach centers. You can find a board-certified music therapist through the American Music Therapy Association's website: https://www.musictherapy.org/about/find/.

Music can also be a way for toddlers to interact with other children. At home, toddlers can participate in dance parties, rhythm band parades (see Chapter 9), and songs during routines. In the car, toddlers can request specific songs from a playlist and sing along with the family. In group settings such as daycare or music and movement classes, toddlers can participate in musical play activities, either informally (playing with others) or formally (led by an adult). You might choose to seek out an early childhood music class during the toddler years; see Chapter 18 for more information.

ACTIVITY 52   Sing a Book

There are so many delightful picture books with song lyrics to sing! Find these by searching "Children's Songs—Texts" in the library catalog or talking to a children's librarian. Some of our favorites are *What a Wonderful World*, by George David Weiss, Bob Thiele, and Ashley Bryan (New York: Atheneum Books, 1995); *Summertime*, by George Gershwin, Dubose Heyward, Dorothy Heyward, Ira Gershwin, and Mike Wimmer (Fullerton, CA: Aladdin Publishing, 2002); *Music Is in Everything*, written by Ziggy Marley and illustrated by Ag Jatkowska (Brooklyn, NY: Akashic Books, 2022); and folk songs with additional verses illustrated by Iza Trapani, such as *I'm a Little Teapot* (Watertown, MA: Charlesbridge, 1998). Find board book versions of your favorites so your child can look at and sing them on their own.

ACTIVITY 53 ▶ Making Soup

One of my favorite music activities with toddlers is "making soup."[12] You can do this while playing on the floor or while your toddler is in a booster or highchair. It is also a fun activity to do in the car—even when I couldn't see my daughter, we interacted as she suggested foods to put in the soup and she did the motions.

It goes like this:

- "Let's make soup! What shall we put in the soup?" -*Get ideas from your child.*
- "Great idea, carrots! Do we need to chop that up?" -*If yes, chant this poem while pretending to chop the ingredient . . .*
   Chip, chop, chippity chop.
   Cut off the bottom and cut off the top.
   What you have left you put in the pot.
   Chip, chop, chippity chop! (~Attribution: American folk chant)
- "Let's put it in!" -*Make a lip bubble sound and motion as you pretend to put the ingredient in.*
- Time to stir! -*Sing a soup stirring song. It could be any melody that you sing without words, just sing la la la or bum bum bum for the words. Choose a short melody because you will be singing it many times.*
- "What else shall we put in the soup?" *Repeat with as many ingredients as your child's attention span allows*
- For ingredients like spices or cheese, you can pretend to sprinkle it in and make ch-ch-ch sounds.
- Non-food ingredients are fun too, like dinosaur-truck-playdoh soup. Children are still using their imagination!
- Remember to add liquids—with a "glug glug glug" sound.

- If the ingredient does not need to be chopped, put it in with a dramatic "splash!"
- As you add more ingredients, say "Oh, it's getting so thick!" and pretend that it's harder to stir. This provides experience with different types of movement (bound vs. free). See Chapter 10 for an explanation of more types of movement to explore.
- Toward the end of the activity, say "Let's taste our soup!" and sing "yum-yum-yum" on slow tones as you taste it. Pause and listen for your toddler to imitate you. Even if your child doesn't imitate you at first, continue to do this step when you do this activity. Eventually they will join in.
- Variations: Make soup with foods that all are one color, like red. Or make "fall soup" with leaves, pumpkins, etc.

ACTIVITY 54   Outdoor Concert

While some toddlers might sit quietly for an indoor concert, such as a sibling's school concert, many will need room to run around or a chance to comment on what they are hearing. If the concert is one that is so loud that a toddler's voice will not be disruptive, it is also probably too loud for the toddler's ears.

Outdoor concerts or live music at restaurants are a good way to introduce young children to music in an environment that works for everyone. Position yourselves in the crowd so your child can see the performers and be comfortable with the volume of the music. If it is particularly loud, sit farther away. You could also use noise-reducing earmuffs designed for toddlers. If possible, talk to the performers before or after the concert. Let your child see the instruments up close before or after the performance. If the performer is busking (playing in a public place with their instrument case open) or playing with a tip jar out, let your child put a few coins or dollars in.

WRAPPING UP CHAPTER 14

There are many ways to parent toddlers musically. Including music in daily routines is a way to help make the tasks easier and potentially more enjoyable. Interacting with your toddler using music is a way to develop a secure attachment. Playing musically with your toddler can provide a fun experience for you both.

FOR FURTHER READING

I Love You Rituals, by Becky A. Bailey (Harper Collins, 2000): includes over 70 activities and games to do with your child for various situations and times of day. Many incorporate music.

The Child as Musician: A Handbook of Musical Development, 2nd ed., edited by Gary McPherson (Oxford University Press, 2016): the chapters in this handbook are written by leading researchers in music education. Each chapter contains summaries of many research studies on a specific area of children's musical development.

CHAPTER 15

WIDENING MUSICAL WORLDS WITH PRESCHOOLERS (AGES 3 TO 5 YEARS)

CHAPTER PREVIEW

- Preschoolers rapidly gain broader musical skills, abilities, and interests.
- It is important to provide opportunities for musical play for preschoolers.
- The preschool years are an optimal time to cultivate interests in musical genres and cultures.
- Music is helpful in routines and relationships with preschoolers and as an opportunity for child agency.

Overview of Musical Development, Ages 3 to 5

As seen in the "Children Are Musical!" chart in the Appendix at the end of the book, children continue to gain musical skills and capabilities during the preschool years. Some children can move to a steady beat or play a steady beat on an instrument like rhythm sticks or a drum, but others are still learning these skills. Most children are still finding their singing voice and beginning to match pitch. It is unusual for preschoolers to sing entire songs in tune and remain in the same key. Preschoolers can be wonderfully inventive with music, as they play with musical sounds.

There are many informal and formal music experiences available for the 3- to 5-year-old age group. If your child attends preschool or daycare, they might have the opportunity to engage in musical play with a music specialist at the school, as well as in their classroom with their teacher. Community music schools may offer musical play classes that help children develop tonal and rhythm skills, musical expression, and creativity through play. Libraries often include music in their story times. Your community may have cultural celebrations and outdoor concerts that provide a great way to interact with music and your family.

When it comes to listening, be ready for your preschooler to want to listen to the same song or album repeatedly. (Our kids once asked for the Rio 2 movie soundtrack four times in a row on a road trip. It felt like a choice between peace in the backseat and our own sanity, and we opted for peace in the backseat). Repeated listening may be a way for preschoolers to seek to master the music they listen to, thus having more control over it. Don't be surprised if your preschooler asks or tells you not to sing along in the car. This is probably not a judgment on your singing ability; I was a vocal major in college and still my children asked me not to sing along. Rather, extra people singing can interfere with the mastery/control experience for preschoolers, especially in an enclosed space.

Considering Music Lessons in the Preschool Years

Some children may be ready to start playing an instrument during the preschool years, calling on your musical parenting resources. You could do this informally, by providing your child with a harmonica, ukulele, keyboard, or piano, and giving time for exploration. You could pair this with observation of an older child, teen, or adult playing the instrument who can serve as a model. There are many online sources, both free and for a cost, for learning instruments.

Another path is more formal lessons, such as Suzuki instrumental lessons. The Suzuki approach was designed by Dr. Shinichi Suzuki[1] (1898–1998) and is based on the belief that all children can learn to play a musical instrument. This approach is well-suited to young beginners. Children can choose from many instruments, depending on the teacher or studio near you. You can find out more about the Suzuki approach and if there is a program in your area at suzukiassociation.org. It is valuable to talk to other parents, especially those with children who have been doing Suzuki for a while, when you are thinking about enrolling your child.

Beginning formal instrumental lessons at any age can be a complicated venture for a family. Beyond the financial and logistical hurdles, there can be several relational components that families might not expect. Practicing with your child, or compelling them to practice, can bring out a side of you and a side of your child that you may not usually see. The relationship between teacher, child, and parent can take time to develop, and finding a good working relationship is important. You might not find a good fit the first time. If things are consistently tense, you can consider trying a different teacher or taking a break for a while. Return to the idea of "why are we doing this?" presented in Chapter 6's discussion of hopes and dreams, and if something is not working, reevaluate and modify the plan. You can read more about considerations for instrumental lessons in Chapter 20. If you do not play an instrument or did not take instrumental lessons as a child, find a friend or family member who did to help you navigate the process.

ACTIVITY 55 Be an Early Childhood Music Researcher

Be a researcher interested in how your child is developing musically. What is your child into right now? What can they do now that they couldn't do before? What have you noticed about their coordination and movement? What are their interests?

Involve your child and other family members. What are the stories you all like to share with others outside of your family related to your child and music—the way she conducted a recording while eating watermelon, or the way he sang the "Star-Spangled Banner" while watching a baseball game? The stories we share and re-share often hold special meaning to us.

Keep track of your observations about your child's musical interactions. If you have questions about their musical development or activities, head to Google Scholar (scholar.google.com). Type your question in the box and read the abstracts of research studies that come up. Remember to be skeptical, as discussed in the opening of Part 3.

Musical Play

The word "play" has a double meaning in this chapter and for many musical scenarios. Playing is the way children interact with their world, inventing, manipulating, and experimenting. Play is an ideal way for children to learn[2]—and adults, as well![3] We also use the term "play" to refer to music—pressing "play" to hear a recording or "playing" an instrument, for example. Just as blended relational musicking and practical musicking can lead to a more satisfying musical experience, incorporating elements of playfulness into the act of playing music can make the musicking more fulfilling.

Musical play could be making up songs while playing with trucks, blocks, or small figures. Children play musically when testing different sounds by hitting various objects with a stick. You might hear your child playing musically with sounds while falling asleep for a nap or at bedtime, experimenting with high and low sounds, different syllables, and sound effects. Continuing to put play and playfulness in the center of musical experiences is crucial with preschoolers. Children learn best through play in many areas of development, including music. Musical play for preschoolers may be characterized by child-initiated or child-influenced activities. Control can be an important part of children's play; they may assign you a role but want to retain creative control themselves. This sort of situation is one in which a parent could shift from a "musical parenting" mindset, with a musical goal in mind, to more of a "parenting musically" mindset. Recognizing the importance of child control first, and musical outcome second, may help a parent make this mental shift. In other situations, your child might need you to take the lead and model musical play, such as in the Dinosaur Opera activity described below.

Musical play can occur anywhere—the kitchen, the family vehicle, the backyard, the toy room. No specific materials are needed, although props like scarves and beanbags may aid expressive movement, and instruments can add to the creative possibilities. Seeing you as a grown-up delighting in your child's play may encourage your child to continue their play.

ACTIVITY 56 ▶ Dinosaur Opera

An opera is a musical form in which almost everything is sung or rapped. To make a dinosaur opera with your preschooler, assemble some dinosaurs (or any other toys) and start singing or rapping the action rather than speaking it. This can be fun, stream-of-consciousness monologue or dialogue to a tune you make up, or you could put words to a song you already know. Your child may already be a pro at making up little songs while playing. If so, follow their lead, and try to use some of the same words and melodies. If this is new, your child might appreciate hearing what you come up with.

This is an activity you can also do in the car as a ritual when you pick your child up from daycare or school. Imagine a dramatic rendition of "Marco, how was schooooool to-day?" from the driver's seat, followed by a sung response: "Ooooooo—kay." "What did you plaaaaay with on the play-ground?" "Scoo-ters!"

One last extension for this idea is to use your "opera voice" during household moments where you need children's attention and might be finding yourself losing patience. I have been known to stand at the bottom of the stairs and SING dramatically, rather than shout, "It's time for DINNNNNNNN-er! Wash your hands and come to the TAAAAAAAA-ble!" It's fun and helps reduce my stress as a parent, while still getting the job done: parenting musically all the way.

Music in Routines with Preschoolers

As your child grows, you can continue the music from past routines as well as add music to new routines. Some families I know like to take well-known tunes ("Baby Shark," for example), and make up new words to the tune to help assist with routine. For instance, "Put on boots doo doo, doo doo doo doo . . ." "Put on coat," "Out the door," "Get in van," "Arm through straps," "Mama buckles you you you you you!"

When I was an elementary school general music teacher, I found that making transitions musical helped the children stay focused and avoid spinning out into chaos. The same can be true at home. Having a few musical routines that you can do on autopilot can help ease stressful moments during the day. Your child will probably start doing the routines on their own as well! One example is the following chant I learned from an elementary music teacher. We found it to be surprisingly effective with my son Kip when he was 4. It goes like this: "Make a circle, don't be late, by the time I count to eight. 1, 2, 3, 4, 5, 6, 7, 8" (origin: American folk chant) ▶. We modified this according to the situation: "Go to the potty, don't be late . . ." and "Eat your green beans, don't be late" and "Pick up the LEGO, don't be late." Kip followed our directions when we chanted the instructions more often than he did when we just spoke them. We used this chant so often that we started counting in languages other than English or substituting silly words, like "by the time I bubble to eight," followed by lip-bubbled versions of the numbers.

Music and Relationships with Preschoolers

One of the ways families use music is to build relationships within the family unit, as well as with extended family, friends, and community. Music can also help a preschool child begin to define himself or herself by expressing musical preferences or engaging in musically expressive activities. Adult-child relationships are fostered through such activities as

- Dance parties
- Lullabies at nap or bedtime
- Singing songs with grandparents via video call
- Listening to music together in the family vehicle and talking about it

Child-child relationships can also grow through music, including

- Siblings singing calm-down songs to one another
- Siblings or playmates singing little songs while playing
- Children having a parade with rhythm instruments around the house or outside
- A younger sibling conducting and giving musical suggestions to an older sibling while she practices the violin.

All of these are examples of relational musicking, where the goal of the music-making is to strengthen relationships. Practical results may also abound!

> As you watch your child interact with others in musical activities, what do you notice about relational qualities such as empathy, eye contact, and attachment? Do you agree with researchers who have found that musical engagement can promote healthy relational interactions?

Cultivating Interest in Musicians and Musical Cultures

Preschoolers have the capacity to develop strong interests and passions (some might say obsessions!). This is a good time to introduce your child to a wide range of musical cultures. Pay attention to which musical sights and sounds most appeal to your child, and then go deep exploring those musical cultures together.

There are many resources available online. I like the Putumayo World Playground recordings because the producers source music from multiple artists for each CD (https://www.putumayo.com/world-playground). This gives you a chance to expose your child to many genres within a theme (region or style of music). There are endless videos of world music cultures on YouTube as well.

ACTIVITY 57   Nurture a Musical Passion

One family I know made a calendar of different genres of music to play during each evening meal while their children were preschoolers, an example of musical parenting related to listening. As their children became more aware of Afro-Pop, Big Band, and Celtic harp music, among many other styles and genres, the children knew to request their favorites when it was their turn to pick.

Your child may want to specialize in a particular style, artist, album, or even song, and listen over and over. This is developmentally appropriate, but it can be hard on the grown-ups. That is another reason to introduce your child to many types of music—you can hope for more variety during the times when you are listening together!

Let's say your child falls in love with sitar (classical Indian) music and can't get enough of it. Check your library for picture books and additional CDs or DVD recordings. Look around for any festivals in your area coming up that feature a sitar player. If you live near a university, you could find out if the music department knows of any sitar players who have public concerts scheduled.

All of this doesn't mean your child will end up playing the sitar, although they might. Diving in and pursuing an interest is a way to show your child that you value their musical tastes, that music adds richness to life, and that music is something we explore together as a family. This type of joint pursuit brings together elements of musical parenting (broadening your child's musical interests), parenting musically (supporting your child's expression of agency), as well as relational musicking (exploring new music together as a family).

WRAPPING UP CHAPTER 15

The preschool years are an exciting time of learning and growth. Music is an essential part of preschoolers' lives. This includes everything from unstructured play that incorporates music to using music in routines. Take time to listen to your child's musical preferences and have fun exploring the music together.

FOR FURTHER READING

Music 3–5, by Susan Young (Routledge, 2009): A comprehensive guide to preschool children's musical experiences and ideas for activities; written for a school setting, but easily transferable to families.

I Can Make Music: Play and Learn Activities to Empower Children Through Music, by Patricia Shehan Campbell and Maja Pitamic (Elwin Street Limited, 2015): A collection of activities for parents and children to do together to explore music and musical expression.

CHAPTER 16

UNCOVERING MUSICAL INTERESTS WITH EARLY ELEMENTARY AGE CHILDREN (AGES 5 TO 9 YEARS)

> **CHAPTER PREVIEW**
> - Children in kindergarten through third grade (approximately ages 5–9) delight in learning music and expressing themselves through music.
> - Music is an excellent tool to help children with other areas of learning and personal growth.
> - Some early elementary aged children may be ready to begin formal instrumental lessons, and others may wait until later.
> - Music is a way to connect relationally with self, family members, those outside the home, the broader world, and the divine.

Overview of Musical Development, Kindergarten to 3rd Grade (Ages 5–9)

During the early elementary years, children continue to expand in all areas of their musical development, as seen in the "Children Are Musical!" chart in the appendix. Children can differentiate between speaking and singing voices. Their vocal range gradually expands. Keep singing higher than you normally would as an adult (above middle C). Children enjoy playing all types of instruments, including instruments they can make themselves (see "Found Sounds," below). You will probably hear your children continue to engage in spontaneous singing during these years. You can encourage musical creativity by providing simple instruments or found sounds and then paying attention to what your children create.

> How is your child's musical expression changing as they grow older? What do you notice about your child's singing and movement? What times of the day or week does your child create music?

When thinking about musical development, music researcher and educator Dr. Edwin Gordon encouraged parents to compare musical development to language development. Gordon believed that children ideally learn music in a similar way to language: first through years of listening, followed by speaking (singing), then reading and writing notated music. Gordon pointed out that school music programs often ask children to read and write standard music notation when they have had little experience listening and "speaking" (singing, clapping, or playing) music. For this reason, it is important for children to have many opportunities to sing, chant, and move to music before they are asked to read or write notation. If children progress too quickly to notation, they may have fewer opportunities or motivation to learn to play by ear (learn music by listening to recordings or a live musician rather than through notation). Playing by ear is a valuable skill and experience.

All children will benefit from continued opportunities to play a range of classroom instruments, such as xylophones, drums, and maracas. Continuing to engage in musical play, including creative activities such as creating songs while engaged in imaginative play, is essential to this age group as well. Some children may be ready to study with a private teacher. If you are considering beginning instrumental lessons, see Chapter 20 for considerations. Other children will not yet be ready to begin lessons. Starting music lessons is a complex decision and there is not one right or wrong time. Think through the family logistics and your child's overall readiness. Talk to a music teacher for extra context. You can also consider group music experiences like children's choruses.

Music and Relationships with Early Elementary Age Children

Music can be a part of five types of relationships: a child and themself, their family, others, the world, and the divine. When children identify songs or pieces they like or do not like, this provides an opportunity for children to express themselves. Naming specific aspects of the songs or pieces is a way to deepen those conversations with your child. For example:

> ADULT: "Tell me about a song you like to listen to."
> CHILD: "I like 'Dos Oruguitas' from *Encanto*.
> ADULT: "Oooh. Yeah. Let's listen to it." (listen while riding in the car, hanging out at home, etc.)
> ADULT: "Such a cool song. So, what do you like about it?"
> CHILD: "It floats."
> ADULT: "Mmm, yeah. It floats. What does it float like?"

Using language like this, affirming the child's perceptions and asking a gentle follow-up, can show your child you are listening as well as help them extend their expressive thinking.

This vignette also provides an example of the second category: family members. As an adult, you could share things after listening like "I love that piece, 'Carol of the Bells'! It's such a pretty melody and then when the other rock instruments come in, they make it so exciting!" Children can also experience relational musicking with family members through many of the activities discussed in Part 2 of this book—singing, playing instruments, dancing, and creating. Associating specific songs or pieces with specific family members can be a special way to deepen relational connections. For example, perhaps your children always listen to Michael Jackson songs in the car with their grandparents. This provides a special connection and something to talk about. As your children grow, when they hear the Michael Jackson songs, they may return to the pleasant memories of their childhood experiences with grandparents. Researchers label this "music-evoked autobiographical memories" and note that music

FIGURE 16.1 Family members having fun dancing together and documenting their musicking. GETTY IMAGES

helps trigger these memories. The memories are often vivid and include positive emotions.[1]

Third, music is a means for connecting children with those outside the family, including friends, school peers, and community members. This could occur through kids talking at school lunch about the music they enjoy. A group of friends can create a shared playlist of songs. This is a good time to be a little extra watchful, monitoring the song sharing to be sure it fits your family expectations. Steer your kids clear of online apps that allow children to connect with strangers. There are online apps and services to help parents manage and supervise online content and devise use by children.

A fourth way to consider relational musicking is as a connection between your child and the world. Understanding oneself as an individual living in relation to time (history) and place (culture and geography) is an important form of self-knowledge. Find a physical map of the world or an online map that your child can mark with locations of home, family and friends, destinations visited, and locations of music they enjoy listening to.

If your child is interested in a certain historical period, find music from that period to listen to together.

Finally, music can be a way for early elementary aged children to have a connection with the divine. Based on your family's or your child's spiritual or religious context, you could facilitate this form of relational musicking through sharing examples. For instance, "The beauty of the organ music and the vibrations I feel in my body with the loud notes is a way that I hear and feel God in the world." Another example is teaching children music that is used in a devotional context, such as a prayer before a meal, a bedtime blessing song, and music associated with religious holidays. Children might associate the experience of singing or playing in a music ensemble, "being part of something bigger," with spiritual beliefs.

Overview of General Music Teaching Methods

General music refers to a music class that incorporates many forms of musicking, such as singing, listening, playing instruments, moving, and creating. If that sounds familiar, it's because this entire book is a form of a general music methods class for you as a family member! You may have heard some terms related to general music teaching that your child might experience at school or in the community as an early elementary aged student. Here is a summary. Knowing a little about each could help you understand communication from teachers. All of these teaching approaches offer teacher certification workshops as well as periodic professional development sessions in which teachers can learn more. Many elementary general music teachers use a combination of these approaches.

Music Learning Theory. Music Learning Theory is an approach developed by American jazz musician and music educator Edwin Gordon (1927–2015). This approach emphasizes the importance of children learning to "audiate," or think in sound. Can you sing "Happy Birthday" in your head? That's audiating. Teachers who use Music Learning Theory often plan lessons using a "whole-part-whole" approach, with students experiencing a song or musical piece, then learning about component parts such as rhythm and pitch, followed by putting it all together again.[2]

Key parent takeaway: Explain the idea of audiation to your family. Ask your child (or other family members) to audiate if they are singing or humming and you need a bit of quiet. It's good for their musical development and gives you an aural break!

Orff-Schulwerk. Orff-Schulwerk refers to an approach to teaching children music pioneered by German composer Carl Orff (1895–1982) and composer and educator Gunild Keetman (1904–1990). This approach is known for an emphasis on the creative process: imitation, exploration, improvisation, and composition. Lessons in Orff-Schulwerk music classrooms often feature collaboratively created music compositions that may use hand-held percussion instruments and barred instruments like xylophones.

Key parent takeaway: Any poem or children's book can be turned into a chant or song. Add body percussion patterns, including stomps, claps, pats, and snaps, to deepen the musical composition.

Kodály. Zoltán Kodály (1882–1967) was a Hungarian composer and educator. His method has a strong emphasis on children learning the folk music of their "mother tongue" (home culture). Teachers who use Kodály curricula adopt a sequential approach to teaching children to sing in tune and read notation.

Key parent takeaway: If your child is struggling to learn a musical concept or gain a musical skill, slow down and think about how to break it into smaller parts. Start with a simpler and more manageable musical task, and then gradually add complexity.

Dalcroze Eurhythmics. Émile Jaques-Dalcroze (1865–1950) was a composer and music educator. His approach to music education centered on the connection between music and movement. "Dalcroze Eurhythmics" refers to a specialized music and movement class that is offered in some communities to young children as well as older children and conservatory students.

Key parent takeaway: Remember that movement is essential to all aspects of music learning and music experience. Think about the ways you model musical movement for your child.

ACTIVITY 58 Investigate Your Child's Musical Opportunities

Find out about the music offerings available to your child. Attend school open houses or parent-teacher conferences and make a point of meeting the music teacher. Ask questions to learn what approaches the teacher uses in class. Look around for free or low-cost opportunities for your child to be involved in short-term or long-term music activities, such as through the library or community recreation center. Consider music, dance, and drama opportunities—all of these contribute to musical development.

As you learn more about your child's music opportunities, you may decide to seek out additional opportunities that will provide alternative experiences. For instance, if the school music program emphasizes singing but students do not have opportunities to play drums or other instruments, you could go to a community drum circle as a family. If the school music teacher does a lot with instruments and rhythm but not as much singing, you could consider a community children's choir.

ACTIVITY 59 Create a Soundscape

When our children are young, it can be interesting to stop and listen to their "soundscape." A soundscape is all the sounds in a child's environment. When they are toddlers, this could include the sounds of their toys, music playing in the background, a sibling talking in the other room, a lawnmower outside, and the chimes and notifications of a cell phone. The various music choices that children have access to are another aspect of soundscape. To read more on this, see Dr. Katherine Palmer's insightful article for families and teachers, "Expanding the Neighborhood: Diversifying Music Making and Listening Inspired by Fred Rogers" (https://www.fredrogersinstitute.org/files/content/katiepalmerwhitepaper2023.pdf).[3]

Adults or children can also intentionally create a soundscape. Just as you might arrange furniture in your home in a certain way and put pictures on the wall and decorative items around the room, you could create a soundscape. You can choose to let the sounds from outside into your home through opening the windows or intentionally block the sounds by using a white noise generator. If you or your child are sensitive to sounds such as the buzzing of lights or appliances, you could seek to reduce those noises. Recorded music played on speakers or a mobile device can be a part of a soundscape. This could be accompanied by other sounds as well, such as jingle bells on a pet's collar or a table-top waterfall.

Ask your early elementary aged child to create a soundscape with you for a special family event, such as a dinner or a holiday celebration. Think together about which sounds to include or exclude. A soundscape could consist of a specific type of music, a fan running in a side room to block other sounds coming from that room, and a special chime your child strikes when it is time to eat.

Exploring soundscapes is also a good opportunity to consider sound sensitivity. Are you or your child sensitive to particular sounds? Or are noisy environments difficult to navigate? As a parent, being aware of your child's sound sensitivities can help you choose activities that are right for your child in their current stage. If you are concerned about sound sensitivity for your child, talk to your child's pediatrician. Autism, ADHD, auditory or sensory processing disorders, and misophonia are all conditions that can cause sound sensitivity. Misophonia is a condition in which individuals have strong aversions to particular sounds (chewing, swallowing, breathing, clock ticking, etc.). On the other hand, if you notice your child has reduced sensitivity to sounds, talk to the pediatrician about potential hearing loss or auditory processing difficulty.

ACTIVITY 60   Found Sounds, Early Elementary Edition

Early elementary aged children will enjoy creating and decorating their own found-sound instruments. For this activity, direct your child to any clean recycled material (plastic containers, water bottles, jugs, cardboard) and household items (rubber bands, dowels, dried beans, stickers, ribbons, tissue paper) you are willing to let them use. Another wonderful source of found sounds is items found in nature, such as dry pine needles, acorns, dry seed pods as shakers, and sticks and rocks for drumming.[4] Let your children create their own instruments or help them if their ideas need adult assistance. Ask your child to play their instruments along with family musicking or music listening. Also invite your child to create their own compositions with their instruments. Children can use their own invented notation (any kind of symbols they choose) to document their compositions.

ACTIVITY 61 Instruments at a Museum

Visit a museum in person or via online exhibits to look at musical instruments from a range of times and places (for example, *Musical Instrument Museum*, Phoenix, Arizona: mim.org and *The Metropolitan Museum of Art*, New York: https://www.metmuseum.org/about-the-met/collection-areas/musical-instruments). Talk with your child about what you see. Pay special attention to the ways the people who created the instruments made them beautiful. Are there carvings and embellishments? Talk about the shape of the instruments. How does the shape affect the sound? Relate back to the instruments your child creates. Were the instruments in the museum made from found items? See the books listed in Further Reading for more ideas about learning about instruments.

WRAPPING UP CHAPTER 16

In this chapter we considered the musical world of early elementary aged students, approximately 5–9 years old, or kindergarten through 3rd grade. While some children may start taking private music lessons during this time period, musical play and informal musicking continues to be important for all children. There are many ways for children to connect relationally with themselves, their family, friends, the world, and the divine through music. Families can incorporate musical exploration through making instruments, creating soundscapes, and exploring instrument exhibits at museums.

FOR FURTHER READING

Before Music: Where Instruments Come From, by Annette Bay Pimentel and Madison Safer (Harry N. Abrams, 2022): presents a wealth of information about instruments both throughout history and around the world, including who makes the instruments and how they are made.

Billy the Kid Makes It Big, by Dolly Parton and MacKenzie Haley (Penguin Workshop, 2023): Dolly Parton shares the story of how bulldog Billy the Kid overcomes bullies to pursue his musical dreams.

The Music Advantage: How Music Helps Your Child Develop, Learn, and *Thrive,* by Anita Collins (Penguin Random House, 2020): interprets a collection of music cognition and neuroscience research to make the case for how music influences many areas of children's development.

CHAPTER 17

NURTURING MUSICAL EXPRESSION WITH LATE ELEMENTARY AGE CHILDREN (AGES 9 TO 12 YEARS)

> **CHAPTER PREVIEW**
> - Children in late elementary school are broadening their interests in many areas.
> - Be ready for your child to have the time and skill to create and invest in their own passion projects during the later elementary school years.
> - Keep making music a part of family life at home even when your child becomes more involved in school or community music activities.
> - Use music in routines to connect with your late elementary school child.

Overview of Musical Development, 4th Through 6th Grade (Ages 9–12)

During the fourth through sixth grade years, children's musical abilities increase, as noted in the "Children Are Musical!" chart in the appendix. Their fine motor skills and vocal range also increase, allowing them to play and sing more complex music of a wider range. Children ages 9–12 can continue to demonstrate innate musicality through learning by ear, teaching themselves music (see Chapter 20), and creating music.

As a parent, be aware that you may feel pressure for your child to specialize in a specific sport or activity as soon as fourth grade (or even before). Travel sports teams, dance teams, and intensive music programs may ask for a time commitment that does not fit your family's priorities. I would encourage you to resist any pressure for specializing as long as possible—ideally, all the way through high school. In Episode 2 of the *Parenting Musically* podcast, Dr. Elizabeth Parker discussed the importance of adolescence as a time for exploration ▶.[1]

Recognize the Vast Potential: Meeting of Time + Skill!

Late elementary school is a particularly exciting time developmentally because of the intersection of children's growing independence and skill level with their plentiful free time. Children this age may have more free time than when they are in middle school and high school, when additional activities, sports, homework, and after-school jobs take up the hours. Late-elementary children also have more skill and independence than they did as younger elementary students.

This combination of time and skill provides a window for creative learning to occur. Children can teach themselves ukulele given a $50 ukulele and access to tutorials online. Or you can buy an affordable build-your-own ukulele kit. Late elementary-age students can learn basic sound editing and begin their own podcast. Using mobile phones, children can film, edit, and share their own creative work. Throw in a green sheet, and children can add green screen video effects.

> Does your child have enough free time to explore creatively? If not, what are some ways to carve out that time? Are there any other supports your child would need?

As a parent or caregiver, there are a few things you can do to create an environment where this extended creativity can occur. First, do not be afraid of letting your children become bored. If a child constantly has other activities, opportunities, and technology at the ready, they will probably not choose to launch a creative venture. But if your child experiences periods of unscheduled time and needs to make their own fun, that is when the magic occurs.

GRAMMY- and Emmy-award winner Ziggy Marley provided an example of this in Episode 1 of the *Parenting Musically* podcast, describing his childhood in Jamaica ▶. He shared that television was only available during limited hours and there were no other screens. Ziggy cited this lack of screens as important to developing his musical creativity as a child: "You had to use your mind, you had to be imaginative to entertain yourself as a child," he explained.[2]

Another way to help children in creative, independent endeavors is to provide a few materials. This could be a musical instrument, a recording device, or musical staff paper. Talk to family and friends to see if anyone has a guitar, ukulele, or music keyboard your child could borrow for a while. Help your child find child-appropriate sites and apps online with information if they would like (how to play chords on the ukulele, for instance).

Third, show interest in your child's project without trying to take over. Remember that the value here is mostly on the child's own agency in the creative process, not in the product. Support your child if they ask for assistance looking information up online or going to the library, but as much as possible, let your child direct the process.

Fourth, celebrate your child's endeavor. Children notice when adults take an interest through taking photos or videos, telling others about something, or just stopping to watch and listen. Hearing me talking to their grandma on the phone and saying, "The kids are doing the funniest, coolest thing! They have this green sheet on the basement wall and are recording songs and dances. . . . I'll ask them to send it to you when they're done!" goes a long way to communicate how I value their process and show my pride in their initiative.

Music and Other Learning

Music instruction may be a way to support other types of learning, such as literacy and math, during the elementary school years. Music also plays an important role in social-emotional development, including the development and expression of empathy, across the lifespan.[3] Research about the impact of music instruction or participation on other domains, such as reading or math, is typically tied to a specific type of instruction or frequency of music instruction. In an introduction to a special issue of the online journal *Frontiers in Psychology*, Welch et al.[4] made the point that research studies about music and other forms of learning and development include a wide range of music experiences and programs. This is not to say that one program is better than another. Rather, it underscores the many ways to be musical. You can read the editorial, along with specific research articles, through the open-access, free journal: https://www.frontiersin.org/articles/10.3389/fpsyg.2020.01246/full.

Recent research on the impact of music and learning points to benefits for children engaged in music programs on their executive functioning (getting things done in an organized way) and academic achievement.[5] A longitudinal study comparing groups of children who were involved in after-school music, after-school sports, or no extracurriculars, found that musical training led to positive neural, behavioral, and musical growth.[6] Music programs emphasizing rhythm have been found to help children with dyslexia.[7]

I encourage you to be the researcher with your child. Researchers have studied what type of music individuals like to listen to while studying.[8] How about in your family—does music help your child concentrate while doing homework? If so, what kind of music—instrumental or vocal? Home language, different language, or no lyrics? Fast or slow?

Researchers have also found that engagement in music can impact the development and expression of empathy, when a child sees or understands someone else's perspective or experience.[9] Do you notice that with your child? Does participating in interactive music experiences, at home or outside the home, seem to influence your child's ability to see things from another's point of view? What about you—does engaging musically with others shift your mood or interactions?

Choosing a Musical Instrument

Many schools start beginners on band and orchestra instruments between 4th and 6th grade, depending on the district. See Chapter 19 for a discussion on how to help your child choose an instrument and factors to be aware of.

Private Lessons?

Along with starting an instrument in school around this time, many children may also begin private lessons on this instrument, perhaps switching from piano to the new instrument. Other children might begin private lessons for the first time on any instrument. For more on thinking through whether private lessons are right for your family, see Chapter 20. Keep in mind that there are many paths to learning a new instrument, not only private lessons.

Community Music Opportunities

In addition to increasing opportunities to learn instruments, sing in choir, and participate in extra-curricular music groups at school, 4th through 6th graders may also have opportunities in the community to participate in school-year groups, classes, and summer camps. If your child is interested in these opportunities, check whether the organization has scholarships to cover the cost of participation. Your school district or state government may also have a special fund to help cover participation costs in community activities. However, it is also important for children this age to have down time. Choose your family activity level carefully and do not be afraid to make adjustments for individual and family benefit.

ACTIVITY 62   Found Sound Instruments, Late Elementary Edition

Children can continue to create their own instruments of increasing complexity in the later elementary years. In addition to crafting the sound-producing aspects, encourage your child to consider the artistic design of their instrument. Many instruments from traditions around the world include hand-crafted details that add to the aesthetic design of the instrument in addition to the sound of it.

Explore the idea of instrument classifications. Why is classification important? Classifying instruments—as well as animals, plants, and Pokémon cards—is a way for children to understand relationships among groups of items. It helps us to see similarities and differences. For instance, exploring the many types of flutes that humans have created over the years and across cultures can be a way of better understanding our connections to others.

Many music teachers use the classification system of woodwinds/brass/percussion/strings. However, this system ignores many of the instruments outside of Western European art music. Instead, I like to teach late elementary school students the Sachs-Hornbostel system of classification. The Sachs-Hornbostel system was designed by ethnomusicologists to be inclusive of all the instruments of the world. It includes categories of chordophones (instruments that produce sound with strings), aerophones (produce sound with air), membranophones (produce sound with membrane, such as a drum), idiophones (produce sound by shaking, hitting, or scraping the instrument itself), corpophones (produce sound with the human body as resonator, like clapping, singing, snapping), and electrophones (produce sound electronically).[10] This system can also include children's homemade instruments that may otherwise defy classification.

With their homemade instruments, encourage your child to create their own musical composition. In elementary general music I invited children to use "invented notation" as a way to visually record their music composition. This could be achieved through symbols, lines, colors, or any representation your child chooses. If you or your child are interested, Google "history of music notation," "piano roll notation," or "Nashville number system" to learn more about notation systems. You might also explore together to find out how musical traditions around the globe transmit and notate music. This can help children realize that musical notation is a tool that some musicians use, and it is one that developed over time and is not the same everywhere. You don't need to be able to read musical notation in order to do this activity.

Music in Routines and Relationships with Late Elementary Schoolers

As children move from 4th through 6th grade, they experience the transition from childhood to tweenhood (tween referring to "between" child and teen). Continuing to use music in your daily routines with these bigger kids can be a way to provide a sense of stability and continuity as many other aspects of their lives are changing. Here the practical musicking and relational musicking meet: it is through the music of routines that you have an excellent opportunity to build your relationship with your older elementary child.

Do you still read to your late elementary kids at bedtime? It is a great practice if it works in your family schedule. Even if you do not have time to read together, take a moment to tuck your big kids in at night and sing a song. Maybe your child will still like to hear the lullabies you sang when they were babies. Or maybe your bedtime song will grow and change as your child does. Think about what songs you want planted deep in your child's heart. These could be tunes from your own childhood, campfire songs that evoke belonging, or choruses that speak of empowerment.

The car can be an important place for relational musicking, as well as connecting with your child in general, when they are in late elementary school. You may find yourself with time together to talk and listen to music on the way to extracurricular activities. Take advantage of this time to invite your big kid to share music they are interested in with you. If you have multiple children in the car, create a schedule so each one gets the opportunity to choose music.

At this age some kids will be hearing about music from friends and starting to explore new music listening themselves. Invite your older elementary child to choose their own music for a few playlists—for example, "getting ready," "chores," and "relaxing." This provides an opportunity for a child's expression of "agency," or power, control, and authority. Experiencing agency is an important part of each stage of childhood, and as parents and caregivers, we seek to find ways for children to express their agency.

Paying attention to what your child selects could also give you a window into their mood or issues they are thinking about. This can lead to important conversations or better understanding on the part of the parent. A colleague of mine shared that any time her teenage daughter wanted to share a song or playlist with her, she said "Yes!" and put her full attention on it. This mom viewed careful attention to her daughter's music choices as a way to better understand her daughter's world and experiences at that moment. By fostering this sharing process when kids are in late elementary, you create a pattern that can continue into the teenage years.

Even as your child is growing older and having the chance to create their own playlists and share "their music" with you, continue to provide times to listen to music together as a family. One of the fathers in my research for *Parenting Musically* realized his family members were only listening to music individually with their ear buds. He bought a Bluetooth speaker so the family could listen to music together and made a point of having his children take turns sharing their tunes. Find times to listen to music that is part of your family's canon, as described in Chapter 3. Keep having dance parties and learn new dance steps as your children get older. On longer car trips have times when parents choose the music, and everyone sings along. Call family members together on birthdays and sing "Happy Birthday" or a different song together.

WRAPPING UP CHAPTER 17

As children continue to grow and develop in elementary school, more opportunities are available to them. Enjoy your child's growing skill and independence as they create instruments, music compositions, dances, and projects. Balance unstructured time for self-discovery with opportunities in the community or online that can provide supplemental information for the passion projects your children create during these years.

FOR FURTHER READING

Help Your Kids with Music: A Unique Step-by-Step Visual Guide, by Carol Vorderman (DK Publishing, 2019): contains an overview of the elements of music (pitch, rhythm, melody, etc.) and comes with an audio app.

The World Atlas of Musical Instruments, by Bozhidar Abrashev and Vladimir Gadjev (H. F. Ullman, 2013): presents over 1,000 illustrations of musical instruments with information, spanning both time and space.

PART 1
MUSIC IS IMPORTANT

PART 2
MANY WAYS TO BE MUSICAL

PART 3
ALL HUMANS ARE MUSICAL

PART 4
EXPRESSING AGENCY AS A FAMILY WITH MUSIC

The goal of Part 4 is to help you navigate music situations with information about formal and informal music education structures. I share information I would share with a friend who is looking for a Music and Movement class, helping a child choose an instrument, or thinking about whether to switch private lesson teachers. I also include some of the conversations happening within the music education profession about making music spaces more equitable and more inclusive.

CHAPTER 18

HOW TO PARTICIPATE IN EARLY CHILDHOOD MUSIC EXPERIENCES

CHAPTER PREVIEW

- Music is important for young children. There are many ways to experience music in early childhood.
- Decisions about whether to go to an early childhood music class, when to begin, and which class to choose all depend on multiple factors. What works for one family might not work for another.
- Young children demonstrate a wide range of participation in early childhood music classes.
- You can incorporate music activities at home, regardless of whether you currently attend a class.

Early Childhood Music Experiences

Early childhood music learning opportunities, such as "music and movement" type classes or library music story times, can be meaningful experiences to share with your little one. A wide range of opportunities is available, from tuition-based programs to free events. Some opportunities occur weekly while others are one-time only. The setting could be in a classroom, a library, or outside. For simplicity, I will refer to these opportunities as "early childhood music classes" in this chapter.

Music education researchers conduct studies in early childhood music class settings as well as home environments. A recent meta-analysis of studies suggested that participation in early childhood music classes may lead to enhanced social-emotional development, but the authors cautioned that more research was necessary.[1] On the other hand, in a longitudinal study of children in Australia, researchers found that at-home music activities led to developmental benefits for children, including social-emotional development.[2]

It is important that I share both research findings with you because I do not want any reader to think that benefits align only with formal early childhood music experiences. There are many ways to be a musical family, and there are many ways to interact with very young children and music. Going to a class is just one of those ways.

This chapter includes recommendations for if you are choosing to seek out an early childhood music class. If the structure of a weekly class does not appeal to you, consider looking for one-time events such as outdoor music festivals or special music events at your local library. You can also do the activities of an early childhood music class at home.

> Does this idea of attending an early childhood music class appeal to you? What do you hope you and your child will get out of the class? Think about your desires as a parent and caregiver as well as what you hope for your child.

When to Start

Think about three main players when it comes to starting an early childhood music class: you, your child, and your family. Would it be helpful for you to get out once a week and meet some other children and families? Do you have a friend or neighbor you could sign up with? Being a parent can be a lot of things, including isolating. If your goal in signing up for the class is in part to meet new parents, recognizing that as a goal can help you decide when the time is right. On the opposite side, if you are feeling overwhelmed by the thought of getting out of the house at a set time or being around other children because of the germ pool or time of year, it is probably good to wait a while. Second, think about your child. Does your child enjoy trying new things? What time of day would be best for your child? Finally, consider the family. What is your family ready for? Is there a class offered close to the time of a preschool drop-off you are already doing? Would a multi-age format work better than single-age group classes?

Many early childhood music classes accept babies as young as six weeks old. Some of my students who began attending at that age slept through class. That is completely fine; their caregiver was still there learning the activities to do later at home. I recommend taking your child's schedule into account, as it relates to your own goals, when deciding when to start.

Call the program if the dates listed online do not currently work in your schedule. If you missed the sign-up, feel free to call the school to ask if you could start partway through the session for a pro-rated (reduced) amount. For example, if the session runs from September to January but you would like to wait and start in November, go ahead and ask. Their answer will probably depend on the overall enrollment in the class and program. It never hurts to ask.

Choosing a Class

If you are interested in finding an early childhood music class, ask families you know in the neighborhood for recommendations. If you follow a neighborhood social media page, that can be a useful source of information. An internet search for "early childhood music class near me" can also help you to identify options. Some of the early childhood music providers near my home offer free demonstration classes at local libraries; this can be a way to get a taste of various programs. As you look for classes, considering asking if you could observe a class.

Look at any information provided by potential classes to see if it aligns with your own reasons for doing a class. For example, if a play-based environment is important to you, look for that in the description. Some classes may be geared toward a specific age group, such as birth to 2 years or 2 to 4 years, while other classes are multi-age (birth to 5 years). If you live in an area with multiple options for classes, choose the class that fits your family.

Paying for the Class

The class you find might be a free class offered by a local library. If the class is tuition-based, they may offer scholarships to families who meet certain financial requirements. Sometimes these scholarships are listed on the main page of the institution or community music school rather than right by the early childhood music program information.

If cost is a barrier, there may also be community resources available that you could apply for to help with the cost of an early childhood music program. The local library is a great place to learn about such opportunities. An additional resource may be early intervention programs. Many young children identified with learning disabilities or developmental delays participate in county intervention programs. These programs could include group class options such as music or scholarships for music classes. If your child is in an intervention program, ask your coordinator about music class options if you think that would be a good fit for your family.

Another idea for paying for class is to ask for the class tuition as a holiday or birthday gift for your child from a relative. If your home is already full of toys and your child's closet full of clothes, a music class gift can be a wonderful experience for your child. If the relative giving the gift lives in town and can bring your child to class some or all of the time, that is an extra special benefit.

At the Class

While you are in class, take the opportunity to learn the activities the teacher is demonstrating. Many programs will provide audio recordings. If they do not, ask if you may audio record the class (with other families' permission as well).

Savor the time with your child. Appreciate that for these 30 or 45 minutes, someone else is in charge. You and your child have the opportunity to be co-learners. Soak up the eye contact and skin contact and enjoyment. Study your child. What kind of music do they respond to the most? What activities are their favorite?

Accept whatever participation your child chooses. I have seen many children who are observers in music class, often to their parents' chagrin at first. Their parents report that the children sing all the way home in the car seat and when they get home, put on a full music class for their stuffed animals. That's okay! Gently engage with your child during class but do not worry or become frustrated if your child chooses the observer role.

If at all possible, put your phone on silent and take off your smart watch if you have one. I have seen far too many parents miss a sweet moment in class because they were glancing at messages on their watch or phone.

Try not to talk to the other parents and caregivers during class unless the teacher invites this. Spend the time before and after class connecting with others but let the music class time be for music. Do build relationships with other families and consider going from class to a playground, museum, or lunch to deepen the relationships.

After Class

Video your child doing songs or activities from music class during the week. Look back on these over time to see how your child is learning and developing. Write down the activities you most enjoyed as a parent. During the week, try some of the activities again. If you don't remember the songs the teacher used, sing your own.

Be an Advocate for Early Childhood Music in Your Community

Much of this chapter relates to tuition-based music classes in the community. Some of these programs could offer scholarships. However, there may be additional barriers to early childhood music class participation for some families (for instance, schedule, transportation, or health concerns for the family). In this section I will suggest ways to be an advocate for early childhood music classes in your community, both the caregiver-child classes we have been discussing and classes for children at daycares or preschools. In this way more children may have the opportunity to participate in a variety of programs.

Perhaps you are in a position to advocate early childhood music experiences in your community. If you are on the board of directors of an early childhood organization, look at the possibility of incorporating early childhood music programming. Check for grants from organizations like the National Association of Music Merchants (NAMM) Foundation and local foundations.

If your children attend daycare or preschool, find out if there is a music specialist who comes for music classes with your child. If there is not currently a music specialist, ask the director what it would take to add music to the weekly schedule. Reach out to local universities to find out if students would volunteer as music teachers if funding is not available.

Talk to the director of Children's Services at your local library. Find out what early childhood music offerings they already have and offer your support in brainstorming, publicizing, or attending future events. Some libraries have small budgets for programming and could host a family workshop on early childhood music with a local early childhood music teacher. You could also ask if area early childhood music programs would consider offering sample classes at the library. This helps advertise for the program and provide an opportunity to some families who may not otherwise encounter the program. If possible, ask the library to schedule the event during evening or weekend hours to include more families.

Many counties have early intervention programs for children under the age of 3 who are diagnosed with developmental delay or disability. My graduate advisor, Dr. Cynthia Crump Taggart, worked with a team in East Lansing, Michigan, to have early childhood music classes added as one of the playgroup options available to families.[3] Identify organizations with music therapy offerings in your area, such as community music schools, performing arts centers, and nonprofits serving individuals with disabilities. Find the people in your area who know how to get grants or access pools of money. Share your success stories about adding music with other parents through social media or word of mouth.

ACTIVITY 63 At-Home Music Class

Whether or not someone participates in early childhood music classes outside of the home, everyone can include music activities in daily life. This could be an integrated part of your day, such as the suggestions in Chapters 13–15—a parenting musically approach. It could also be a "music class" time that you set aside to try several activities in a row—this is more of a musical parenting approach.

For this at-home activity, gather the following: scarves or bandanas, beanbags, a stuffed animal, a drum or bowl and mallet or wooden spoon, and recorded music. Announce, "It's time for music class!"

- Sing a hello song to your child, yourself, and any stuffed animals who would like to participate.
- Make "soup" (see full description in Chapter 14, Activity 53)
- Put a scarf or bandana on everyone's head, sway to music (you can sing a tune or play a recorded tune), and at the end, sing "Where's [name]?" Respond (or wait for your child to respond) with "There's [name]!" (see Chapter 13, Activity 44)
- Create "Fireworks" with scarves: Bounce the scarves up and down in your hand while chanting "Let's make some fireworks, high up in the sky. Let's make some fireworks, watch the colors fly!" Then toss the scarves in the air and say "Wooooooooooo!" with a high voice. Repeat with various versions (big, little, high, low, fast, slow, silly, tired).
- Move & freeze to some favorite music. If your child is old enough, let them control the pause button.

FIGURE 18.1 Mother and child engaging in music play at home. GETTY IMAGES

- Balance a bean bag or stuffed animal on various body parts (head, elbow, knee, foot) while moving with continuous fluid movement (see more on the importance of this movement in Chapter 10). Sing while moving. Pause in the middle or at the end of the song, and sing "Ah-chooo!" as the beanbag slips to the floor. Sing using the dominant and tonic notes, or fifth and first scale degree of the melody. This helps your child build a sense of tonality. (see Chapter 13, Activity 45)
- Move like animals around the room, calling out animals with different types of movements, such as birds, snakes, giraffes, elephants, and fish.
- Play drums or bowls, either with your hands or with mallets (wooden spoons work well). Drum while singing a song or put on some recorded music to drum along to.
- Rock or row: If you child is an infant, place them on their back and gently circle their legs. With toddlers, sit facing your child, join hands, and slowly rock forward and back (seated). Sing a slow, gentle song.

You could keep the props for music class in a special bag and let your child decide when to have a music class. You can also encourage your child to host a music class for their stuffed animals.

WRAPPING UP CHAPTER 18

Formal early childhood music classes work for some families and not for others. Do not feel guilty if you choose not to participate in an early childhood music class. There are many other ways to engage in music with your young child. If you do choose to attend an early childhood music class, be attentive and open-minded about how your child is participating. Incorporate early childhood music activities regularly in your home.

FOR FURTHER READING

Music Play: The Early Childhood Music Curriculum Guide for Parents, Teachers, and Caregivers, vol. 1, by Wendy H. Valerio, Alison M. Reynolds, Beth M. Bolton, Cynthia C. Taggart, and Edwin Gordon (Chicago: GIA Publications, 1998), provides an overview of young children's music development and an assortment of songs and chants with activities to try with your little ones. A CD is also included with the songs and chants.

CHAPTER 19

HOW TO HELP YOUR CHILD CHOOSE AN INSTRUMENT OR VOICE PART

CHAPTER PREVIEW

- Choosing an instrument or voice part to study informally or formally is an exciting decision.
- Music education research offers valuable information when it comes to choosing instruments or voice parts.
- Family members can support their child's instrument or voice part selection process by introducing children to instruments in recordings or at live events and tracking children's responses and preferences.
- Families can help promote greater equity and access in school music education programs.

Do you play an instrument? Is there an instrument you have always wanted to learn? Did you sing in a choir in school? As you read this chapter, think about learning an instrument or joining a community choir yourself. It's never too late!

Three (of Many) Potential Paths to Starting an Instrument

Consider three of the paths children can take toward starting to play an instrument. In this chapter, "instrument" refers to something beyond the rhythm instruments discussed in Chapter 9. Instruments here include piano, keyboard, guitar, wind instruments, string instruments, and percussion. This could be anything from a harmonica to a flute to a bagpipe, a drum kit to a violin to an electric guitar. Children may also choose voice as their instrument and choir as their ensemble.

Path one: your child is given an instrument by a family member or friend. Perhaps the family member or friend teaches your child the instrument. This could be supplemented by YouTube videos or private lessons from a music teacher.

Path two: you or your child decide it is time to start learning an instrument. You choose an instrument, rent or buy one, find a teacher, and start lessons.

Path three: it is beginning-instrument time at your child's school (often 4th, 5th, or 6th grade). Your child completes a process guided by the music teachers toward selecting a band or orchestra instrument or voice (choir).

Types of Ensembles Commonly Offered in Schools

Music programs vary widely across the country. Many elementary and middle schools have beginning bands and choirs, and some also have beginning orchestras. Depending on the music department structure, all children might be required to choose a band or orchestra instrument. In other schools, choir and visual arts might also be options. Still other schools may have multiple types of choirs offered.

Some schools limit the instruments students can choose as beginners. For instance, in band, the choices might be flute, clarinet, trumpet, trombone, and baritone. Additional instruments, including saxophone, French horn, tuba, percussion, oboe, bassoon, and bass clarinet may be added in later years. Other schools start beginners on a wider range of instruments. For orchestra, the instruments are violin, viola, cello, and bass. Voice parts in choir from highest to lowest are soprano, alto, tenor, and bass.

Students may be able to join both choir and an instrumental ensemble, or they may have to choose between them. If students are required to choose, there could be extracurricular opportunities that provide additional experiences. For instance, a student might be in choir but also play an instrument in a before-school jazz band.

Equity Note: School Music Participation for Children with Disabilities

If your school offers ensembles, your child wants to play an instrument or be in choir at school, and you have concerns about accessibility or accommodations, talk to the teacher early. Set up a team meeting with the teacher, school social worker, occupational therapist, paraprofessional, and a music therapist if available. Some music teachers may not have had extensive coursework in their undergraduate degree about how to make accommodations for instrumentalists and vocalists with physical differences. Nevertheless, your child has the right to learn music. There are many people in the music education profession working to find ways to provide accommodations and to better equip teachers. Work with your local teacher and school so your child can participate. Talk to other parents in your district or in neighboring districts to find out what is working for their children. Join a social media support group and ask for ideas.

ACTIVITY 64   Attend an "Instrument Petting Zoo"

If you have the opportunity, attend an instrument petting zoo in your community. These are typically sponsored by a community music school or community arts organization such as a symphony orchestra. Some schools may also offer instrument petting zoos. There are instruments available for children to touch and try.

Alternatively, seek out opportunities for your child to see an instrumentalist or vocalist performing up close. This could be at a restaurant, outdoor music festival, house of worship, birthday party, parade, fair, or sporting event. With permission, bring your child close to the performer. If you have baby-sitters who play musical instruments, ask them to bring their instruments and play for your children.

Research on Instrument Selection

Researchers who study how children choose instruments have found that it is a complex decision process.[1] Some children choose an instrument because they like the sound, others make the choice based on their friend's choices. Some researchers have suggested that if a child likes the sound of an instrument, they are more likely to practice.[2] Gender stereotypes persist in some communities or schools when it comes to instruments.[3] Asking your child questions about why they are interested in certain instruments can help uncover any stereotypes that might be influencing them.

If you ask children in your neighborhood why they chose their instrument, you might hear a wide range of reasons, such as

- I wanted an instrument with a small case.
- I liked how shiny it is.
- We had a clarinet in the attic, so I chose that.
- I chose it so I could sit by my friends.
- The teacher said I would be good at this because I have long arms.

As you read these, you may notice that none of the reasons are about the sound of the instrument or the type of music the instrument plays. If your child suggests the above reasons, you could say "Yes, I like how shiny it is too. Let's listen to some recordings and you can tell me what you like about them. Let's listen to a few other instruments too."

In beginning choirs, there are sometimes just two voice parts, altos and sopranos. The choir teacher may rotate children through the voice parts. If your child has sung alto throughout middle school and high school and would like to try soprano, request a conversation with the choral instructor about this. It is possible that the choir teacher has asked your child to sing alto because your child is particularly good at reading music and singing harmony. The teacher might assign vocal parts based on vocal range or timbre, as well.

ACTIVITY 65 Explore Your Child's Instrument Timbre (Sound Quality) Preference

Timbre refers to sound quality or sound color, such as bright or mellow, airy or buzzy. This is an activity that can be done with any age child. Play a wide range of music for your child or take your child to live music events and pay attention to their response. Does your child gravitate toward certain instruments or sounds? Does your child prefer lower or higher sounds? Do they respond to brighter sound qualities or timbres, like trumpet, or more mellow sounding instruments, like the guitar? Is your child captivated by the sight of certain instruments?

Your child's interests and tastes will probably change over the years. Opening the conversation about what types of sounds they most enjoy can help when it is time to choose an instrument to learn. It is important to base the decision about instrument choice on multiple conversations and encounters. In education we talk about assessments being "snapshots"—each test, rating, or check-in is one look at how children are doing. We seek to base evaluations on many data points. Similarly, work to base the instrument selection on multiple opportunities to listen or try instruments, not a single "my friends are all playing clarinet and so I will too!" moment.

Beware: Do not let your child trick you. A child I know recently told his mother he did not like the high sound of his violin and thus did not want to practice. It turns out he just did not want to practice and figured out that telling her this would give her pause because of the discussion of the importance of a child liking the sound of the instrument. Later he was singing and playing very, very high notes of his own accord. It is also possible that a child will say they do not like the sound of themselves practicing as a beginner, although they liked hearing the instrument in general and played by other people. That is normal—it takes a while to develop pleasing tone. Encourage your child to play the notes that they can play most beautifully as a reminder of what they are working toward.

Roles of Child, Family, and Teacher in Instrument Selection

In a school-organized instrument selection process, the child's role is to be open-minded in choosing an instrument. Encourage your child to pay attention to their own reactions and responses to the instruments presented by the teachers. Your child might want to sign up for the same instrument as friends. However, be sure your child understands the importance of personally enjoying the sound and the instrument.

As a family member, your role is to encourage your child's open-mindedness and participation in the process. Communicate with the teacher if there is any extra information, such as if you have spent time already discovering your child's instrument timbre preference or if you have access to a certain instrument. Teachers will be interested in hearing if other family members play certain instruments and whether a child has other musical learning experience, such as piano lessons or community choir. Families can also take their child to visit a local music store to try instruments.

If your child is leaning toward an instrument that is out of your price range, ask the school music director if they have any school-owned instruments your child can borrow. Find out if family or friends have an instrument you can borrow. Checking on a neighborhood giveaway or buy-sell social media page is another good way to find an instrument. Local music stores also have instrument rental programs.

The music teacher's role begins with communicating with families and children about the range of possible instruments for beginners. Many districts offer a narrower range of instruments at the entry level and add others later. Teachers also typically provide information about the instruments, give instrument demonstrations, and do "instrument fittings." This is where children hold specific instruments and teachers look for physical characteristics that could help a child be successful, including their stature and their facial features. Teachers might also suggest instruments so the ensemble is somewhat balanced and not made up of only flutes or only cellos. It's valuable for parents to know this so they understand why a teacher may guide their child away from a first-choice instrument. If this happens, you might be okay with it. But if not, set up a meeting with the teacher and hear the teacher's advice. Take their advice seriously, especially as it pertains to finding the right "fit" for your child's instrument. If your child still has a strong preference for a different instrument, explore with the teacher whether this is a possibility.

The types of instruments available to study in your school music program will vary based on your community. It could be band instruments only, or band and orchestra. There could also be the choice to study popular music instruments, mariachi band, steel drum, guitar, or ukulele. If your child is interested in learning an instrument not offered in the school music program, consider whether also learning a school instrument could provide a beneficial supplement. For instance, maybe your child would focus on guitar learning at home and play the trombone at school. This can be beneficial as your child would have the opportunity to play in an ensemble, learn to read notation, and explore different types of music.

Promote Equity in Your School Music Program

Band, Orchestra, and Choir Boosters are common organizations at schools. These are groups of parents and teachers who work toward raising money for special costs of the program, such as uniforms or travel. Booster groups volunteer for special events and serve as liaisons between teachers and families of ensemble members. The Boosters can also be a group focusing on equity in a school music program.

When promoting equity, it is important to think about these groups:

- Children from racial or ethnic groups who may be excluded due to historical inequity, cultural stereotypes, or systemic factors;
- Children with disabilities who may be excluded due to perceived barriers such as ability to read music, remain still during a performance, or complete a marching band drill pattern;
- Children from low socioeconomic status (SES) who may be excluded due to the perceived cost of participation or the logistics (if they do not have a ride to evening events, for example),
- Children who identify as gender-expansive or transgender who may be excluded from choral participation due to gendered voice classification or face difficulties in any ensemble due to gendered performance attire expectations.

If you look at the school music programs in your community and you see inequities, an important question to ask is whether the current music curriculum is serving your community. A vital area of conversation in the music education profession is how to better reach students with our curriculum. The traditional band, choir, and orchestra model that is prevalent in many communities is being supplemented with guitar choirs, steel pan ensembles, rock bands, digital production, and more. When considering equity in music education, the first question is whether there is any music curriculum or program whatsoever in a school or district. Next, is the curriculum itself hospitable to all students? Talking with your school music teachers, administrators, and other parents is a way to investigate this. Your teachers are likely champions for equity within the music program. Ask how you can best support their efforts, perhaps through letters to administration and school board.

Within any school music curriculum, keep an eye out for how participation could be challenging for students. Ask questions about how the school is opening opportunities for children who may not be able to afford instruments, uniform fees, or trips. Join the music boosters or music support group to work with other family members on making more opportunities available. Find out how a child with attention-deficit/hyperactivity disorder (ADHD) or autism could be included and successful in marching band. Ask whether the ensemble directors would be willing to adjust their performance schedule to respect the religious holidays that are observed by families in the community.

The Boosters groups could make a list of aspects of the school music program that may foster inequities and a list of potential solutions. For example:

Observation	Potential Action Steps
Instrument selection requires parent signature on handout or attendance at concert or meeting	Provide multiple opportunities for parents to receive information and talk to teachers, including all-school events like conferences and open houses. Hold a virtual (Zoom or Google Meet) instrument information meeting.

The children in our school who receive free and reduced lunch are not choosing band and orchestra.	Fundraise for scholarships for instrument rental. Hold a community "used instrument drive" asking for tax-deductible donations of instruments for the school to lend out.
We notice that the school music program is racially segregated.	Look at the curriculum. Is it centered on music for and by white people? How can the curriculum be expanded to be more inclusive? Are there community stakeholders who can advise on curricular selections, both repertoire and class offerings?
Only a few children in our district who have Individualized Education Plans (IEPs) or 504 plans are enrolled in school music.	Look for models of success, either in your district or in neighboring districts. Harness the power of social media to find examples of how districts make this work. Is there a paraprofessional who stays with the ensemble? Do the music educators need support to obtain additional professional development on inclusive practices in the ensemble?
The school ensembles have gendered expectations for concert attire.	Find an inclusive model by Googling "inclusive choir uniform" (or band/orchestra). Additional resource: *Honoring Trans and Gender Expansive Students in Music Education* by Dr. Matthew L. Garrett and Dr. Joshua Palkki (Oxford University Press, 2021).

There is substantial research evidence to suggest that participating in school music programs may bring a range of musical and extramusical benefits.[4] If school music and extracurricular music programs are not currently available to all children in your community or district, find others to work together on this cause with you to help it happen.

WRAPPING UP CHAPTER 19

In this chapter, I shared ideas related to choosing instruments. For some families, choosing an instrument or voice part coincides with deciding to be part of a middle school or high school music program. Participating in school music, as well as extracurricular music opportunities and informal musicking, can carry big benefits for our children. It is important that these opportunities are accessible to all children in our communities. Family members can work with music educators and administrators to increase equity in music programs.

FOR FURTHER READING

Raising Musical Kids, 2nd ed., by Robert A. Cutietta (Oxford University Press, 2014): provides instructive information for many musical milestones. Check Chapter 8 of Cutietta's book for more advice on helping your child choose an instrument.

Teaching Music to Students with Special Needs: A Label-Free Approach, 2nd ed., by Alice M. Hammel and Ryan M. Hourigan (Oxford University Press, 2017): presents information about the legal rights of all students to engage in music education, and all education settings, in the least restrictive environment.

https://nafme.org/wp-content/uploads/2020/06/Local-Advocacy-Action-Plan.pdf—This is a step-by-step advocacy plan created by the National Association for Music Education (NAfME). While it is designed for music teachers, this offers valuable insights for families who wish to help advocate music programs in their area.

https://www.nammfoundation.org/why-music-matters%20%20—A list of resources and links curated by the NAMM Foundation (National Association of Music Merchants). Research studies related to specific age groups are linked at the bottom of the webpage. If you need direction for your advocacy efforts, this is a good place to look.

CHAPTER 20

HOW TO HELP YOUR CHILD DEVELOP MUSICAL SKILLS

> **CHAPTER PREVIEW**
> - There are many ways to develop musical skills.
> - It is important to match your goals/your child's goals with the opportunities in your community.
> - When investigating ways to help your child develop musical skills, consider family logistics and budget.
> - General music classes in elementary schools can be a form of music educational equity, providing access for all children to develop musical skills.

Many Ways to Develop Musical Skills

One of the themes of this book is "not one right way." There is not one correct way to make music a part of your family life, to start a child learning a musical instrument, or to have the child participate in a formal school music program. There are many ways to do each of those things. What works for a while might not work when life circumstances change or children grow older. It is important that we remain flexible and pay attention to when a change is needed.

> What are some other areas of parenting for which there is not one right way? How does reminding yourself of this affect how you make decisions as a parent?

Developing musical skills is one of those things that might seem to follow a right way, but there are many ways to do so. Some people can assume that taking lessons with a private lesson teacher for a weekly fee is the best way to help children develop musical skills. However, in this chapter we will discuss many ways to help acquire musical skills: self-teaching, learning online, learning from family or friends, group instruction, community classes, and private lessons.

Hopefully you live in an area that provides music instruction as part of the school curriculum, and hopefully your child is developing musical skills in that setting as well. See the end of this chapter for some thoughts on how to be an advocate for general music programs in elementary schools.

"Teaching Themselves Music" and Learning Online

In my research on children's music learning in The Gambia, West Africa, I found that the children I observed were able to teach themselves music through a process of learning, observing, and doing. I found that the rich musical environment, expectation to be musical, and motivation to learn contributed to their success in teaching themselves music.[1] I noticed that the children had a strong motivation to learn the musical games they played together. The children were determined to learn the complex rhythms, motions, and chants that went with the games. Their focus and attention were self-directed in such a way that they worked hard to figure things out and be part of the game.

Children can teach themselves a wide range of musical skills, repertoire, and technology through listening, observing, and trying. Online tutorials and videos can also be helpful for music learning. Dr. Lucy Green, a music educator and researcher in England, interviewed popular musicians about their music learning.[2] She found that popular musicians learned informally, their passion to learn combined with techniques such as aural imitation and experimentation.

> How can we as families foster our children's motivation to learn a musical skill, piece of repertoire, or instrument? What have you noticed about your own child or children when it comes to motivation?

ACTIVITY 66 Be an Observer of Your Child's Motivation

Take a step back and consider what motivates your child to engage in musical activities. Certain music? Certain instruments? Being part of a group? Being like older siblings? Does your child seem to be motivated by the chance to spend time with others while doing music (relational musicking)? Or do you notice your child more excited by specific goals (practical musicking)?

Now consider your child's motivational style more broadly. Does your child thrive on competition? When you suggest an activity to your child, do they tend to try it or shy away from it? In other words, does your child prefer to come up with their own initiatives? Take this knowledge and let it guide you when you interact with your children and their potential pursuit of musical skills.

Be ready for motivational styles to change as children grow and go through various developmental phases. Kids know how to keep us on our toes!

Learning from a Family Member or Friend

An opportunity may arise for your child to learn musical skills or a specific instrument from a family member or friend. Depending on the mentor, this can dictate the choice of instrument. For instance, if Grandpa plays guitar and is willing to teach your child, then guitar it is! Learning from a friend or family member can provide a special kind of relational musicking for your child and their close teacher.

Group Instruction and Community Classes

Many communities offer beginning music classes, such as group piano or guitar classes. These could be facilitated through after-school programs, community music schools, community recreation programs, music stores, or local universities. Group opportunities may provide logistical convenience and may be less expensive than private lessons. If your child learns well in a group setting, this could be a good option.

Community-based children's choruses are another prime venue for children to develop musical skills. Singing in a choir can lead your child to sing in tune, learn repertoire, and enjoy performing. Singing in choir can also help a child develop musicality and a sense of pitch that can help in learning other instruments.

Many communities have El Sistema-inspired after-school music programs. El Sistema is a classical music program developed in 1975 by Venezuelan musician and economist José Antonio Abreu (1939–2018). His goal was to bring social change and individual self-actualization through children's involvement with classical music. The community-based programs feature musical instruction, both group and individual. Other common elements are care for the whole child and emphasis on personal development.[3] You can learn more by viewing the Ted Talk titled "The El Sistema Music Revolution." El Sistema programs are typically low- or no-tuition, relying on community funding and charitable donations to cover operating costs. You can look for El Sistema programs in your community by searching for "El Sistema _____" (fill in the blank with your city or region).

Taking Lessons with a Teacher

In addition to the possibilities of learning informally, with a friend or family member, and through community classes, taking one-on-one lessons with a teacher can be a way for children to develop musical skills. Here are some aspects to this experience to consider.

In person or online? You know your child best and whether they will learn better in-person or online. Some teachers recommend starting in person so the teacher can help with physical setup of how to hold the instrument, posture, and embouchure (mouth shape). Online lessons might be a good option for a student who is past the beginner phase. It is also convenient to have the option to do an online lesson occasionally if a family member is sick or the teacher is traveling. Talk to your teacher about this as an option.

Looking for a teacher. Talk to friends in the neighborhood and school music educators to find out who the teachers are in your area. Consider whether you want to bring your child to someone's home, to a music studio or school, or if you prefer the teacher to come to your home. Find out the price range in your area—this varies widely by region and by the level of experience of the teacher. Is it important for your child to have performance opportunities, such as a recital?

Another factor to consider is how the teacher can be a role model for your child. I interviewed James Rhodes, a Suzuki viola and violin teacher, for Episode 5 of the *Parenting Musically* podcast. He described how a music teacher is different from a parent. He suggested that a music teacher is not a school teacher, a therapist, or a grandparent, but in some ways a combination of those three ▶.[4] You could also think about whether certain demographics or characteristics are important to you. For instance, maybe you think your child would respond better to a younger teacher. Or perhaps your child learns best from teachers who are very structured and organized.

Selecting a teacher. My best piece of advice is to ask for a sample lesson with a potential teacher. This gives you and your child a chance to meet the teacher, as well as for the teacher to meet you as a family. Watch how the teacher interacts with your child. If you feel comfortable, briefly share your musical hopes and dreams (see Chapter 6) as related to the lessons with the teacher. This could occur before or during the sample lesson. For example, when writing to ask for a sample lesson, you could say, "Dear Mr. Smith, we received your name and email address from our neighbors, the Wrights. We are looking for a guitar teacher for our 8-year-old child. We are looking for someone who is playful, creative, and flexible as a teacher. Our hopes for the lessons are for our child to learn to play chords and learn music by ear, as well as to learn to play classical guitar style. Do you have any openings in your studio? If so, would you consider allowing us to sign up for a sample lesson? Please let us know if this would work, and what your sample lesson fee is."

If, based on the sample lesson, the teacher does not seem like the right fit, thank them and move on. It is easier to take several sample lessons in the beginning than to switch later, although switching is also an option.

Switching teachers. If lessons are not going well, one possibility to explore is whether switching teachers would make a difference. I know many families who have switched teachers for a variety of reasons. The best-case scenario would be to talk openly with your teacher if you are considering this. You could say something like, "Mrs. Jones, we so appreciate your work with our child. You may have noticed that she is struggling lately, and we know you've tried a lot of different things. We're just wondering about your thoughts here. Our child wants to quit. How do you see it? Do you think trying a different teacher can be a possibility?" Your teacher might even recommend someone who has a different teaching style than they have themselves.

If having a conversation like this would prove too awkward, another approach is to seek the opportunity for a sample lesson with a different teacher. One way this could naturally occur is through a summer camp that includes private lessons. Your child may have the opportunity to take a trial lesson with one of the summer camp teachers. Through doing this you may find that a different approach or style works better for your child. You could then approach that teacher about lessons or find someone with similar characteristics.

Having a conversation about taking a break or stopping lessons. If lessons are not going well, another possibility is that it is time to take a break or consider stopping lessons. This can be a complicated decision for families. Maybe one parent stopped taking lessons as a child and regrets stopping, while the other parent continued in lessons and did not enjoy the experience. It is important to acknowledge one's own childhood experiences but also set them aside when considering the child's unique situation and experience. James Rhodes described the importance of talking with the teacher, parent, and child together when deciding what to do, "leaving that space to openly, honestly have a conversation to see what's best for the child and what's best for the family. But when we have those conversations there's always a solution. Talking together leaves that space for that solution to become present."[5] The solution could be pausing lessons, switching to every other week, or looking for a new teacher. You know your child best and whether it is important to push ahead or to pause.

I find it reassuring to remember that "all is not lost" if a child stops music instruction. This is a phrase one of my research participants used when reflecting on the long trajectory of her children's musical involvement. Children can continue to play their instruments and develop their skills, including learning informally and creating their own music. In talking with other adults, you may find that some of your friends who value and engage in music as adults took only a few or no private music lessons. Perhaps their family moved frequently, which made it hard to establish relationships with private lesson teachers. Maybe they dabbled as a child, taking several years of lessons on several different instruments. Researchers have found that children—and professional musicians!—can learn informally, through processes like learning by ear, experimentation, and self-guided learning.[6] Online resources are also viable ways to learn music.[7] Tuition-based private music lessons may play a role but are not a necessary part of a musical childhood or a musical home.

Bartering for lessons. You might also have the opportunity to barter for lessons with a music teacher. If you find a teacher you are interested in working with and their fees do not fit your budget, ask them if you trade services—lawn work, hair cutting, house cleaning, childcare, etc.

I interviewed Maggie Baird, mother to GRAMMY award-winning musicians Billie Eilish and FINNEAS, on the topic of children, music lessons, practicing, and home music environment. She shared that Billie and FINNEAS took several piano lessons when they were children. Maggie and her husband, Patrick O'Connell, bartered services in exchange for the lessons, because money was tight. When it became apparent the children were not invested in the lessons, Maggie and Patrick offered their children the option of stopping. Billie and FINNEAS decided to stop.[8] Those formal lessons were not necessary to their musical growth and expression, which was nurtured within their home musical environment created by Maggie and Patrick. Maggie described how Billie and FINNEAS learned a few music theory basics from herself and Patrick, and then spent time on their own with YouTube videos exploring piano and guitar. Maggie noted that her children's musical skill acquisition was influenced by the increasing availability of online resources and technological tools. Their story, like many others, highlights informal learning strategies as a way for some children to acquire musical skills and knowledge.

Advocate General Music Programs in Elementary Schools

General music in elementary schools is different from middle school and high school bands, choir and orchestra, because typically all students participate in elementary general music. Often only around 20% to 25% of high schoolers in the United States continue in school music.[9] Become familiar with the general music offerings at your children's schools. If there is a program offered, find out how many times a week children come to music class and for how many minutes.

Families and community members can support general music programs and general music teachers. Reach out to the teachers in your district to ask for ways you can help. Some possibilities are visiting class to share a song, instrument, or tradition; helping to format and print concert programs; assisting with larger events like school musicals; and helping with classroom projects like making instruments.

Pay close attention to any schedule changes the district or school makes to see if the number of minutes of music is cut. Occasionally a district, when faced with a financial crisis or in response to educational trends (increased science and technology instruction, for instance), will talk about cutting the elementary music program. They will probably not announce this to parents; you may need to check school board minutes or be in touch with music teachers to know if something is afoot. It is critical to speak up and become involved in any way you are comfortable if you hear that your district is considering such a change. You could start with an email to the school board or administration. For example:

> Dear Members of the School Board and Members of the Administration,
>
> Our family are strong supporters of [School District]. We count ourselves blessed that our children have the opportunity to learn from the passionate, generous educators of this district.
>
> I am writing to express my deep concern about the proposal to reduce the amount of general music offered at the elementary school level from the current once-a-week, 42 minutes to a once-per-7 days rotation in order to facilitate the addition of technology awareness classes.
>
> We are concerned about this proposal for the following reasons:
>
> - In searching peer-reviewed educational literature, I could not find any research supporting this schedule. I would be glad to receive any research you are working from.
> - It is not in the best interest of the children. The elementary years are critical to musical development.
> - Reducing elementary general music reduces educational equity for children. General music is the time that all children have the opportunity to develop musical skills and have musical experiences, regardless of their future enrollment. The children of our district deserve high-quality arts education.
>
> Thank you for your consideration,
>
> [Signature]

Talk to other parents and teachers to find out the best next steps to continue advocating the program. Once a program is cut back or eliminated altogether, it is hard to bring it back. Now is the time to fight. General music is a critical setting for laying a foundation for lifelong musicking. It is the only formal music education that many children receive, so offering general music is important from an equity perspective. General music provides an opportunity for all students to build their musical skills and experience group musicking, regardless of whether students choose to continue in school music at the secondary level.

WRAPPING UP CHAPTER 20

We have looked at many ways for children to develop musical skills. As in other areas of musical parenting, there is no one best way for children to learn music. Think about the goals you and your child have and match them to the opportunities that are available. If possible, be an advocate for general music instruction in elementary schools. This helps provide a chance for all children to develop musical skills.

FOR FURTHER READING

Look for biographies of musicians, written for adults or children: pay attention to what musicians say about how they learned music as a way to see the many pathways to building musical skills.

How Popular Musicians Learn: A Way Ahead for Music Education, by Lucy Green (Ashgate Publishing, 2002): rich interviews with popular musicians between the ages of 15 and 50. Reading these interviews may give you new insights into motivating your child.

CHAPTER 21

HOW TO APPROACH MUSICAL PRACTICE IN HEALTHY WAYS

> **CHAPTER PREVIEW**
> - There are many strategies for making musical practice work for your child and your family.
> - Musical practice can be a point of conflict for families.
> - Cultural beliefs influence a family's experience and expectations around musical practice.
> - Music aptitude, personality, and learning styles play a role in a child's experience of practicing.
> - Work to maintain a positive relationship with your child when encountering difficulty during musical practice.

Finding Your Family Peace with Musical Practicing

If I were reading this book, this is the chapter I would turn to first. Of all the topics about families and music that I have heard families discuss over the years, practicing at home is the dilemma that comes up most frequently and is accompanied by complex emotional interactions. Regular music practice is an expectation of many school music ensembles and private lessons. Your school music teacher and private lesson teachers will have practice guidelines. Here are some Practice Principles that come from my own experience as a musician, parent, music educator, and researcher of families and music. See chapters 8 and 9 in Dr. Robert

Cutietta's "Raising Musical Kids" (Oxford: Oxford University Press, 2014) for additional practice suggestions.

Practice Principles

1. There is no one right way to practice. Your teacher or the methodology you take lessons in might suggest that you practice every day, or at a certain time of day, or for a certain amount of time. The more parents I talk to in my research, the more I realize that not everyone practices the same way. Find what works for your family and do not lose time worrying further.
2. Intrinsic motivation, or the child wanting to practice of their own accord in order to get better at music, is a lovely goal to pursue. But it is not uncommon for that to be take months or years to occur. If your child needs some extrinsic motivation to support their practice early on (stickers, a star chart leading to a special outing, etc.), that is fine. If screen time is a limited commodity in your house and therefore motivating, that can be a great one (for every minute of practice, the child gets a minute of screen time).
3. Talk about the level of frustration or discomfort that your child can tolerate while you and your child are both calm, sitting away from the instrument. This could vary based on their personality, age, and what else is happening—if it is a stressful time at school, perhaps they will slide back on the frustration level. For example:

    PARENT: Wow, you seemed pretty frustrated yesterday when you were practicing. Are you okay with that?
    CHILD: Yeah. I like to get my feelings out while I practice. I'm fine.
    PARENT: Okay. Could you give me a signal if you're really REALLY frustrated? Like "That's it, I need a break!"
    CHILD: Okay.

    This signal could be useful in other situations as well, such as homework or interactions with siblings.
    It is also possible that the frustration could be tied to something else happening, and just coming out while the child is practicing.

This is a very important conversation to have because it models a process you want your child to be able to engage in throughout their life. Here is an example that could occur in a different place and at a different time than when the child practices. The car is a good place for conversations like this:

> PARENT: Hey sweetie, I noticed you've been getting super frustrated while you practice lately. Can you tell me more about that?"
> CHILD: I don't know.
> PARENT: Is your teacher assigning too much to work on? Is it too hard?
> CHILD: No.
> PARENT: Any ideas why you're getting frustrated?
> CHILD: I don't know. [Pause]. When I get home from school I just want to hang out for a while, not practice right away.

In this vignette, the parent has received some important information about how the child feels. Other possible things they could have discovered were hunger, distraction, or tiredness being an issue at practice time.

4. Remember that things will change. Just when you find a good groove for musical practicing—the right time of day, the right amount of time—your schedule will change or the difficulty of the material will change. Be ready to keep helping your child find their musical balance for a while, until they can find it on their own. Remember, again, what a great life skill this is: being able to adjust to challenges.
5. Be on guard against perfectionism. Practicing music can naturally lead to perfectionism, or a determination not to make mistakes. It is hard to go through life without making mistakes, however. Trying to do so is frustrating and can lead to an unwillingness to take healthy risks. Keep an eye on potential perfectionism as it relates to music. Encourage your child to sight-read pieces and enjoy playing some pieces without learning them all the way to a performance level. Seek out musical models who enjoy musicking without the need for perfection. Look for activities that can balance out the nitty-gritty work that may go along with musical practice. You can model this yourself by saying "Let's go bowling! I know I'm not a great bowler

but it's still fun for me" or "You know, I just love coloring in this geometric coloring book. It doesn't have to be perfect. I'm doing this to relax and enjoy."

Here are four scenarios related to practice, followed by discussion of the issues related to each scenario and how to proceed.

Scenario 1: "Am I scarring her for life?"

I've heard from parents who say their children like going to lessons, but fuss and cry while practicing. "Am I scarring her for life?" a worried colleague asks.

Acquaintances on the playground who hear that I research families and music have told me that they are worried about their children's emotional experience while practicing, using words like "it's torture" and "scarred for life." They describe children who are happy to go to lessons but then sit at the piano or with their instrument and cry with frustration. Others resist practicing.

There are many possibilities to explain this discomfort or distress with practice. Erin Hopkins, a music educator and researcher who focuses on neurodiversity and music education, suggests one possibility:

> For kids who have executive functioning differences due to conditions like ADHD or autism, or who experience high levels of anxiety, resistance to practice could be related to difficulties with task initiation. For example, there can be a mental "wall" preventing them from being able to open their instrument case, or it could be almost physically painful to try to press the first piano key. One way to ease into practicing could be to start with the fun, easy stuff. Playing a favorite TV or video game theme song, or starting way back at the beginning of the method book with music they mastered long ago can help them to get the ball rolling in a motivating and low-stress way. Once the barrier to playing the instrument is broken, then it can be much easier to turn toward working on the practice goals of the week.[1]

If you are concerned for your child's well-being and noticing something in relation to musical practice, please talk to your child's pediatrician about it.

Second, if you think what is happening is "within normal limits"[2] then start with this idea: "This is so super hard. It would be weird if you could do it without trying." Here's an example, and this conversation could be spread out over several sessions. It might also need to occur regularly over a period of months and years. Know your own child—this can be a better conversation to have separate from practice time, as in the examples above. You could then remind your child of the idea when the big feelings hit during practice.

> PARENT: Hey there. This is so hard. Wow, super hard song here. Isn't this so hard?
> CHILD: (sniffling) Yes.
> PARENT: But let me ask you something. Wouldn't it just be so strange, so bizarre, if you could do this super hard thing without any practice? You know I couldn't just sit down and play a new song on a new instrument, right?
> CHILD: No?
> PARENT: Remember two weeks ago you couldn't play [name previous song], and it was so hard and you cried, but now you can?
> CHILD: Yes.
> PARENT: You're doing something really hard here. When I'm doing something really hard and I get frustrated, it helps me to squeeze a ball and breathe through my nose. Would you like a squeezie ball to keep by the piano?

This type of conversation is one that you can return to many times, in different learning contexts, as your child grows. This is a beautiful example of the blend of musical parenting and parenting musically: your child is learning self-regulation and coping through musical practice.

Third, consider setting up a situation where the child has some control. Perhaps you could say, "It seems like you love your instrument, but practicing is really rough. We've committed to lessons for this school year, but we can talk again in May about whether you want to continue. Until then, here are some choices you can make: practice in the morning or evening? Practice before or after screen time? Practice 15 min every day or 20 min five days a week?" Ask your child to draw up a practice plan. Let them know that if they do not follow through (too tired after screen time, for example), you will need to help reset the schedule for a while.

Fourth, be flexible yourself! Better to miss a day or two of practice if your child has an especially busy or stressful day, than to quit altogether. Remember, we're in this for the long game.

ACTIVITY 67   Consider Your Own Practicing History

What is your own history of musical practice, if any? Write down, or talk to a friend, about your own experiences. Did you set a little timer for 30 minutes every morning and practice without a complaint? Did your parents force you to practice by withholding privileges until practice was done? Were you lonely while you practiced, and as a result, gave up musical study? My professor of music education in my undergraduate program, Dr. Dale Topp, urged us to consider how difficult solo practice is for students who are extroverted. Notice if your child prefers to have others around while they practice.

Whatever your own practicing story is, it may be important to acknowledge it. The children in our lives are their own unique individuals. Just because practicing at 6:30 A.M. worked well for you as a child, it might not be best for your own child. If you carry distress from your memories of practicing in childhood, consider talking with a counselor or therapist about it.

Scenario 2: Revisiting "Battle Hymn of the Tiger Mother"

> *An acquaintance at the pool laughs self-consciously while she shares that she and her daughter yell at each other while her daughter, an award-winning young trumpet performer, practices. "I guess I am a Tiger Mother," she says. "But I know she can be exceptional. She needs to take her practicing more seriously." Once their neighbors got worried due to the yelling and called the police.*

In Yale law professor Amy Chua's controversial memoir, *Battle Hymn of the Tiger Mother*, Chua detailed her rigidly disciplined parenting style.[3] She expected her daughters to practice their instruments for many hours a day, including on weekends and vacations. Chua's self-described parenting style was informed by elements of her upbringing she associated with her Chinese heritage. Chau's book received, and continues to receive, a wide range of responses. Some readers are outraged by what they see as harsh and overly authoritarian parenting. Others say that the typical American parent is too lax, and more of Chua's no-excuses, high-expectations-style parents are needed.

A middle ground is proposed by Dr. Shimi Kang in her book *The Dolphin Way: A Parent's Guide to Raising Healthy, Happy, Motivated Kids—without Turning into a Tiger*.[4] Kang recommends the metaphor of the playful, social, balanced dolphin as inspiration for parenting rather than a tiger. While Dr. Kang does not directly address musical practice, she does emphasize the importance of play to human development. Keeping the "play" in "playing music" is important when thinking about musical practice.

Scenario 3: A Reminder About Music Aptitude

> *A teenager rolls his eyes and he notes that his younger sister practices about 15 minutes a week, total, and has great lessons and feedback from their piano teacher, while he had to put in at least 30 min a day in order to prepare when he was at her learning level.*

Scenario 3 has a direct connection to the concept of music aptitude, described further in Chapter 2.[5] In this scenario the younger sister likely has a higher music aptitude than her older brother. That explains her ability to adequately prepare for her lesson with very little practice, while her brother had to work at it to get the same result.

Please note two things here. Even though the teenager may have a lower music aptitude, that does not mean there is a limit on how well he can play piano or how far he can go with it. The music aptitude relates to how quickly he learns. It can be helpful for you as a parent to share this concept with him. You could even frame it like this: "I read about something called music aptitude. It's like a music learning speed limit. I think you and your sister might have different music learning speeds. But look—you've stuck with it all these years. Look how much you've learned and how beautifully you play. See how you use your piano music for your own enjoyment and also to help others when you play at the nursing home or accompany the choir. You've developed such important skills besides the piano playing too, like breaking down a hard project or showing up every day. I'm so proud of you."

The second thing to note is that for the child with higher aptitude, you might want to ask the teacher for more challenging material so more practice is required. Or you and your child might be more than happy to let it come easily and without much practice. Making an informed and reflective decision is the important part, whatever you decide.

Scenario 4: Monitoring Your Relationship with Your Child

A parent moans that practice used to be fine but now has become unmanageable, and they worry for their relationship with their child. Better to quit the lessons than to wreck the parent-child closeness?

A positive parent-child relationship is central in the vignette in Scenario 3. Having a conversation like the one with the teenager above is an example of both musical parenting and parenting musically. On the musical parenting side, you are helping your child develop musical skills by giving them greater understanding of their own learning process. You're also helping your child see how music lessons fit into the wider picture of their development as a person. I expect that this conversation would also serve to strengthen a positive relationship between a parent and child.

Musical practice can unfortunately also become a wedge in the parent-child relationship. Fighting over how much or whether a child has practiced and a parent over-commenting on a child's practice (shouting "That C was too sharp!" from the other room) are two ways the relationship can be weakened. If you notice this occurring, talk with your child. It's possible your child needs a change in the lessons, such as how much music is prepared each week, the difficulty of music (either too easy or too hard could lead to resistance), or type of music. Your child might also want a different form of support from you. Some kids appreciate your quiet presence in the room while they practice, with you working on your laptop. Or your child might want you to be more involved in helping listen for wrong notes or figure out difficult rhythms. If you consistently find that monitoring or encouraging musical practice is getting in the way of a healthy relationship with your child, look for someone else to be the Practice Person. For instance, you could enlist a grandparent or additional adult as the Practice Person for your child. Whether this person is in town or far away, you could ask them to be in charge of asking your child about practice, listening to some practice (in person or via videocall), and providing feedback. The feedback does not need to be technical! In some cases, having an outside person could be just what your child needs.

If music practice has become difficult and the above suggestions do not help, brainstorm together with your child's teacher and your child. Maybe your child needs a two-week practice pause but will continue to go to lessons. Or it is also possible your child needs a break from lessons for a time. This is not a failure on anyone's part. See Chapter 20 for more on taking a break.

Your relationship with your child is more important than how much they practice or whether they stay in music lessons at a given point in time. I have never interviewed a parent who said they regretted prioritizing their relationship with their child over music practice. This is not to say that the minute the going gets tough, you should quit lessons. Be ready for some friction in your relationship over the topic of practice. Pull out your parental wisdom and try different strategies. But if the disagreements over practicing invade other areas of your relationship with your child and do not resolve, make a change.

ACTIVITY 68   Make a List of Practice Strategies

The next two sections present a dozen ideas for making practice more manageable, both for the child and for the other members of the household. As a parent, try some of these strategies, as well as those recommended by your teacher. Keep track of what works. Write a list of strategies on a note and post it on the fridge or keep a memo in your phone. If practice time starts to get stressful, try a new approach.

A Treasure Trove of Tricks and Tips

Over the years of practicing with my own children, and talking to others about practice, I've gathered some practice tricks and tips. Some things work for an extended period of time, but many of these only work for a while, until the novelty wears off. It's useful in parenting to have a whole range of strategies for various scenarios. The same is true for the musical parenting task of encouraging kids to practice.

"**Is that the radio?**" Once when my daughter was practicing, I called from the other room, "Hey hey hey. Why are you playing the radio right now? You're supposed to be practicing!" She was delighted with the idea that her playing was so good, we thought we heard the radio playing. This has evolved into "What? I thought Linnea (oldest sibling) is at school. But I hear her practicing violin!" when it is the youngest brother practicing in the other room.

"**I just love that piece.**" If your child enjoys your presence during practicing, try to be nearby while they practice. Share comments like "Oh, that's my favorite song this week!" or "You've really grown this week." If grandparents or family friends visit, offer your child the chance to practice for them. A grandmother, Nancy, shared that *her* grandmother used to say "Oh, I just love to hear you play that piece. Will you play it again for me?" This was a way to both express appreciation to the child and to motivate the child to play the piece again. Nancy said she used this line many times with her own grandchildren.[6]

"**Practice Uno.**" Once while desperate to make practice more positive, I grabbed a deck of Uno cards, and we made up a game as we went. For each card we turned over, I quickly assigned a meaning. "It's a . . . 5! That means we play this tricky measure 5 times!" or "Oh no, a WILD card. You get to play any song you know!" The playful and random nature of this game provided a welcome diversion. You can do something similar with a pair of dice. Or you could make your own set of practice cards to achieve something similar. Some children may be more willing to practice specific songs, scales, and exercises that are chosen at random (by cards or dice) than what is listed in order in a practice notebook.

Power of routine. If your child and your family do well with routines, then sticking to a common practice time that is linked to another part of the day can serve you well. For instance, if there is time before school, your child could get ready, practice, then have free time before school.

"Margin minutes." When my oldest was 9 our goal was for her to get ready for school and practice violin with very few reminders from me in the morning. We set up a system that for every minute before school time that she was ready, she earned two screen time minutes. We called these "margin minutes" to teach the idea of being ready with time to spare ("margin").[7] Our younger kids misheard us and called them Martian Minutes! Our oldest became more and more efficient in getting ready and completing her practice, and they all still talk about margin.

Silent practice. If family members are sleeping or your living situation is not conducive to practice, ask your child to audiate (think in sound) their music and move their fingers along with the music notation. They could also listen to recordings.

Child's practice journal. Let your child pick out a notebook to keep a practice journal. Depending on their age, you or they could write down what songs they played that day, tricky things they are working on, and fun songs they would like to learn.

Kids track parent. While writing this book I asked my children to "dare" me to complete a certain number of hours working on the book for one week. Each day they asked me repeatedly if I had met my goal for that day. They seemed to enjoy the role reversal of checking up on whether I had done my homework. Choose something musical, work, or fitness-related that you are working on and let your children help keep track of how you are doing.

Strategies for the Rest of the Household

My parents put in a sound-blocking French door when my brothers and I were in late elementary school to muffle the sound of piano, trumpet, flute, and vocal practice in the living room. This might not be possible in your living situation, but here are some strategies for the rest of the household while a child is practicing. This does not just apply to a beginner's practice; listening to an excellent high school musician practice scales and repeat short phrases of their practice over and over to attain excellence can be disruptive to concentration or conversation.

- If you have little ones in the house, work with the older children to schedule practice at times that work with the younger siblings' sleep schedules. You can ask for no practice during naps or during the half hour after a child falls asleep. Alternatively, your younger children may be soothed listening to their sibling practice and like to hear it as they fall asleep.
- Many instruments have practice mutes. The musician can use one and still work on most aspects of their technique and musical expression, but the sound is reduced.
- If you have some family members trying to do work or homework while someone is practicing, consider earplugs, over-the-ear sound protection, or noise-cancelling headphones for the ones who are working.
- Weather-permitting and if it will not bother the neighbors, allow your child to practice outside for brief practice sessions.

ACTIVITY 69 Keep a Parent Observation Journal of Practicing

Sometimes teachers ask children to keep a practice log with what they worked on during practice. But for this activity, your job is to note the time of day, child's mood or condition (mellow, energetic, etc.), location, length of practice, how it went, and any other details that can help you watch for patterns. After a week or two, look over the journal to see if you notice any similarities on the days when practice went better or worse. One family I worked with struggled to get through the lesson material each evening. They noticed their child had extra time in the mornings before school and switched to practicing then. What had taken 20 minutes and frustration in the evening was covered in 10 minutes cheerfully in the morning.

WRAPPING UP CHAPTER 21

If you feel conflicted about music practice, you are in good company. In this chapter we talked about some of the influences on musical practice. I shared some of my survival tips. Musical practice is an area at the intersection of musical parenting and parenting musically. As a parent you probably want your child to practice in order to develop musical skills. Making practice successful and maintaining a positive relationship can be a challenging parenting task. Hang in there. It gets easier for many families. Sometimes it gets harder after it gets easier. But then it gets easier again!

FOR FURTHER READING

Time to Practice: A Companion for Parents, by Carrie Reuning-Hummel (Sound Carries Press, 2006): writing from a Suzuki perspective, the author shares advice as well as journal exercises for the parent.

The Dolphin Way: A Parent's Guide to Raising Healthy, Happy, Motivated Kids—Without Turning into a Tiger, by Shimi Kang (Penguin Group, 2014): outlines an approach to parenting that is neither "jellyfish" (permissive) or "tiger parenting" (aggressive).

Loretta: Ace Pinky Scout, by Keith Graves (Scholastic Press, 2002): In this picture book, the main character, Loretta, deals with failure, perfectionism, and getting back up again.

CHAPTER 22

HOW TO SUSTAIN MUSICAL INVOLVEMENT

CHAPTER PREVIEW

- Be flexible when thinking about your child's music involvement for the "long game."[1]
- Be an advocate for your school music program as well as for flexibility for students within the program.
- Awareness of practical and relational musicking can help sustain involvement.
- Remember there are many ways to be musical. Perhaps your child will transfer their musical skills learned in childhood to other forms of musicking as a young adult.
- Model musical engagement as an adult.

> What have been some of the musical highlights of your family life? How about your personal musical life?

Musical Involvement for the "Long Game"

If you have set a course for your family with music—a tradition of making playlists for road trips, or time and space for musical creativity, or a healthy approach to practicing an instrument—you might wonder how to sustain that musical involvement across the years. Maybe you value the musicking that is occurring right now, in beginning lessons or ensembles, for instance. But you might also hope and dream that your child will "stick with it" and be able to enjoy playing or singing or dancing in the years to come. These aspects of family musical life could encompass musical parenting-type activities, like lessons or ensemble participation, as well as activities representing parenting musically, like using music during routines.

Follow your child's interest. Researchers have found that if the child likes the timbre (sound) of the instrument, they may be more likely to be successful.[2] Common sense suggests that if the child gets to choose the instrument, they will be more invested as well. If you always wanted to learn to play the violin, then do it yourself. Don't make your child do it to fulfill your own childhood dreams, if your child doesn't want to.

Be flexible. A friend's daughter played the violin, then added clarinet for a year before switching to bassoon, which she played well for three years. The COVID-19 pandemic hit and there was less energy for extra lessons, so she stopped playing bassoon and concentrated on her violin. The time with the clarinet and bassoon was enjoyable and she could return to it in the future, but trying to keep all of the instruments moving forward would have been overly taxing. Playing the bassoon in this case was not practical musicking, nor did it meet relational musicking goals. By staying flexible through adding and dropping instruments, the child and her parents met her musical goals.

Be an advocate. Many school music programs and private lessons are set up in a way that works for the dominant group of people. For instance, school band programs tend to cater to beginners in late elementary school or early middle school and have no on-ramps for beginners later (in high school, for instance). But this does not work for everyone. Some individuals wait until they are retired and join New Horizons ensembles, groups geared toward adults,[3] because they always wanted to play an instrument or sing. If your child is a sophomore and wants to join the band playing a brass instrument, but has not had lessons or played before, have your child talk to the school band director. Ask what it would take to join, ask to borrow a school instrument, and ask for a recommendation of a peer to give introductory lessons. Talking with your child's music instructor is important to check expectations.

Consider the many ways to be musical. There are many ways to be musical, many ways to experience music, and many pathways to musical experiences. These can be understood as fitting into categories of practical musicking, relational musicking, or a blend of the two. Sometimes as parents we hear external messages that one way is better than the others or will lead to better outcomes for our child. We might think that the more our child achieves in music (according to someone else's standard), the better their experience is or the more worthwhile the endeavor. The problem with this thinking is that it is all based on someone else's determination of what is valuable or worthwhile. While there is a body of research with various ages of children linkng musical experiences to benefits in other areas of development, this research is not conclusive or limited to specific musical genres or levels of achievement. A child who plays fourth chair French horn in the concert band may have a healthier experience with music, balanced between practical and relational musicking, than the first chair student who is pressured by teachers and family. The child who was fourth chair can go on to play in a community band because she loves the sound of the French horn and the parts she plays in the ensemble, while the more driven student may never touch her horn again after leaving college because it would require two hours of practice per day to stay at a level with which she was satisfied with her tone. Which family's musical parenting goals were realized?

In other cases, music might be a child's main interest and identity-driver. Encouraging your child to develop their musical skills to the highest level, seek out extracurricular opportunities, and possibly consider competitions are all part of musical parenting for a child like this. Some additional specific resources are found in the books *The Music Parents' Survival Guide: A Parent-to-Parent Conversation* by Amy Nathan (Oxford University Press, 2014) and *Raising Musical Kids* by Robert Cutietta (Oxford University Press, 2014).

Think about what you really hope for your child and talk to your child about their dreams. Music is something that can provide enjoyment, self-understanding, flow experiences (more on those below), social opportunities, and an emotional outlet throughout the decades of life. The many outcomes of musical experiences can be understood by considering the goals of musical parenting or parenting musically. What is it that your child wants from music? What are your hopes and dreams for your child musically? How can you make decisions during the childhood years to help set that up for your family? See Chapter 6 for a Hopes and Dreams inventory.

The participants in my research for the book *Parenting Musically* whose children sustained musical involvement over many years were the ones who identified both musical parenting reasons and parenting musically reasons for musical involvement. For instance, the Petersons wanted their children to learn to play stringed instruments (violin, viola, cello). This would equip them to play with their extended family for holiday family orchestra as well as to play in their school ensembles and chamber ensembles. These are musical parenting reasons and led them to organize practice, pay for lessons, attend recitals, and send the kids to music camp. However, the parents also articulated their strong desire for the children to learn organizational skills and perseverance, which the parents thought would then transfer to other areas of their children's lives. The great thing about having reasons from both musical parenting and parenting musically is that when one portion of the project is not going well—say, a child is struggling to learn a new piece and wants to quit; or it is early on in the lessons and the instrumental tone is not pleasing—the parents can remember "We're doing this for another reason—to build perseverance!" This double reasoning can be so helpful when children or parents pass through a "this is so hard, we want to quit" phase. These phases are very common.

A Note About Regret

All of this talk about sustaining musical involvement could evoke a twinge of regret for some. It is possible that some readers may be regretting quitting their own musical lessons or ensemble participation or allowing their child to do so. Or maybe you see your child about to make the decision to quit lessons and worry that they will regret it.

First, regret itself is not usually a useful emotional place to stay—as someone told me once, it is a profound waste of psychological energy. But if you are feeling regret, it can be instructive to consider briefly why you quit. Did you have to choose between music and another activity? Was there a mismatch with a teacher's personality and your own? Was it due to financial constraints? Articulating why you made the decision may bring a measure of peace, if you realize it was a decision that contributed to your overall well-being or that of your family at the time.

Next, think about what you want from music now. It is never too late to learn a new instrument or musical practice. There are many ways to learn: from a friend or family member, using online tutorials, in a group class, or through lessons. You probably can't go back to be in the high school marching band now, but you could play in a community band. You could also probably volunteer with the marching band—the marching band directors who I know are always looking for band camp mentors and football game chaperones.

Psychology Related to Motivation

Sustaining musical involvement comes with ups and downs. It may be helpful for you to learn a little about motivation and psychology to smooth the way with the ups and downs of musical involvement across the years. Here are two concepts to keep in mind:

Locus of control. Psychologists talk about "locus of control"—whether a child believes something is in their control or not.[4] For instance, if your child has just started playing the flute and cannot make the right sound with the mouthpiece, do they yell in frustration? If so, they may be operating from an external locus of control and think that there is nothing they can do to learn how to play on the mouthpiece. If your response is, "Hm, yeah, I can't do that either. It takes a while and bunch of tries to figure out how to make the sound," that helps to bring the child back to an internal locus of control, realizing that their actions (practicing) can influence the outcome.

Flow. Another useful concept to know as a parent is psychologist Mihaly Csikszentmihaly's idea of *flow*.[5] *Flow* is an ideal state characterized by self-optimization, losing track of time, and sense of fulfillment. According to Csikszentmihaly (1934–2021), one of the goals of life (and parenting) is to experience flow and guide our children to do so. In order to experience flow, we try to match the challenge with the ability level—so the experience is neither boring nor utterly frustrating. When you find that balance of ability and challenge, you can experience flow. There are many activities that can lead to flow experiences, and music is one of them. As you've read this paragraph, you've probably thought of activities in which you as well as your children have experienced flow—maybe when they are building with LEGO blocks, or you are baking bread, or when you are kayaking as a family. Thinking about pursuing flow experiences in music may help you as a family make decisions about musical involvement or steer toward or away from specific opportunities.

Modeling Musical Engagement

A final important consideration in sustaining musical involvement is to model musical engagement yourself as an adult. One year a friend of mine mentioned that her family was struggling with various aspects of her son's cello lessons and practice.[6] They decided to take the money they were spending on the cello lessons and put it towards piano lessons for her instead. She commented that she thought taking piano lessons herself could help her kids' musical development, a musical parenting consideration. It was a beautiful plan on many levels—her children saw her take on a challenge: practicing piano and going to lessons. They heard her work over and over on specific measures of music. They sat near her or on her lap or built train tracks around her while she practiced. The children learned that for the 15 minutes of practicing they were not to disturb their mom unless for emergencies. Years later, several of her kids take lessons and are involved in music ensembles and musical theater, and she has developed the piano skills that had been mostly untouched since middle school.

There are many other ways to show musical engagement as an adult besides taking lessons:

- Creating playlists of "my music" that your children notice you listening to for your own purposes (while working, while cleaning, while exercising)—showing them that you enjoy listening to music with them, and you also listen to music for yourself;
- Practicing karaoke songs at home and then performing at a family party;
- Playing in a garage band, even if the music contains lyrics your children are not allowed to hear (I give this example because I have several friends who do this);
- Taking a beginning tap dance class for adults;
- Singing in a choir at your house of worship;
- Delighting in the release of new music from an artist you follow, and listening intently to the release, pointing out highlights and connections to your children.

FIGURE 22.1 Father providing a musical model for his child while engaging in musical play. GETTY IMAGES

All of these ideas and more can help model a sustained musical involvement yourself, which may be the most powerful way of promoting sustained musical involvement for your children.

What Really Matters?

Let's go back to my question at the beginning of the chapter about musical highlights. As a music major in college, I had the opportunity to participate in some complex, highly polished, artistically pleasing musical experiences. However, one of my most treasured musical memories is singing around a campfire with individuals with developmental disabilities at a camp for which I was a counselor. Hearing our group's singing, and seeing the interactions around the campfire, I was reminded that musical experiences are much more than the production of sounds. Thomas Turino[7] and Tia De Nora[8] are among the music scholars who write eloquently about the importance of human relationships and individual experience within musical interactions. De Nora provides examples and analysis of the many ways individuals use music in their lives. Turino explains the difference between "presentational performance" (musicians on stage, audience in chairs) and "participatory performance" (audience is part of performance). Turino's and DeNora's books highlight the many types of musical performances and experiences, as well as the many types of meaning humans find in and through music. Discussing ideas of musical meaning and diverse experiences with your family could help your children to clarify and claim the role of musicking in their lives.

WRAPPING UP CHAPTER 22

Balancing relational and practical musicking may help align musical hopes and dreams with motivation. Keeping in mind the many ways to be musical and modeling lifelong musicking and musical enjoyment yourself will help sustain your family's musical involvement for the "long game."

FOR FURTHER READING

Flow: The Psychology of Optimal Experience, Mihaly Csikszentmihaly (Harper & Row, 1990): describes psychologist Csikszentmihaly's concept of flow as a form of self-actualization.

The Music Parents' Survival Guide: A Parent-to-Parent Conversation, Amy Nathan (Oxford University Press, 2014): shares perspectives from parents about the standard music system in the United States of lessons, ensembles, and college auditions.

EPILOGUE

PARENTING MUSICALLY AND MUSICAL PARENTING IN CONTEXT

This book is full of ideas about how to engage in musical parenting (doing things to help your child grow musically) as well as parenting musically (using music to help get things done). Musical parenting and parenting musically are activities that happen in the home as well as in school and community settings.

Be aware of ways that you could be an advocate for more music for all the children in your community. As recommended in each chapter of Part 4, get to know the programs in your community and find ways to rally support as needed. Since you're reading this book, I'm guessing that you are interested in making music an important part of your child's life. Perhaps you have some additional resources or energy that you could contribute to helping increase music access for all children in your community.

Get to know music educators in your community. Ask them what local, state, or national issues are impacting how they teach music. If time allows, get involved in arts advocacy at any level possible. Express your appreciation to the music educators in your community working to bring music into children's lives.

As your children grow, you'll notice that some of the ways you interact musically may shift. You might not sing lullabies to an older child—although your teenager can appreciate having you sing or hum to them if they are having trouble falling asleep. Instead of creating playlists for your child, your teenager can start creating and sharing playlists with you. Pay attention to these playlists: teenagers communicate through the music they share with us. Rather than seeking out outdoor concerts for your rambunctious toddler, you can spend hours on the computer to get tickets for a popular musician's concert tour for your teenager and yourself.

The ideas in this book form a spiral, and you can return to the ideas and activities at various points in your family's journey and in your children's development. Keep asking questions about your child's hopes and dreams for music. Keep thinking about how to include music in family life to deepen your family's experience of musicking. Keep enjoying music together and making music a meaningful part of your family's life. Remember that music is important, there are many ways to be musical, all humans are musical, and you have the knowledge, skills, and desire to make music a meaningful part of your family's life.

ACTIVITY 70   Write a Parenting Musically Manifesto

A manifesto is a visual reminder of your values and your intended engagement or action.[1] For this activity, write down phrases or ideas that remind you of what you believe is most important when it comes to music and your family. You could do this yourself or involve your family members. Create a design for your statements and hang it somewhere to remind you of what is important for your own parenting musically journey.

A Parenting Musically Manifesto by The Koops Family

Music helps us connect.

We can all keep learning and enjoying music.

We express our music in many ways.

Practicing can be hard. That's normal.

Music is important.

We are a musical family.

We play music for joy.

There is not one right way to do music.

We have everything we need to make music.

Music is for everyone.

We want to help others have access to music education.

APPENDIX

Children Are Musical!

Children are musical beings and will surprise you with their musical ability and complexity! Here are a few common **milestones** and **suggested activities** organized by category of musicking, but remember that every child is different, and their musical development varies widely based on home environment and musical exposure.

Chart Sources: *Music in Childhood*, by Patricia Shehan Campbell and Carol Scott-Kassner (Cengage, 2018) and *Music Play: The Early Childhood Music Curriculum Guide for Parents, Teachers, and Caregivers*, vol. 1, by Wendy H. Valerio, Alison M. Reynolds, Beth M. Bolton, Cynthia C. Taggart, and Edwin Gordon (GIA Publications, 1998)

Age	Singing	Movement	Beat	Creativity	Instruments	Listening
Prenatal	Beginning mid-second trimester, baby can hear sounds. Sing to baby!	Mid-second trimester, baby detects dance-like movements				Most music played while baby is in womb will be calming after birth
Newborn (0–3 months)	Familiar voices are soothing; singing calms baby and grown-up	Baby's reflex movement can be observed; rock, sway, bounce baby gently	Baby shows general response to various musical tempi	Baby is absorbing musical environment	Rattles on wrists or booties	Provide diverse listening diet, especially familiar music played during pregnancy

Age	Singing	Movement	Beat	Creativity	Instruments	Listening
Infant (3–12 months)	Sing in higher range, making eye contact with baby	Rock, sway, bounce, dance, twirl with baby in adult's arms; baby will kick, roll, squirm on the floor	Baby will have a general response to various musical tempi	Respond to baby's early vocal utterances by echoing and pausing. Note how the utterances are musical (with pitch and rhythmic content)	Plastic-covered jingle bells, large shakers, drums	Adult should provide diverse listening diet
Young Toddler (12–24 months)	Pitch songs D–A above middle C; provide a variety of tonalities and meters; include chanting; songs with and without words	Toddler walks, crawls, bounces, twirls, dances	Toddler rocks, waves, bounces, taps rhythm, sometimes with the beat. Often imitates dance moves done by adults.	Toddler plays with pitch and rhythm to create "little songs" or "spontaneous songs"	Tambourines, rhythm sticks, hand drums with mallets	Provide diverse listening diet; watch and listen for children to express preferences
Older Toddler (24–36 months)	Continue using higher pitch and variety; sing songs from many cultures	Child learns to skip, gallop, swim, march, jump; experiment with Laban elements (flow, weight, space, time)	Adult may see increased accuracy of child keeping steady beat, particularly if beat is close to child's heartbeat (faster than adult heartbeat)	Child's "little songs" become more complex, include fragments of known songs	Xylophones, maracas, rhythm instruments, keyboards	Provide diverse listening diet; give child control of song choice and stop/starting during Dance and Freeze

3–4 years	Follow child's interests; create songs together; create new words for known tunes	Continue all of the above; add movement with a partner (sibling, playmate or parent) and in a group	Many children can keep a steady beat with body percussion or on an instrument, but some are still developing beat competency	Adult provides improvised commentary/free-play dialogue that is sung; new words to known tunes; instrumental compositions if opportunity allows	Tone bells, electronic instruments (iPad apps), keyboards	Provide diverse listening diet; expect children to want to "master" things by listening repeatedly
4–5 years	Child's range is expanding, but keep most songs above middle C; encourage healthy vocal production (no shout-singing)	Explore far ends of Laban continua (flow, weight, space, and time); simple circle dances	Provide continued beat development activities with faster and slower beats and different meters	Encourage unbounded creativity with vocal songs and instruments by providing space and time to explore. Use "noticing" comments instead of "judging" comments.	Informal exploration of instruments available at home and school. Some children may be ready for violin, viola, cello, guitar, or piano lessons	Introduce new genres
5–6 years	Child experiments with using speaking voice and singing voice to learn how to differentiate	Introduce folk dances, galloping, beginning to skip	Have child echo rhythm patterns	Provide opportunities for child to create songs and dances. Child's musical creativity influenced by known songs	Child will continue to explore instruments with increasing accuracy	Take turns as family members choosing which music to listen to

Age	Singing	Movement	Beat	Creativity	Instruments	Listening
6–7 years	Child's range may expand down to middle C and up to b above middle C	Adult introduces folk dances, line dances, skipping	Child will perform and create rhythm patterns of increasing complexity	Create music together through call and response (take turns being leader)	Encourage children to create found sound instruments	Consider music as a way for your child to differentiate from siblings and from you
8–9 years	Singing range may expand to B below Middle C to e in upper octave; comfortable singing range is C to c. Try singing harmony lines or bass lines	Child may be able to conduct with accuracy; follow all types of dance	Child may be ready to perform and create rhythm patterns of increasing complexity	Adult should encourage use of apps for creativity (see Chapter 11)	Adult can provide opportunities to try instruments such as recorder	Encourage child to take ownership of listening by curating playlists
9–12 years	Range may expand to G below Middle C to g in upper octave; comfortable singing range is C to c. Continue to experiment with harmony or rounds	Try any type of dance as a family	Child may be performing and creating rhythm patterns of increasing complexity	Child may enjoy opportunities to record and share musical compositions	Some children may choose an instrument to learn at school	Monitor children's online music use while encouraging music listening habits

NOTES

INTRODUCTION
1. Lisa Huisman Koops, *Parenting Musically* (New York: Oxford University Press, 2020).
2. Mayumi Adachi and Sandra E. Trehub, "Musical Lives of Infants," in *The Oxford Handbook of Music Education*, ed. Gary E. McPherson and Graham F Welch (Oxford: Oxford University Press, 2012).
3. Kate E. Williams et al., "Associations between Early Shared Music Activities in the Home and Later Child Outcomes: Findings from the Longitudinal Study of Australian Children," *Early Childhood Research Quarterly* 31 (April 1, 2015): 113–24, https://doi.org/10.1016/j.ecresq.2015.01.004.
4. Alexis Anja Kallio, "Decolonizing Music Education Research and the (Im)Possibility of Methodological Responsibility," *Research Studies in Music Education* 42, no. 2 (July 1, 2020): 177–91, https://doi.org/10.1177/1321103X19845690.

CHAPTER 1
1. Beatriz Ilari, "Musical Parenting and Music Education: Integrating Research and Practice," *Update: Applications of Research in Music Education* 36, no. 2 (February 1, 2018): 45–52, https://doi.org/10.1177/8755123317717053.
2. Urie Bronfenbrenner, *Making Human Beings Human: Bioecological Perspectives on Human Development* (Thousand Oaks, CA: Sage, 2005).
3. Thanks to Kelsey Kordella Giotta, middle school music educator and research assistant for *Parenting Musically*, for articulating this way of differentiating the two ideas.
4. Christopher Small, *Musicking*, Music/Culture (Middleton, CT: Wesleyan University Press, 1998).
5. Lucy Green, *Music, Informal Learning and the School: A New Classroom Pedagogy*, 1st ed. (London: Routledge, 2008).

CHAPTER 2

1. Shinichi Suzuki, *Nurtured by Love*, rev. ed. (Van Nuys, CA: Alfred Music, 2013).
2. Patricia Shehan Campbell, *Teaching Music Globally: Experiencing Music, Expressing Culture* (Oxford, UK: Oxford University Press, 2004).
3. Edwin E. Gordon, *A Music Learning Theory for Newborn and Young Children* (Chicago: GIA Publications, 2003).
4. Cynthia Crump Taggart, "Developmental Music Aptitude" (lecture, Michigan State University, East Lansing, MI, September 4, 2003).

CHAPTER 3

1. Nikki Bush, "Stretch Your Vision and Parent for the Long Game," *Creative Parenting Blog* (blog), January 20, 2017, https://nikkibush.com/stretch-vision-parent-long-game/; Anne Clarkson, "Parenting Futures: Playing the Long-Game in Parenting Your Teen," *Parenthetical* (blog), 2017, https://parenthetical.wisc.edu/parenting-futures-playing-the-long-game-in-parenting-your-teen/; Jessica Lahey, "Parenting, Not for the Moment, but for the Long Haul," *Motherlode Blog* (blog), June 10, 2015, https://parenting.blogs.nytimes.com/2015/06/10/parenting-not-for-the-moment-but-for-the-long-haul/.
2. Eun Cho and Beatriz Ilari, "Mothers as Home DJs: Recorded Music and Young Children's Well-Being During the COVID-19 Pandemic," *Frontiers in Psychology* 12 (2021), https://www.frontiersin.org/articles/10.3389/fpsyg.2021.637569.
3. Kelly Jakubowski and Anita Ghosh, "Music-Evoked Autobiographical Memories in Everyday Life," *Psychology of Music* 49, no. 3 (May 1, 2021): 649–66, https://doi.org/10.1177/0305735619888803; Elizabeth Hellmuth Margulis, *Psychology of Music: A Very Short Introduction* (Oxford: Oxford University Press, 2019).
4. Lisa Huisman Koops, "Musical Tweens: Child and Parent Views on Musical Engagement in Middle Childhood," *Music Education Research* 20 (August 8, 2018): 412–26, https://doi.org/10.1080/14613808.2018.1491541.

CHAPTER 4

1. Terese M. Volk, *Music, Education, and Multiculturalism: Foundation and Principles.* (New York: Oxford University Press, 1998).
2. David J. Hargreaves, Adrian C. North, and Mark Tarrant, "Musical Preference and Taste in Childhood and Adolescence," in *The Child as Musician* (Oxford: Oxford University Press, 2006), https://doi.org/10.1093/acprof:oso/9780198530329.003.0007.
3. https://sites.google.com/view/crewsertechge2017/roll-the-dice.
4. Lisa Huisman Koops (host), "Mandy Smith (Rock & Roll Hall of Fame)," *Parenting Musically*, n.d., https://podcasters.spotify.com/pod/pod/show/parentingmusically/episodes/Episode-9-Mandy-Smith-Rock--Roll-Hall-of-Fame-e1vliuj.

CHAPTER 5

1. Eva Kahana et al., "Grandparent-Grandchild Relationships: A Proposed Mutuality Model with a Focus on Young Children and Adolescents," in *Grandparenting: Influences on the Dynamics of Family Relationships* (New York: Springer, 2019), 61–80, https://doi.org/10.1891/9780826149855.0004.
2. Carol S. Dweck, *Mindset: The New Psychology of Success* (New York: Random House, 2006).
3. Albert Bandura, "Self-Efficacy: Toward a Unifying Theory of Behavioral Change," *Psychological Review* 84 (1977): 191–215, https://doi.org/10.1037/0033-295X.84.2.191.
4. Lisa Huisman Koops (host), "Songstress Jo, Nicole Ochenduski, and Nate Kruse (CWRU)," *Parenting Musically*, n.d., https://podcasters.spotify.com/pod/show/parentingmusically/episodes/Episode-10-songstress-jo--Nicole-Ochenduski--and-Nate-Kruse-CWRU-e219v7p.

CHAPTER 6

1. See Chapter 17 for a discussion on research studies regarding music participation and learning in areas outside of music.
2. Music therapy is defined as "clinical & evidence-based use of music interventions to accomplish individualized goals within a therapeutic relationship by a credentialed professional who has completed an approved music therapy program" ("AMTA Official Definition of

Music Therapy." American Music Therapy Association. Accessed January 25, 2024. https://www.musictherapy.org/about/musictherapy/.)

CHAPTER 7

1. Graham F Welch, "Singing and Vocal Development," in *The Child as Musician: A Handbook of Musical Development*, ed. Gary McPherson, 2nd ed. (Oxford: Oxford University Press, 2016), 441–61.
2. Lori Custodero, "Intimacy and Reciprocity in Improvisatory Musical Performance," in *Communicative Musicality: Exploring the Basis of Human Companionship*, ed. Stephen Malloch and Colwyn Trevarthen (New York: Oxford University Press, 2009), 513–29.
3. Thanks to Dr. Aimée Gaudette-Leblanc for this important point: Fostering secure attachment with singing relies on matching the singing to the situation. If a parent sings an energetic play song to a child who is sad in order to distract the child without eventually attending to the reason for the sadness, the parent-child relationship suffers. See Aimée Gaudette-Leblanc et al., *The Implications of Participation in a Music Early Learning Program for Parent-Child Relationships and Child's Socioemotional Functioning : A Randomized Control Trial*, 2023 for a more in-depth discussion.
4. Samuel A. Mehr et al., "Form and Function in Human Song," *Current Biology: CB* 28, no. 3 (February 5, 2018): 356-368.e5, https://doi.org/10.1016/j.cub.2017.12.042.
5. Laura K. Cirelli, Zuzanna B. Jurewicz, and Sandra E. Trehub, "Effects of Maternal Singing Style on Mother–Infant Arousal and Behavior," *Journal of Cognitive Neuroscience* 32, no. 7 (July 1, 2020): 1213–20, https://doi.org/10.1162/jocn_a_01402.
6. Patricia Shehan Campbell and Carol Scott-Kassner, *Music in Childhood: From Preschool through the Elementary Grades*, 4th ed. (Boston: Cengage Learning, 2018).
7. My thanks to my brother, Andy Huisman, for this suggestion he learned from singing with his sons.
8. Bridget Sweet, *Thinking Outside the Voice Box: Adolescent Voice Change in Music Education* (New York: Oxford University Press, 2019).

9. Lisa Huisman Koops (host), "JOHNNYSWIM & Beatriz Ilari (USC)," *Parenting Musically*, n.d., https://podcasters.spotify.com/pod/show/parentingmusically/episodes/Episode-13-JOHNNYSWIM-and-Beatriz-Ilari-USC-e22kptg.
10. Marci Rosenberg and Wendy D. LeBorgne, *The Vocal Athlete: Application and Technique for the Hybrid Singer*, 2nd ed. (San Diego: Plural Publishing, 2019).
11. Marilee David, *The New Voice Pedagogy* (Lanham, MD: Scarecrow Press, 2008).

CHAPTER 8

1. Small, *Musicking*.
2. Koops, "Musical Tweens."
3. Erin Hopkins, "Musical Stimming in Autistic Adults" (Case Western Reserve University Music Graduate Student Association Conference, Cleveland, Ohio, 2023).
4. Erin Hopkins in written discussion with the author, May 2023. You can read more of Erin's work at her website, www.neurodivergentmusiceducation.com/
5. Diana Boer and Amina Abubakar, "Music Listening in Families and Peer Groups: Benefits for Young People's Social Cohesion and Emotional Well-Being across Four Cultures," *Frontiers in Psychology* 5 (2014), https://www.frontiersin.org/article/10.3389/fpsyg.2014.00392.
6. Lisa Huisman Koops (host), "Risa & John Goerhke," *Parenting Musically*, n.d., https://podcasters.spotify.com/pod/pod/show/parentingmusically/episodes/Episode-12-Risa--John-Goehrke-Rock--Roll-Hall-of-Fame-e227to4.
7. Lisa Huisman Koops, "Songs from the Car Seat: Exploring the Early Childhood Music-Making Place of the Family Vehicle," *Journal of Research in Music Education* 62 (2014): 52–65, https://doi.org/10.1177/0022429413520007.
8. Thanks to music education scholar Erin Hopkins for sharing this insight about car musicking.
9. Lisa Huisman Koops (host), "Jason Hanley (Rock & Roll Hall of Fame)," *Parenting Musically*, n.d., https://podcasters.spotify.com/pod/show/parentingmusically/episodes/Episode-7-Jason-Hanley-Rock--Roll-Hall-of-Fame-e1vlgbn.

CHAPTER 9

1. Ernest D. Brown Jr., "African American Instrument Construction and Music Making," in *African American Music: An Introduction*, ed. Mellonee V. Burnim and Portia K. Maultsby (New York: Routledge, 2006), 23–33.
2. Jane Frazee, *Orff Schulwerk Today: Nurturing Musical Expression and Understanding* (New York: Schott, 2007).
3. John Blacking, *How Musical Is Man?* (Seattle: University of Washington Press, 1973).
4. Kenneth R. Ginsburg and Martha M. Jablow, *Building Resilience in Children and Teens: Giving Kids Roots and Wings*, 2nd ed. (Itasca, IL: American Association of Pediatrics, 2011).

CHAPTER 10

1. Daniel J. Levitin, "Dancing in the Seats," *New York Times*, October 26, 2007.
2. Anthony Seeger, "Music and Dance," in *Companion Encyclopedia of Anthropology: Humanity, Culture and Social Life*, ed. Tim Ingold (New York: Routledge, 2002), 720–39.
3. Small, *Musicking*.
4. Sharon G. Davis, "Children, Popular Music, and Identity," in *The Child as Musician: A Handbook of Musical Development*, ed. Gary E. McPherson, 2nd ed. (New York: Oxford University Press, 2016), 266–83.
5. Laurel J. Trainor and Laura Cirelli, "Rhythm and Interpersonal Synchrony in Early Social Development," *Annals of the New York Academy of Sciences* 1337, no. 1 (2015): 45–52, https://doi.org/10.1111/nyas.12649.
6. Eden Davies, *Beyond Dance: Laban's Legacy of Movement Analysis* (Abingdon, UK: Routledge, 2007).
7. Wendy H. Valerio et al., *Music Play: The Early Childhood Music Curriculum Guide for Parents, Teachers, and Caregivers*, vol 1 (Chicago: GIA Publications, 1998).
8. Lisa Huisman Koops, Christa Kuebel, and Sarah Starr Alleman Smith, "Mama's Turn: A Mother's Musical Journey," *Research Studies in Music Education* 39 (December 1, 2017): 209–25, https://doi.org/10.1177/1321103X17711629.

CHAPTER 11

1. Margaret S. Barrett, "Musical Narratives: A Study of a Young Child's Identity Work in and through Music-Making," *Psychology of Music* 39 (2010): 403–23, https://doi.org/doi:10.1177/0305735610373054; Meryl Sole, "Crib Song: Insights into Functions of Toddlers' Private Spontaneous Singing," *Psychology of Music* 45, no. 2 (March 1, 2017): 172–92, https://doi.org/10.1177/0305735616650746.
2. Patricia Shehan Campbell, *Songs in Their Heads: Music and Its Meaning in Children's Lives*, 2nd ed. (Oxford: Oxford University Press, 2010); Jan S. Knudsen, "Children's Improvised Vocalisations: Learning, Communication and Technology of the Self," *Contemporary Issues in Early Childhood* 9, no. 4 (2008): 287–96, https://doi.org/10.2304/ciec.2008.9.4.287; Kathryn Marsh, *The Musical Playground: Global Tradition and Change in Children's Songs and Games* (New York: Oxford University Press, 2008).
3. *Do Schools Kill Creativity?*, accessed April 23, 2021, https://www.ted.com/talks/sir_ken_robinson_do_schools_kill_creativity.
4. Lisa Huisman Koops, "'Now Can I Watch My Video?': Exploring Musical Play through Video Sharing and Social Networking in an Early Childhood Music Class," *Research Studies in Music Education* 34 (2012): 15–28, https://doi.org/10.1177/1321103X12442994.
5. Ruth Richards, ed. *Everyday Creativity and New Views of Human Nature: Psychological, Social and Spiritual Perspectives*. Washington, DC: American Psychological Association, 2007.
6. Felicity A. Baker, "What About the Music? Music Therapists' Perspectives on the Role of Music in the Therapeutic Songwriting Process," *Psychology of Music* 43, no. 1 (January 1, 2015): 122–39, https://doi.org/10.1177/0305735613498919; Felicity A. Baker and Julie Ballantyne, "'You've Got to Accentuate the Positive': Group Songwriting to Promote a Life of Enjoyment, Engagement and Meaning in Aging Australians," *Nordic Journal of Music Therapy* 22, no. 1 (February 1, 2013): 7–24, https://doi.org/10.1080/08098131.2012.678372.
7. Lisa Huisman Koops (host), "Justin Andrews (Otis Redding Foundation) and David Thompson (Glen Oak High School)," *Parenting Musically*, n.d., https://podcasters.spotify.com/pod/show/parentingmusically/episodes/Episode-8-Justin-Andrews-Otis-Redding-Foundation--David-Thompson-GlenOak-High-School-e20duc8.

8. Andrew R. Brown and S. Alex Ruthmann, *Scratch Music Projects* (New York: Oxford University Press, 2020).
9. Gordon, *A Music Learning Theory for Newborn and Young Children.*
10. That is a fun game to play on a long road trip, though– speak to the other people in the car only using phrases from the children's books you all have memorized due to extensive re-reading.

PART 3
1. Sandra E. Trehub, N. Ghazban, and M. Corbeil, "Musical Affect Regulation in Infancy," *Annals of the New York Academy of Sciences* 1337, no. 1 (2015): 186–92, https://doi.org/10.1111/nyas.12622.

CHAPTER 12
1. Olena Chorna et al., "Neuroprocessing Mechanisms of Music During Fetal and Neonatal Development: A Role in Neuroplasticity and Neurodevelopment," *Neural Plasticity* 2019 (March 20, 2019): e3972918, https://doi.org/10.1155/2019/3972918.

CHAPTER 13
1. Courtney B. Hilton et al., "Acoustic Regularities in Infant-Directed Speech and Song Across Cultures," *Nature Human Behaviour* 6, no. 11 (November 2022): 1545–56, https://doi.org/10.1038/s41562-022-01410-x; Ran Yan et al., "Across Demographics and Recent History, Most Parents Sing to Their Infants and Toddlers Daily," *Philosophical Transactions of the Royal Society B: Biological Sciences* 376, no. 1840 (November 2021): 20210089, https://doi.org/10.1098/rstb.2021.0089.
2. Sandra D. Trehub and Franziska Degé, "Reflections on Infants as Musical Connoisseurs," in *The Child as Musician: A Handbook of Musical Development*, ed. Gary E. McPherson, 2nd ed. (Oxford: Oxford University Press, 2015), 31–51.
3. Lisa Huisman Koops (host), "Chelsea Crowell, Rodney Crowell & Laura Cirelli (University of Toronto)," *Parenting Musically*, n.d., https://podcasters.spotify.com/pod/pod/show/parentingmusically/episodes/Episode-11-Chelsey-Crowell--Rodney-Crowell--and-Laura-Cirelli-University-of-Toronto-e21ohak.

4. *Communicative Musicality: Exploring the Basis of Human Companionship*, Communicative Musicality: Exploring the Basis of Human Companionship (New York: Oxford University Press, 2009).
5. Hilton et al., "Acoustic Regularities in Infant-Directed Speech and Song Across Cultures."
6. Alison M. Reynolds and Suzanne L. Burton, "Serve and Return: Communication Foundations for Early Childhood Music Policy Stakeholders," *Arts Education Policy Review* 118, no. 3 (July 3, 2017): 140–53, https://doi.org/10.1080/10632913.2016.1244779.
7. Yan et al., "Across Demographics and Recent History, Most Parents Sing to Their Infants and Toddlers Daily."
8. Samuel A. Mehr and Elizabeth S. Spelke, "Shared Musical Knowledge in 11-Month-Old Infants," *Developmental Science* 21, no. 2 (2018): e12542, https://doi.org/10.1111/desc.12542.
9. David Gerry, Andrea Unrau, and Laurel J. Trainor, "Active Music Classes in Infancy Enhance Musical, Communicative and Social Development," *Developmental Science* 15, no. 3 (2012): 398–407, https://doi.org/10.1111/j.1467-7687.2012.01142.x.
10. Trainor and Cirelli, "Rhythm and Interpersonal Synchrony in Early Social Development."
11. Gerry, Unrau, and Trainor, "Active Music Classes in Infancy Enhance Musical, Communicative and Social Development."
12. Anna Fiveash et al., "Processing Rhythm in Speech and Music: Shared Mechanisms and Implications for Developmental Speech and Language Disorders," *Neuropsychology* 35 (2021): 771–91, https://doi.org/10.1037/neu0000766.
13. These activities and more can be found in *Music Play: The Early Childhood Music Curriculum Guide for Parents, Teachers, and Caregivers*, vol. 1, by Wendy H. Valerio, Alison M. Reynolds, Beth M. Bolton, Cynthia C. Taggart, and Edwin Gordon (Chicago: GIA Publications, 1998).
14. Jeffrey H. Kahn et al., "Regulating Sadness: Response-Independent and Response-Dependent Benefits of Listening to Music," *Psychology of Music* 50, no. 4 (July 1, 2022): 1348–61, https://doi.org/10.1177/03057356211048545.

15. Suvi Saarikallio, "Music as Emotional Self-Regulation Throughout Adulthood," *Psychology of Music* 39, no. 3 (2011): 307–27, https://doi.org/10.1177%2F0305735610374894.
16. Cirelli, Jurewicz, and Trehub, "Effects of Maternal Singing Style on Mother–Infant Arousal and Behavior."
17. Trehub and Degé, "Reflections on Infants as Musical Connoisseurs."
18. Gordon, *A Music Learning Theory for Newborn and Young Children*.

CHAPTER 14

1. Valerio et al., *Music Play: The Early Childhood Music Curriculum Guide for Parents, Teachers, and Caregivers*, vol 1.
2. Sole, "Crib Song."
3. Knudsen, "Children's Improvised Vocalisations: Learning, Communication and Technology of the Self."
4. Gordon, *A Music Learning Theory for Newborn and Young Children*.
5. Jane Edwards, *The Oxford Handbook of Music Therapy* (New York: Oxford University Press, 2016).
6. Lisa Huisman Koops (host), "Pua Pèa & Claire Morison," *Parenting Musically*, n.d., https://podcasters.spotify.com/pod/pod/show/parentingmusically/episodes/Episode-4-Pua-Pea--Claire-Morison-e1meicb.
7. Erika Christakis, "The Dangers of Distracted Parenting," *The Atlantic*, June 16, 2018, https://www.theatlantic.com/magazine/archive/2018/07/the-dangers-of-distracted-parenting/561752/.
8. Lisa Huisman Koops and Kimberly Tate, "A Framework for Considering Teacher-Child Musical Interactions in the Early Childhood Classroom," *Early Child Development and Care* 191, no. 12 (September 10, 2021): 1956–71, https://doi.org/10.1080/03004430.2020.1862820.
9. Laura K. Cirelli and Sandra E. Trehub, "Familiar Songs Reduce Infant Distress," *Developmental Psychology* 56 (2020): 861–68, https://doi.org/10.1037/dev0000917.
10. Lisa Huisman Koops (host), "Kenitha Roberts & Lisa Damour," *Parenting Musically*, n.d., https://podcasters.spotify.com/pod/show/parentingmusically/episodes/Episode-3-Kenitha-Roberts--Lisa-Damour-e1lrue5.

11. Jane Edwards, "The Use of Music Therapy to Promote Attachment between Parents and Infants," *The Arts in Psychotherapy* 38, no. 3 (July 1, 2011): 190–95, https://doi.org/10.1016/j.aip.2011.05.002; Stine L. Jacobsen, Cathy H. McKinney, and Ulla Holck, "Effects of a Dyadic Music Therapy Intervention on Parent-Child Interaction, Parent Stress, and Parent-Child Relationship in Families with Emotionally Neglected Children: A Randomized Controlled Trial," *Journal of Music Therapy* 51, no. 4 (December 1, 2014): 310–32, https://doi.org/10.1093/jmt/thu028.
12. This activity and more can be found in *Music Play: The Early Childhood Music Curriculum Guide for Parents, Teachers, and Caregivers*, vol. 1, by Wendy H. Valerio, Alison M. Reynolds, Beth M. Bolton, Cynthia C. Taggart, and Edwin Gordon (Chicago: GIA Publications, 1998).

CHAPTER 15

1. Suzuki, *Nurtured by Love*.
2. Sandra Russ, *Pretend Play in Childhood: Foundation of Adult Creativity* (Washington, DC: American Psychological Association, 2013).
3. Stuart Brown and Christopher Vaughan, *Play: How It Shapes the Brain, Opens the Imagination, and Invigorates the Soul* (New York: Avery, 2009).

CHAPTER 16

1. Jakubowski and Ghosh, "Music-Evoked Autobiographical Memories in Everyday Life."
2. Patricia Shehan Campbell and Carol Scott-Kassner, *Music in Childhood: From Preschool through the Elementary Grades*, 4th edition (Boston: Cengage Learning, 2018).
3. Katherine Palmer, "Expanding the Neighborhood: Diversifying Music Making and Listening Inspired by Fred Rogers" (Latrobe, PA: Fred Rogers Institute, 2023), https://www.fredrogersinstitute.org/files/content/katiepalmerwhitepaper2023.pdf.
4. My thanks to Stacey Kolthammer, a music educator and Montessori teacher, for these ideas on gathering items from nature for found sound instruments.

CHAPTER 17

1. Lisa Huisman Koops (host), "Maggie Baird & Elizabeth Parker," *Parenting Musically*, n.d., https://podcasters.spotify.com/pod/pod/show/parentingmusically/episodes/Episode-2-Maggie-Baird--Elizabeth-Cassidy-Parker-e1fp08f.
2. Lisa Huisman Koops (host), "Ziggy Marley & Vanessa Bond," *Parenting Musically*, n.d., https://podcasters.spotify.com/pod/show/parentingmusically/episodes/Episode-1-Ziggy-Marley--Vanessa-L--Bond-e1foteg.
3. Tal-Chen Rabinowitch, Ian Cross, and Pamela Burnard, "Long-Term Musical Group Interaction Has a Positive Influence on Empathy in Children," *Psychology of Music* 41, no. 4 (July 1, 2013): 484–98, https://doi.org/10.1177/0305735612440609.
4. Graham F. Welch et al., "Editorial: The Impact of Music on Human Development and Well-Being," *Frontiers in Psychology* 11 (2020), https://www.frontiersin.org/articles/10.3389/fpsyg.2020.01246.
5. Steven J. Holochwost et al., "Music Education, Academic Achievement, and Executive Functions," *Psychology of Aesthetics, Creativity, and the Arts* 11 (2017): 147–66, https://doi.org/10.1037/aca0000112.
6. Assal Habibi et al., "Music Training and Child Development: A Review of Recent Findings from a Longitudinal Study," *Annals of the New York Academy of Sciences* 1423, no. 1 (2018): 73–81, https://doi.org/10.1111/nyas.13606.
7. James L. Reifinger, "Dyslexia in the Music Classroom: A Review of Literature," *Update: Applications of Research in Music Education* 38, no. 1 (October 1, 2019): 9–17, https://doi.org/10.1177/8755123319831736.
8. Anastasia Kotsopoulou and Susan Hallam, "The Perceived Impact of Playing Music While Studying: Age and Cultural Differences," *Educational Studies* 36, no. 4 (October 1, 2010): 431–40, https://doi.org/10.1080/03055690903424774.
9. Rabinowitch, Cross, and Burnard, "Long-Term Musical Group Interaction Has a Positive Influence on Empathy in Children."
10. Bonnie C. Wade, *Thinking Musically: Experiencing Music, Expressing Culture*, 3rd ed. (New York, NY: Oxford University Press, 2013).

CHAPTER 18

1. Aimée Gaudette-Leblanc et al., "Participation in an Early Childhood Music Programme and Socioemotional Development: A Meta-Analysis," *International Journal of Music in Early Childhood* 16, no. 2 (September 1, 2021): 131–53, https://doi.org/10.1386/ijmec_00032_1.
2. Williams et al., "Associations between Early Shared Music Activities in the Home and Later Child Outcomes."
3. Cynthia Crump Taggart, Jenny Alvarez, and Kathy Schubert, "The Role of Early Childhood Music Class Participation in the Development of Four Children with Speech and Language Delay," in *Learning from Young Children: Research in Early Childhood Music*, ed. Suzanne L. Burton and Cynthia Crump Taggart (Washington, DC: Rowman & Littlefield Education, 2011), 245–58.

CHAPTER 19

1. Gary E. McPherson, "From Child to Musician: Skill Development During the Beginning Stages of Learning an Instrument," *Psychology of Music* 33, no. 1 (January 1, 2005): 5–35, https://doi.org/10.1177/0305735605048012.
2. Edwin E. Gordon, "A Study of the Characteristics of the Instrument Timbre Preference Test," *Bulletin of the Council for Research in Music Education*, no. 110 (1991): 33–51.
3. John Eros, "Instrument Selection and Gender Stereotypes: A Review of Recent Literature," *Update: Applications of Research in Music Education* 27, no. 1 (November 1, 2008): 57–64, https://doi.org/10.1177/8755123308322379.
4. Anita Collins, *The Music Advantage: How Learning Music Helps Your Child's Brain and Wellbeing* (Sydney: Allen & Unwin, 2020); Graham F. Welch et al., "Editorial: The Impact of Music on Human Development and Well-Being," *Frontiers in Psychology* 11 (2020), https://www.frontiersin.org/articles/10.3389/fpsyg.2020.01246.

CHAPTER 20

1. Lisa Huisman Koops, "'Deñuy Jàngal Seen Bopp'(They Teach Themselves): Children's Music Learning in The Gambia," *Journal*

of Research in Music Education 58 (2010): 20–36, https://doi.org/10.1177/0022429409361000.
2. Lucy Green, *How Popular Musicians Learn: A Way Ahead for Music Education* (Farnham, UK: Ashgate Publishing, 2002).
3. Beatriz Ilari et al., "The Development of Musical Skills of Underprivileged Children Over the Course of 1 Year: A Study in the Context of an El Sistema-Inspired Program," *Frontiers in Psychology* 7 (2016), https://www.frontiersin.org/articles/10.3389/fpsyg.2016.00062.
4. Lisa Huisman Koops (host), "Making Music Lessons Work for Your Family," *Parenting Musically*, n.d., https://podcasters.spotify.com/pod/show/parentingmusically/episodes/Episode-5-James-Rhodes-Bonus-Episode-Making-Music-Lessons-Work-for-Your-Family-e1qheca.
5. Koops (host), *Making Music Work for Your Family*.
6. Green, *How Popular Musicians Learn*.
7. Janice Waldron, "YouTube, Fanvids, Forums, Vlogs and Blogs: Informal Music Learning in a Convergent on- and Offline Music Community," *International Journal of Music Education* 31, no. 1 (February 1, 2013): 91–105, https://doi.org/10.1177/0255761411434861.
8. Koops (host), "Maggie Baird & Elizabeth Parker."
9. Kenneth Elpus and Carlos R. Abril, "Who Enrolls in High School Music? A National Profile of U.S. Students, 2009–2013," *Journal of Research in Music Education* 67, no. 3 (October 1, 2019): 323–38, https://doi.org/10.1177/0022429419862837.

CHAPTER 21

1. Erin Hopkins in written discussion with the author, May 2023.
2. This is a helpful phrase to use with children and teach them as they enter tween and teen years. Within normal limits, or WNL, is a medical term meaning that a blood test or other medical indicator came back as normal. If a child is describing discomfort of any kind (conflict with friends, headache, frustrated with practice), ask "Is it within normal limits? Do you need help resolving this?"
3. Amy Chua, *Battle Hymn of the Tiger Mother* (New York: Penguin Group, 2011).

4. Dr Shimi Kang, *The Dolphin Way: A Parent's Guide to Raising Healthy, Happy, and Motivated Kids--Without Turning into a Tiger*, 1st ed. (New York: TarcherPerigee, 2014).
5. Gordon, *A Music Learning Theory for Newborn and Young Children*.
6. Koops, *Parenting Musically*.
7. Richard A. Swenson, *Margin: Restoring Emotional, Physical, Financial, and Time Reserves to Overloaded Lives* (Colorado Springs: NavPress, 2004).

CHAPTER 22

1. Nikki Bush, "Stretch Your Vision and Parent for the Long Game," *Creative Parenting Blog* (blog), January 20, 2017, https://nikkibush.com/stretch-vision-parent-long-game/; Anne Clarkson, "Parenting Futures: Playing the Long-Game in Parenting Your Teen," *Parenthetical* (blog), 2017.
2. Gordon, "A Study of the Characteristics of the Instrument Timbre Preference Test."
3. The New Horizons International Music Association promotes music ensembles for adults: https://newhorizonsmusic.org/about.
4. Herbert M. Lefcourt, ed., *Locus of Control: Current Trends in Theory & Research*, 2nd ed. (New York: Psychology Press, 2017).
5. Mihaly Csikszentmihalyi, *Flow: The Psychology of Optimal Experience* (New York: Harper Perennial, 1990).
6. Her journey is documented in Koops et al., 2017.
7. Thomas Turino, *Music as Social Life: The Politics of Participation* (Chicago: University of Chicago Press, 2008).
8. Tia De Nora, *Music in Everyday Life* (Cambridge: Cambridge University Press, 2000).

CHAPTER 23

1. Charlotte Burgess-Auburn, *You Need a Manifesto: How to Craft Your Convictions and Put Them to Work* (Berkeley, CA: Ten Speed Press, 2022).

BIBLIOGRAPHY

Adachi, Mayumi, and Sandra E. Trehub. "Musical Lives of Infants." In *The Oxford Handbook of Music Education*, edited by Gary E. McPherson and Graham F Welch. Oxford: Oxford University Press, 2012.

"AMTA Official Definition of Music Therapy." American Music Therapy Association. Accessed January 25, 2024. https://www.musictherapy.org/about/musictherapy/

Baker, Felicity A. "What About the Music? Music Therapists' Perspectives on the Role of Music in the Therapeutic Songwriting Process." *Psychology of Music* 43, no. 1 (January 1, 2015): 122–39. https://doi.org/10.1177/0305735613498919.

Baker, Felicity A., and Julie Ballantyne. "'You've Got to Accentuate the Positive': Group Songwriting to Promote a Life of Enjoyment, Engagement and Meaning in Aging Australians." *Nordic Journal of Music Therapy* 22, no. 1 (February 1, 2013): 7–24. https://doi.org/10.1080/08098131.2012.678372.

Bandura, Albert. "Self-Efficacy: Toward a Unifying Theory of Behavioral Change." *Psychological Review* 84 (1977): 191–215. https://doi.org/10.1037/0033-295X.84.2.191.

Barrett, Margaret S. "Musical Narratives: A Study of a Young Child's Identity Work in and Through Music-Making." *Psychology of Music* 39 (2010): 403–23. https://doi.org/doi:10.1177/0305735610373054.

Blacking, John. *How Musical Is Man?* Seattle: University of Washington Press, 1973.

Boer, Diana, and Amina Abubakar. "Music Listening in Families and Peer Groups: Benefits for Young People's Social Cohesion and Emotional Well-Being Across Four Cultures." *Frontiers in Psychology* 5 (2014). https://www.frontiersin.org/article/10.3389/fpsyg.2014.00392.

Bond, Vanessa L. (in press). *Inspiring Musical Play in Elementary General Music Through Loose Parts*. Tecumseh, MI: Conway Publications.

Bronfenbrenner, Urie. *Making Human Beings Human: Bioecological Perspectives on Human Development.* Thousand Oaks, CA: Sage, 2005.

Brown, Andrew R., and S. Alex Ruthmann. *Scratch Music Projects.* New York: Oxford University Press, 2020.

Brown, Stuart, and Christopher Vaughan. *Play: How It Shapes the Brain, Opens the Imagination, and Invigorates the Soul.* New York: Avery, 2009.

Burgess-Auburn, Charlotte. *You Need a Manifesto: How to Craft Your Convictions and Put Them to Work.* Berkeley, CA: Ten Speed Press, 2022.

Bush, Nikki. "Stretch Your Vision and Parent for the Long Game." *Creative Parenting Blog* (blog), January 20, 2017. https://nikkibush.com/stretch-vision-parent-long-game/.

Butterfield, M., and Claudia Boldt. *Dance Like a Flamingo.* London: Welbeck Editions, 2020.

Campbell, Patricia Shehan. *Songs in Their Heads: Music and Its Meaning in Children's Lives.* 2nd ed. Oxford: Oxford University Press, 2010.

Campbell, Patricia Shehan. *Teaching Music Globally: Experiencing Music, Expressing Culture.* Oxford: Oxford University Press, 2004.

Campbell, Patricia Shehan, and Carol Scott-Kassner. *Music in Childhood: From Preschool Through the Elementary Grades.* 4th ed. Boston: Cengage Learning, 2018.

Cho, Eun, and Beatriz Ilari. "Mothers as Home DJs: Recorded Music and Young Children's Well-Being During the COVID-19 Pandemic." *Frontiers in Psychology* 12 (2021). https://www.frontiersin.org/articles/10.3389/fpsyg.2021.637569.

Chorna, Olena, M. Filippa, J. Sa De Almeida, L. Lordier, M. G. Monaci, P. Hüppi, D. Grandjean, and Andrea Guzzetta. "Neuroprocessing Mechanisms of Music During Fetal and Neonatal Development: A Role in Neuroplasticity and Neurodevelopment." *Neural Plasticity* 2019 (March 20, 2019): e3972918. https://doi.org/10.1155/2019/3972918.

Christakis, Erika. "The Dangers of Distracted Parenting." *The Atlantic*, June 16, 2018. https://www.theatlantic.com/magazine/archive/2018/07/the-dangers-of-distracted-parenting/561752/.

Chua, Amy. *Battle Hymn of the Tiger Mother.* New York: Penguin Group, 2011.

Cirelli, Laura K., Zuzanna B. Jurewicz, and Sandra E. Trehub. "Effects of Maternal Singing Style on Mother–Infant Arousal and Behavior." *Journal of Cognitive Neuroscience* 32, no. 7 (July 1, 2020): 1213–20. https://doi.org/10.1162/jocn_a_01402.

Cirelli, Laura K., and Sandra E. Trehub. "Familiar Songs Reduce Infant Distress." *Developmental Psychology* 56 (2020): 861–68. https://doi.org/10.1037/dev0000917.

Clarkson, Anne. "Parenting Futures: Playing the Long-Game in Parenting Your Teen." *Parenthetical* (blog), 2017. https://parenthetical.wisc.edu/parenting-futures-playing-the-long-game-in-parenting-your-teen/.

Collins, Anita. *The Music Advantage: How Learning Music Helps Your Child's Brain and Wellbeing*. Sydney: Allen & Unwin, 2020.

Csikszentmihalyi, Mihaly. *Flow: The Psychology of Optimal Experience*. New York: Harper Perennial, 1990.

Custodero, Lori. "Intimacy and Reciprocity in Improvisatory Musical Performance." In *Communicative Musicality: Exploring the Basis of Human Companionship*, edited by Stephen Malloch and Colwyn Trevarthen, 513–29. New York: Oxford University Press, 2009.

Cutietta, Robert A. *Raising Musical Kids: A Guide for Parents*. 2nd ed. New York, NY: Oxford University Press, 2013.

David, Marilee. *The New Voice Pedagogy*. Lanham, MD: Scarecrow Press, 2008.

Davies, Eden. *Beyond Dance: Laban's Legacy of Movement Analysis*. Abingdon, UK: Routledge, 2007.

Davis, Sharon G. "Children, Popular Music, and Identity." In *The Child as Musician: A Handbook of Musical Development*, edited by Gary E. McPherson, 2nd ed., 266–83. Oxford: Oxford University Press, 2016.

De Nora, Tia. *Music in Everyday Life*. Cambridge: Cambridge University Press, 2000.

Do Schools Kill Creativity? Accessed April 23, 2021. https://www.ted.com/talks/sir_ken_robinson_do_schools_kill_creativity.

Dweck, Carol S. *Mindset: The New Psychology of Success*. New York: Random House, 2006.

Edwards, Jane. *The Oxford Handbook of Music Therapy*. New York: Oxford University Press, 2016.

Edwards, Jane. "The Use of Music Therapy to Promote Attachment Between Parents and Infants." *Arts in Psychotherapy* 38, no. 3 (July 1, 2011): 190–95. https://doi.org/10.1016/j.aip.2011.05.002.

Elpus, Kenneth, and Carlos R. Abril. "Who Enrolls in High School Music? A National Profile of U.S. Students, 2009–2013." *Journal of Research in Music Education* 67, no. 3 (October 1, 2019): 323–38. https://doi.org/10.1177/0022429419862837.

Brown, Ernest D., Jr. "African American Instrument Construction and Music Making." In *African American Music: An Introduction*, edited by Mellonee V. Burnim and Portia K. Maultsby, 23–33. New York: Routledge, 2006.

Eros, John. "Instrument Selection and Gender Stereotypes: A Review of Recent Literature." *Update: Applications of Research in Music Education* 27, no. 1 (November 1, 2008): 57–64. https://doi.org/10.1177/8755123308322379.

Fiveash, Anna, Nathalie Bedoin, Reyna L. Gordon, and Barbara Tillmann. "Processing Rhythm in Speech and Music: Shared Mechanisms and Implications for Developmental Speech and Language Disorders." *Neuropsychology* 35 (2021): 771–91. https://doi.org/10.1037/neu0000766.

Frazee, Jane. *Orff Schulwerk Today: Nurturing Musical Expression and Understanding*. New York: Schott, 2007.

Garrett, Matthew L., and Joshua Palkki. *Honoring Trans and Gender-Expansive Students in Music Education*. New York: Oxford University Press, 2021.

Gaudette-Leblanc, Aimée, Hélène Boucher, Flavie Bédard-Bruyère, Jessica Pearson, Jonathan Bolduc, and George M. Tarabulsy. "Participation in an Early Childhood Music Programme and Socioemotional Development: A Meta-Analysis." *International Journal of Music in Early Childhood* 16, no. 2 (September 1, 2021): 131–53. https://doi.org/10.1386/ijmec_00032_1.

Gaudette-Leblanc, Aimée, Jonathan Bolduc, Sébastien Boucher, Julie Raymond, Andrea Creech, and George Tarabulsy. "The Implications of Participation in a Music Early Learning Program for Parent-Child Relationships and Child's Socioemotional Functioning : A Randomized Control Trial." Research poster presented at the Society for Research in Child Development Biennial Meeting, Salt Lake City, Utah, 2023.

Gerry, David, Andrea Unrau, and Laurel J. Trainor. "Active Music Classes in Infancy Enhance Musical, Communicative and Social Development." *Developmental Science* 15, no. 3 (2012): 398–407. https://doi.org/10.1111/j.1467-7687.2012.01142.x.

Gershwin, George, Dubose Heyward, Dorothy Heyward, Ira Gershwin, and Mike Wimmer. *Summertime*. Fullerton, CA: Aladdin Publishing, 2002.

Ginsburg, Kenneth R., and Martha M. Jablow. *Building Resilience in Children and Teens: Giving Kids Roots and Wings*. 2nd ed. Itasca, IL: American Association of Pediatrics, 2011.

Gordon, Edwin E. *A Music Learning Theory for Newborn and Young Children*. Chicago: Gia Publications, 2003.

Gordon, Edwin E. "A Study of the Characteristics of the Instrument Timbre Preference Test." *Bulletin of the Council for Research in Music Education*, no. 110 (1991): 33–51.

Green, Lucy. *How Popular Musicians Learn: A Way Ahead for Music Education*. Farnham, UK: Ashgate, 2002.

Green, Lucy. *Music, Informal Learning and the School: A New Classroom Pedagogy*. London: Routledge, 2008.

Habibi, Assal, Antonio Damasio, Beatriz Ilari, Matthew Elliott Sachs, and Hanna Damasio. "Music Training and Child Development: A Review of Recent Findings from a Longitudinal Study." *Annals of the New York Academy of Sciences* 1423, no. 1 (2018): 73–81, https://doi.org/10.1111/nyas.13606.

Hanley, Jason. *We Rock!* Beverly, Mass: Quarry Books, 2015.

Hargreaves, David J., Adrian C. North, and Mark Tarrant. "Musical Preference and Taste in Childhood and Adolescence." In *The Child as Musician*. Oxford: Oxford University Press, 2006. https://doi.org/10.1093/acprof:oso/9780198530329.003.0007.

Hilton, Courtney B., Cody J. Moser, Mila Bertolo, Harry Lee-Rubin, Dorsa Amir, Constance M. Bainbridge, Jan Simson, et al. "Acoustic Regularities in Infant-Directed Speech and Song Across Cultures." *Nature Human Behaviour* 6, no. 11 (November 2022): 1545–56. https://doi.org/10.1038/s41562-022-01410-x.

Holochwost, Steven J., Cathi B. Propper, Dennie Palmer Wolf, Michael T. Willoughby, Kelly R. Fisher, Jacek Kolacz, Vanessa V. Volpe, and Sara R. Jaffee. "Music Education, Academic Achievement, and Executive Functions." *Psychology of Aesthetics, Creativity, and the Arts* 11 (2017): 147–66. https://doi.org/10.1037/aca0000112.

Hopkins, Erin. "Musical Stimming in Autistic Adults." Presented at the Case Western Reserve University Music Graduate Student Association Conference, Cleveland, Ohio, 2023.

Ilari, Beatriz. "Musical Parenting and Music Education: Integrating Research and Practice." *Update: Applications of Research in Music Education* 36, no. 2 (February 1, 2018): 45–52. https://doi.org/10.1177/8755123317717053.

Ilari, Beatriz, Patrick Keller, Hanna Damasio, and Assal Habibi. "The Development of Musical Skills of Underprivileged Children Over the Course of 1 Year: A Study in the Context of an El Sistema-Inspired Program." *Frontiers in Psychology* 7 (2016). https://www.frontiersin.org/articles/10.3389/fpsyg.2016.00062.

Jacobsen, Stine L., Cathy H. McKinney, and Ulla Holck. "Effects of a Dyadic Music Therapy Intervention on Parent-Child Interaction, Parent Stress, and Parent-Child Relationship in Families with Emotionally Neglected Children: A Randomized Controlled Trial." *Journal of Music Therapy* 51, no. 4 (December 1, 2014): 310–32. https://doi.org/10.1093/jmt/thu028.

Jakubowski, Kelly, and Anita Ghosh. "Music-Evoked Autobiographical Memories in Everyday Life." *Psychology of Music* 49, no. 3 (May 1, 2021): 649–66. https://doi.org/10.1177/0305735619888803.

Kahana, Eva, Boaz Kahana, Timothy Goler, and Jeffrey Kahana. "Grandparent-Grandchild Relationships: A Proposed Mutuality Model with a Focus on Young Children and Adolescents." In *Grandparenting: Influences on the Dynamics of Family Relationships*, 61–80. New York: Springer, 2019. https://doi.org/10.1891/9780826149855.0004.

Kahn, Jeffrey H., Kendall Ladd, Destiny A. Feltner-Williams, Amanda M. Martin, and Brooke L. White. "Regulating Sadness: Response-Independent and Response-Dependent Benefits of Listening to Music." *Psychology of Music* 50, no. 4 (July 1, 2022): 1348–61. https://doi.org/10.1177/03057356211048545.

Kallio, Alexis Anja. "Decolonizing Music Education Research and the (Im)Possibility of Methodological Responsibility." *Research Studies in Music Education* 42, no. 2 (July 1, 2020): 177–91. https://doi.org/10.1177/1321103X19845690.

Kang, Shimi. *The Dolphin Way: A Parent's Guide to Raising Healthy, Happy, and Motivated Kids-Without Turning into a Tiger*. 1st ed. New York: TarcherPerigee, 2014.

Knudsen, Jan S. "Children's Improvised Vocalisations: Learning, Communication and Technology of the Self." *Contemporary Issues in Early Childhood* 9, no. 4 (2008): 287–96. https://doi.org/10.2304/ciec.2008.9.4.287.

Koops (host), Lisa Huisman. "Chelsea Crowell, Rodney Crowell & Laura Cirelli (University of Toronto)." *Parenting Musically*, n.d. https://podcasters.spotify.com/pod/pod/show/parentingmusically/episodes/Episode-11-Chelsey-Crowell--Rodney-Crowell--and-Laura-Cirelli-University-of-Toronto-e21ohak.

Koops (host), Lisa Huisman. "Jason Hanley (Rock & Roll Hall of Fame)." *Parenting Musically*, n.d. https://podcasters.spotify.com/pod/show/parentingmusically/episodes/Episode-7-Jason-Hanley-Rock--Roll-Hall-of-Fame-e1vlgbn.

Koops (host), Lisa Huisman. "JOHNNYSWIM & Beatriz Ilari (USC)." *Parenting Musically*, n.d. https://podcasters.spotify.com/pod/show/parentingmusically/episodes/Episode-13-JOHNNYSWIM-and-Beatriz-Ilari-USC-e22kptg.

Koops (host), Lisa Huisman. "Justin Andrews (Otis Redding Foundation) and David Thompson (Glen Oak High School)." *Parenting Musically*, n.d. https://podcasters.spotify.com/pod/show/parentingmusically/episodes/Episode-8-Justin-Andrews-Otis-Redding-Foundation--David-Thompson-GlenOak-High-School-e20duc8.

Koops (host), Lisa Huisman. "Kenitha Roberts & Lisa Damour." *Parenting Musically*, n.d. https://podcasters.spotify.com/pod/show/parentingmusically/episodes/Episode-3-Kenitha-Roberts--Lisa-Damour-e1lrue5.

Koops (host), Lisa Huisman. "Maggie Baird & Elizabeth Parker." *Parenting Musically*, n.d. https://podcasters.spotify.com/pod/pod/show/parentingmusically/episodes/Episode-2-Maggie-Baird--Elizabeth-Cassidy-Parker-e1fp08f.

Koops (host), Lisa Huisman. "Making Music Lessons Work for Your Family." *Parenting Musically*, n.d. https://podcasters.spotify.com/pod/show/parentingmusically/episodes/Episode-5-James-Rhodes-Bonus-Episode-Making-Music-Lessons-Work-for-Your-Family-e1qheca.

Koops (host), Lisa Huisman. "Mandy Smith (Rock & Roll Hall of Fame)." *Parenting Musically*, n.d. https://podcasters.spotify.com/pod/pod/show/parentingmusically/episodes/Episode-9-Mandy-Smith-Rock--Roll-Hall-of-Fame-e1vliuj.

Koops (host), Lisa Huisman. "Pua Pèa & Claire Morison." *Parenting Musically*, n.d. https://podcasters.spotify.com/pod/pod/show/parentingmusically/episodes/Episode-4-Pua-Pea--Claire-Morison-e1meicb.

Koops (host), Lisa Huisman. "Risa & John Goerhke." *Parenting Musically*, n.d. https://podcasters.spotify.com/pod/pod/show/parentingmusically/episodes/Episode-12-Risa--John-Goehrke-Rock--Roll-Hall-of-Fame-e227to4.

Koops (host), Lisa Huisman. "Songstress Jo, Nicole Ochenduski, and Nate Kruse (CWRU)." *Parenting Musically*, n.d. https://podcasters.spotify.com/pod/show/parentingmusically/episodes/Episode-10-songstress-jo--Nicole-Ochenduski--and-Nate-Kruse-CWRU-e219v7p.

Koops (host), Lisa Huisman. "Ziggy Marley & Vanessa Bond." *Parenting Musically*, n.d. https://podcasters.spotify.com/pod/show/parentingmusically/episodes/Episode-1-Ziggy-Marley--Vanessa-L--Bond-e1foteg.

Koops, Lisa Huisman. "'Deñuy Jàngal Seen Bopp'(They Teach Themselves): Children's Music Learning in The Gambia." *Journal of Research in Music Education* 58 (2010): 20–36. https://doi.org/10.1177/0022429409361000.

Koops, Lisa Huisman. "Musical Tweens: Child and Parent Views on Musical Engagement in Middle Childhood." *Music Education Research* 20 (August 8, 2018): 412–26. https://doi.org/10.1080/14613808.2018.1491541.

Koops, Lisa Huisman, "'Now Can I Watch My Video?': Exploring Musical Play through Video Sharing and Social Networking in an Early Childhood Music Class," *Research Studies in Music Education* 34 (2012): 15–28, https://doi.org/10.1177/1321103X12442994.

Koops, Lisa Huisman. *Parenting Musically*. New York: Oxford University Press, 2020.

Koops, Lisa Huisman. "Songs from the Car Seat: Exploring the Early Childhood Music-Making Place of the Family Vehicle." *Journal of Research in Music Education* 62 (2014): 52–65. https://doi.org/10.1177/0022429413520007.

Koops, Lisa Huisman, Christa Kuebel, and Sarah Starr Alleman Smith. "Mama's Turn: A Mother's Musical Journey." *Research Studies in Music Education* 39 (December 1, 2017): 209–25. https://doi.org/10.1177/1321103X17711629.

Koops, Lisa Huisman, and Kimberly Tate. "A Framework for Considering Teacher-Child Musical Interactions in the Early Childhood Classroom." *Early Child Development and Care* 191, no. 12 (September 10, 2021): 1956–71. https://doi.org/10.1080/03004430.2020.1862820.

Kotsopoulou, Anastasia, and Susan Hallam. "The Perceived Impact of Playing Music While Studying: Age and Cultural Differences." *Educational Studies* 36, no. 4 (October 1, 2010): 431–40. https://doi.org/10.1080/03055690903424774.

Lahey, Jessica. "Parenting, Not for the Moment, but for the Long Haul." *Motherlode Blog* (blog), June 10, 2015. https://parenting.blogs.nytimes.com/2015/06/10/parenting-not-for-the-moment-but-for-the-long-haul/.

Lefcourt, Herbert M., ed. *Locus of Control: Current Trends in Theory & Research*. 2nd ed. New York: Psychology Press, 2017.

Levitin, Daniel J. "Dancing in the Seats." *New York Times*, October 26, 2007.

Malloch, Stephen and Colwyn Trevarthen, eds. *Communicative Musicality: Exploring the Basis of Human Companionship*. New York: Oxford University Press, 2009.

Margulis, Elizabeth Hellmuth. *Psychology of Music: A Very Short Introduction*. Oxford: Oxford University Press, 2019.

Marley, Ziggy and Ag Jatkowska. *Music Is in Everything*. Brooklyn, NY: Akashic Books, 2022.

Marsh, Kathryn. *The Musical Playground: Global Tradition and Change in Children's Songs and Games*. New York: Oxford University Press, 2008.

McPherson, Gary E. "From Child to Musician: Skill Development During the Beginning Stages of Learning an Instrument." *Psychology of Music* 33, no. 1 (January 1, 2005): 5–35. https://doi.org/10.1177/0305735605048012.

McPherson, Gary E. *The Child as Musician: A Handbook of Musical Development.* Oxford University Press, 2016.

Mehr, Samuel A., Manvir Singh, Hunter York, Luke Glowacki, and Max M. Krasnow. "Form and Function in Human Song." *Current Biology: CB* 28, no. 3 (February 5, 2018): 356-368.e5. https://doi.org/10.1016/j.cub.2017.12.042.

Mehr, Samuel A., and Elizabeth S. Spelke. "Shared Musical Knowledge in 11-Month-Old Infants." *Developmental Science* 21, no. 2 (2018): e12542. https://doi.org/10.1111/desc.12542.

"Musical Instruments." Metropolitan Museum of Art, New York. Accessed May 19, 2023. https://www.metmuseum.org/about-the-met/collection-areas/musical-instruments

"Musical Instrument Museum." Musical Instrument Museum, Phoenix, Arizona. Accessed May 19, 2023. https://www.mim.org

Nathan, Amy. *The Music Parents' Survival Guide: A Parent-to-Parent Conversation.* Oxford, UK: Oxford University Press, 2014.

Palmer, Katherine. "Expanding the Neighborhood: Diversifying Music Making and Listening Inspired by Fred Rogers." Latrobe, PA: Fred Rogers Institute, 2023. https://www.fredrogersinstitute.org/files/content/katiepalmerwhitepaper2023.pdf.

Rabinowitch, Tal-Chen, Ian Cross, and Pamela Burnard. "Long-Term Musical Group Interaction Has a Positive Influence on Empathy in Children." *Psychology of Music* 41, no. 4 (July 1, 2013): 484–98. https://doi.org/10.1177/0305735612440609.

Reifinger, James L. "Dyslexia in the Music Classroom: A Review of Literature." *Update: Applications of Research in Music Education* 38, no. 1 (October 1, 2019): 9–17. https://doi.org/10.1177/8755123319831736.

Reynolds, Alison M., and Suzanne L. Burton. "Serve and Return: Communication Foundations for Early Childhood Music Policy Stakeholders." *Arts Education Policy Review* 118, no. 3 (July 3, 2017): 140–53. https://doi.org/10.1080/10632913.2016.1244779.

Richards, Ruth, ed. *Everyday Creativity and New Views of Human Nature: Psychological, Social and Spiritual Perspectives.* Washington, DC: American Psychological Association, 2007.

Rosenberg, Marci, and Wendy D. LeBorgne. *The Vocal Athlete: Application and Technique for the Hybrid Singer*. 2nd ed. San Diego: Plural Publishing, 2019.

Russ, Sandra. *Pretend Play in Childhood: Foundation of Adult Creativity*. Washington, DC: American Psychological Association, 2013.

Saarikallio, Suvi. "Music as Emotional Self-Regulation Throughout Adulthood." *Psychology of Music* 39, no. 3 (2011): 307–27. https://doi.org/10.1177%2F0305735610374894.

Seeger, Anthony. "Music and Dance." In *Companion Encyclopedia of Anthropology: Humanity, Culture and Social Life*, edited by Tim Ingold, 720–39. New York: Routledge, 2002.

Small, Christopher. *Musicking*. Music/Culture. Middleton, CT: Wesleyan University Press, 1998.

Sole, Meryl. "Crib Song: Insights into Functions of Toddlers' Private Spontaneous Singing." *Psychology of Music* 45, no. 2 (March 1, 2017): 172–92. https://doi.org/10.1177/0305735616650746.

Suzuki, Shinichi. *Nurtured by Love*. Rev. ed. Van Nuys, CA: Alfred Music, 2013.

Sweet, Bridget. *Thinking Outside the Voice Box: Adolescent Voice Change in Music Education*. Oxford University Press, 2019.

Swenson, Richard A. *Margin: Restoring Emotional, Physical, Financial, and Time Reserves to Overloaded Lives*. Colorado Springs: NavPress, 2004.

Taggart, Cynthia Crump. "Developmental Music Aptitude." Lecture, Michigan State University, East Lansing, MI, September 4, 2003.

Taggart, Cynthia Crump, Jenny Alvarez, and Kathy Schubert. "The Role of Early Childhood Music Class Participation in the Development of Four Children with Speech and Language Delay." In *Learning from Young Children: Research in Early Childhood Music*, edited by Suzanne L. Burton and Cynthia Crump Taggart, 245–58. Washington, DC: Rowman & Littlefield Education, 2011.

Trainor, Laurel J., and Laura Cirelli. "Rhythm and Interpersonal Synchrony in Early Social Development." *Annals of the New York Academy of Sciences* 1337, no. 1 (2015): 45–52. https://doi.org/10.1111/nyas.12649.

Trapani, Iza. *I'm a Little Teapot*. Watertown, MA: Charlesbridge, 1998.

Trehub, Sandra D., and Franziska Degé. "Reflections on Infants as Musical Connoisseurs." In *The Child as Musician: A Handbook of*

Musical Development, edited by Gary E. McPherson, 2nd ed., 31–51. Oxford: Oxford University Press, 2015.

Trehub, Sandra E., N. Ghazban, and M. Corbeil. "Musical Affect Regulation in Infancy." *Annals of the New York Academy of Sciences* 1337, no. 1 (2015): 186–92. https://doi.org/10.1111/nyas.12622.

Turino, Thomas. *Music as Social Life: The Politics of Participation.* Chicago: University of Chicago Press, 2008.

Valerio, Wendy H., Alison M. Reynolds, Beth M. Bolton, Cynthia C. Taggart, and Edwin Gordon. *Music Play: The Early Childhood Music Curriculum Guide for Parents, Teachers, and Caregivers*, vol 1. Chicago: GIA Publications, 1998.

Volk, Terese M. *Music, Education, and Multiculturalism: Foundation and Principles.* New York: Oxford University Press, 1998.

Wade, Bonnie C. *Thinking Musically: Experiencing Music, Expressing Culture*, 3rd ed. New York: Oxford University Press, 2013.

Waldron, Janice. "YouTube, Fanvids, Forums, Vlogs and Blogs: Informal Music Learning in a Convergent on- and Offline Music Community." *International Journal of Music Education* 31, no. 1 (February 1, 2013): 91–105. https://doi.org/10.1177/0255761411434861.

Weiss, George David, Bob Thiele, and Ashley Bryan. *What a Wonderful World.* New York: Athenum Books, 1995.

Welch, Graham F. "Singing and Vocal Development." In *The Child as Musician: A Handbook of Musical Development*, edited by Gary McPherson, 2nd ed., 441–61. Oxford: Oxford University Press, 2016.

Welch, Graham F., Michele Biasutti, Jennifer MacRitchie, Gary E. McPherson, and Evangelos Himonides. "Editorial: The Impact of Music on Human Development and Well-Being." *Frontiers in Psychology* 11 (2020). https://www.frontiersin.org/articles/10.3389/fpsyg.2020.01246.

Williams, Kate E., Margaret S. Barrett, Graham F. Welch, Vicky Abad, and Mary Broughton. "Associations Between Early Shared Music Activities in the Home and Later Child Outcomes: Findings from the Longitudinal Study of Australian Children." *Early Childhood Research Quarterly* 31 (April 1, 2015): 113–24. https://doi.org/10.1016/j.ecresq.2015.01.004.

Yan, Ran, Ghazal Jessani, Elizabeth S. Spelke, Peter de Villiers, Jill de Villiers, and Samuel A. Mehr. "Across Demographics and Recent History, Most Parents Sing to Their Infants and Toddlers Daily." *Philosophical Transactions of the Royal Society B: Biological Sciences* 376, no. 1840 (November 2021): 20210089. https://doi.org/10.1098/rstb.2021.0089.

FOR FURTHER READING

CHILDREN'S BOOKS OR PICTURE BOOKS—GENERAL

Cheaper by the Dozen, by Frank B. Gilbreth Jr. and Ernestine Gilbreth Carey (Thomas Y. Crowell Co, 1948).

Dance Like a Flamingo, written by Moira Butterfield and illustrated by Claudia Boldt (Welbeck Editions, 2020).

Giraffes Can't Dance, written by Giles Andreae and illustrated by Guy Parker-Rees (Orchard Books, 1999).

Loretta: Ace Pinky Scout, by Keith Graves (Scholastic Press, 2002).

Y is for Yet: A Growth Mindset Alphabet, by Shannon Anderson and Jake Souva (Free Spirit, 2020).

CHILDREN'S BOOKS OR PICTURE BOOKS—MUSIC

Around the World in 80 Musical Instruments, by Nancy Dickmann and Sue Downing (Welbeck Editions, 2022).

Before Music: Where Instruments Come From, by Annette Bay Pimentel and Madison Safer (Harry N. Abrams, 2022).

Billy the Kid Makes It Big, by Dolly Parton and MacKenzie Haley (Penguin Workshop, 2023).

Music and How It Works: A Complete Guide for Kids, by Charlie Morland (Penguin Random House, 2020).

Music Is in Everything, written by Ziggy Marley and illustrated by Ag Jatkowska (Akashic Books, 2022).

My Family Plays Music, by Judy Cox and Elbrite Brown (Holiday House, 2003).

Rubber-Band Banjos and a Java Jive Bass: Projects and Activities on the Science of Music and Sound, by Alex Sabbeth (Jossey-Bass, 1997).

The World Atlas of Musical Instruments, by Bozhidar Abrashev and Vladimir Gadjev (H. F. Ullman, 2013).

MUSIC BOOKS—GENERAL INTEREST

Music Is My Life, by Myles Tanzer and Ali Mac (Quarto Publishing, 2020).

Why You Love Music: From Mozart to Metallica, the Emotional Power of Beautiful Sounds, by John Powell (Little, Brown, 2016).

MUSIC EDUCATION RESEARCH BOOKS

Adolescents on Music: Why Music Matters to Young People in Our Lives, by Elizabeth Cassidy Parker (Oxford University Press, 2020).

The Child as Musician: A Handbook of Musical Development (2nd ed.), edited by Gary McPherson (Oxford University Press, 2016).

Children's Home Musical Experiences Across the World, edited by Beatriz Ilari and Susan Young (Indiana University Press, 2016).

Honoring Trans and Gender-Expansive Students in Music Education, by Matthew L. Garrett and Josh Palkki (Oxford University Press, 2021).

How Popular Musicians Learn: A Way Ahead for Music Education, by Lucy Green (Ashgate Publishing, 2002).

The Musical Child, by Joan Koenig (Houghton Mifflin Harcourt, 2021).

The Music Advantage: How Music Helps Your Child Develop, Learn, and Thrive, by Anita Collins (Penguin Random House, 2020).

Parenting Musically, by Lisa Huisman Koops (Oxford University Press, 2020).

Songs in Their Heads, by Patricia Shehan Campbell (Oxford University Press, 2010).

Thinking Outside the Voice Box: Adolescent Voice Change in Music Education, by Bridget Sweet (Oxford University Press, 2019).

MUSIC EDUCATION RESOURCE BOOKS

Help Your Kids with Music: A Unique Step-by-Step Visual Guide, by Carol Vorderman (DK Publishing, 2019)

I Can Make Music: Play and Learn Activities to Empower Children Through Music, by Patricia Shehan Campbell and Maja Pitamic (Elwin Street Limited, 2015).

Music 3–5, by Susan Young (Routledge, 2009).

Music Learning Today: Digital Pedagogy for Creating, Performing, and Responding to Music, 2nd ed., by William I. Bauer (Oxford University Press, 2020).

Music Play: The Early Childhood Music Curriculum Guide for Parents, Teachers, and Caregivers, vol. 1, by Wendy H. Valerio, Alison M. Reynolds, Beth M. Bolton, Cynthia C. Taggart, and Edwin Gordon (GIA Publications, 1998).

Raising Musical Kids, 2nd ed., by Robert A. Cutietta (Oxford: Oxford University Press, 2014).

Roots and Branches: A Legacy of Multicultural Music for Children, by Patricia Shehan Campbell, Ellen McCullough-Brabson, and Judith Cook Tucker (World Music Press, 1994).

Teaching Music to Students with Special Needs: A Label-Free Approach, 2nd ed., by Alice M. Hammel and Ryan M. Hourigan (Oxford University Press, 2017).

The Music Parents' Survival Guide: A Parent-to-Parent Conversation, Amy Nathan (Oxford University Press, 2014).

Time to Practice: A Companion for Parents, by Carrie Reuning-Hummel (Sound Carries Press, 2006).

TIPS: The Child Voice, edited by Maria Runfola and Joanne Rutkowski (Rowman & Littlefield, 2010)

The Ways Children Learn Music: An Introduction and Practical Guide to Music Learning Theory, by Eric Bluestine (GIA Publications, 2000).

We Rock: A Fun Family Guide for Exploring Rock Music History, by Jason Hanley (Quarry Books, 2015).

MUSICOLOGY AND ETHNOMUSICOLOGY RESEARCH BOOKS

Music as Social Life: The Politics of Participation, by Thomas Turino (University of Chicago Press, 2008).

Music in Everyday Life, by Tia DeNora (Cambridge University Press, 2000).

Musicking, by Christopher Small (Wesleyan University Press, 1998).

OTHER BOOKS

Brain-Compatible Dance Education, by Anne Green Gilbert (National Dance Association, 2006).

Gift from the Sea, by Anne Morrow Lindbergh (Pantheon Books, 2003).

PARENTING BOOKS

Baby 411, by Dr. Ari Brown and Denise Fields (Windsor Peak Press, 2022).

The Dolphin Way: A Parent's Guide to Raising Healthy, Happy, Motivated Kids—without Turning into a Tiger, by Shimi Kang (Penguin Group, 2014).

I Love You Rituals, by Becky A. Bailey (Harper Collins, 2000).

Mom Brain: Proven Strategies to Fight the Anxiety, Guilt, and Overwhelming Emotions of Motherhood—and Relax into Your New Self, by Ilyse Dobrow DiMarco (Guilford Press, 2021).

Slow Family Living: 75 Ways to Slow Down, Connect, and Create More Joy, by Bernadette Noll (Penguin Publishing Group, 2013)

PSYCHOLOGY BOOKS

Flow: The Psychology of Optimal Experience, by Mihaly Csikszentmihaly (Harper & Row, 1990).

Growth Mindset, by Carol Dweck (Random House, 2006).

Pretend Play in Childhood: Foundation of Adult Creativity, by Sandra Russ (American Psychological Association, 2014)

Psychology of Music: A Very Short Introduction, by Elizabeth Hellmuth Margulis (Oxford University Press, 2019).

WEBSITES

The Rock & Roll Hall of Fame: (https://www.rockhall.com/rock-hall-edu)

Musical Instrument Museum: (https://www.mim.org/educator-resources/)

Metropolitan Museum of Art: https://www.metmuseum.org/about-the-met/collection-areas/musical-instruments

Carnegie Hall: (https://kids.carnegiehall.org/)

Auckland (New Zealand) Philharmonic Orchestra: (https://www.apo.co.nz/community-education/families/apo-whoa/)

Fred Rogers Institute: https://www.fredrogersinstitute.org/resources

Mama Lisa's World: International Music & Culture, by Lisa Yannucci (https://www.mamalisa.com/)

Putumayo World Playground Recordings: www.putumayo.com/world-playground

Suzuki Association of the Americas: www.suzukiassociation.org

American Music Therapy Association: https://www.musictherapy.org/about/musictherapy/

Erin Hopkins, Neurodiversity in Music Education: https://www.neurodivergentmusiceducation.com/

Advocacy plan created by the National Association for Music Education (NAfME): https://nafme.org/wp-content/uploads/2020/06/Local-Advocacy-Action-Plan.pdf

Resources and links from NAMM Foundation (National Association of Music Merchants): https://www.nammfoundation.org/why-music-matters%20%20—

INDEX

For the benefit of digital users, indexed terms that span two pages (e.g., 52–53) may, on occasion, appear on only one of those pages.

Abreu, José Antonio, 194
advocacy, 52, 177–78, 197–99, 214, 221
agency, 37, 71–72, 87, 102, 146, 148, 165, 169
ages and stages
   prenatal, 115–18
   infant (birth to 12 months), 119–29
   toddler (12 to 36 months), 130–44
   preschool (3 to 5 years), 145–52
   early elementary (5 to 9 years), 153–62
   late elementary (9 to 12 years), 163–70
American Music Therapy Association, 231n.2–32
Andrews, Justin, 103
audiating, 88, 128, 157–58, 210

Bach, J. S., 108
Baird, Maggie, 197
be a researcher of your child, 36, 75–77, 102, 113, 119, 130, 147, 154, 164, 166, 176, 191, 192–93, 211
Beatles, The, 22, 108
benefits of music engagement, 2, 189, 194, 214–15
   cognitive benefits, 165–66
   emotional benefits, 119–20, 166
   of musical creativity, 102–3
   of dancing, 92
   of joint music listening, 71–74
   of playing instruments, 81
   of singing, 62
   social benefits, 121–22
   stress reduction for parents, 115, 119–20, 124, 126–27, 149
Blacking, John, 84–85
blended goals in musicking, 17, 51, 148, 204, 215–16, 220
Bolton, Beth M., 225

Bond, Vanessa L., 102
Bronfenbrenner, Urie, 15
Brown, Andrew R., 107

Carnegie Hall, 91
Cash, Johnny, 74
Cash, Rosanne, 74
Campbell, Patricia Shehan, 25–26, 225
"Cathy's Clown," 74–75
Chua, Amy, 206
Cho, Eun, 33
Christakis, Erika, 135
Cirelli, Laura, 140
Collins, Anita, 122
communicative musicality, 62, 120, 121–22, 135
community music,
   concerts, 38–39, 52, 143
   ensembles, 63–64, 167
   libraries, 146, 175, 176, 178
   museums, 40, 161
   music landmark, 40
conducting, 87–88, 150
COVID-19 pandemic, 1, 18–19, 39, 79, 84, 214
creative musicking,
   composition, 103–5
   digital musical gift, 108–9
   fostering creativity, 100, 102, 153–54, 164–65
   improvisation, 105
   loops, 106–7
   producing music, 106
   song-writing, 107–8
   writing new lyrics for an existing tune, 1, 102, 127, 136, 139, 149
Crowell, Chelsea, 74–75, 121
Crowell, Rodney, 74–75, 121

Cutietta, Robert, 200–1, 215
Csikszentmihaly, Mihaly, 217

Dalcroze, Émile Jaques–, 158
Dalcroze Eurhythmics, 158
dancing
   creative movement, 92–95
   cultural context, 91
   family dance or secret handshake, 98
   home dance party, 95–96
   Laban effort elements, 92–93, 93f, 96
   Laban movement activities, 94–95
   ways to learn dances, 98
   with babies, 120
   with older kids, 96–97
   with props, 91–99
Damour, Lisa, 140–41
De Nora, Tia, 219–20
Degé, Franziska, 121
developmental delay, 1–2, 19, 31–32, 134–35, 176, 178
digital keepsake email account, 67, 123, 133
dinosaurs, 104–5, 131–32, 149
disabilities, 178, 183, 187, 219–20
"Dos Oruguitas," 155

early childhood music classes, 51, 173–78
early childhood play–based curriculum,
early intervention program, 1–2
ecological systems theory, 15
Eilish, Billie, 108, 197
El Sistema, 194
emotional intelligence, 55
Encanto, 36, 76–78, 155
enculturation,
enjoyment, 27, 44, 52, 62, 77, 81, 92, 102–3, 115, 130, 132, 170, 177, 202–3, 220, 222
equity in music programs, 183, 187–89
executive functioning, 55, 166, 203
expectation to be musical, 28, 192
extended family, 25f, 32, 37–38, 42, 44–47, 50
extramusical goals, 2, 50, 55, 189

false assumptions about musicking, 5–7
   "I can't dance," 91–92

"I don't have a good voice, I shouldn't sing," 61–62
"I'm not musical," 25, 26
kids should only listen to kids' music, 37
family functioning and well–being, 4, 15, 164
family logistics and decisions about activities, 174–75, 216
family musical canon, 30–34
   boo–boo song, 22, 140
   calm down song, 150
   mad song, 27
   goodbye song, 138–40
   tidying song, 138
family musical web, 47, 54
Family Musicking Framework, 17–18, 18f, 20, 22
"Family Time," 64
feedback on children's musicking, 46–47, 69, 132, 148, 165, 209
   "noticing" comments, 44–45, 46–47
financial aid for music opportunities, 167, 175–76
FINNEAS, 197
"For the First Time in Forever," 1
formal music learning, 17

Gambia, The, 8, 192
Garrett, Matthew L., 66, 188
Gaudette–LeBlanc, Aimée, 232
Giotta, Kelsey Kordella, 229
Goehrke, John, 73
Goehrke, Risa, 73
grandparents
   child interviewing grandparents, 78
   creating music for grandchildren, 100–1, 101f, 127–28
   learn a dance from, 97
   long-distance musicking, 1, 18–19, 106, 125, 127–28, 150
   musical gift for grandparents, 108–9
   musical role models, 44, 117
   musicking with grandchildren, 43–44
   providing opportunities, 44, 155–56
   supportive listeners, 42–43, 44–46, 209
"Grandma Bonnie's Lullaby," 100–1, 101f

Gordon, Edwin, 26, 108, 134, 154, 157–58, 225
Green, Lucy, 17, 192
growth mindset, 44–45

Hamilton, 71–72, 73
Hanley, Jason, 77
"Happy Birthday", 157–58, 170
"Hokey Pokey," 136
"Hokey Poky What a Mess," 138
Hopkins, Erin, 72, 203
Huisman, Andy, 232
Huisman, Bonnie, 101*f*

"I Walk the Line," 74
"I Walk the Line (Revisited)," 74
Ilari, Beatriz, 33
informal music learning, 17, 68, 141, 146, 192, 196, 197
instruments, *see* playing instruments
invented notation, 160–61, 168

Jackson, Michael, 155–56
JOHNNYSWIM, 67
"Jump Then Fall," 64
Jurassic Park, 117

Kang, Shimi, 206
Keetman, Gunild, 158
Kodály, Zoltán, 158
Kodály approach, 158
Koops, Jed, 138
Kolthammer, Stacey, 239

Louis Armstrong Park, 40

manifesto, 222
Marley, Ziggy, 64, 165
McPherson, Gary, 122
Morison, Claire, 134–35
motivation, 193
"Mozart effect", 6, 116
multi-generational, 87
"music for music's sake", 103
music and language, 108, 134–35
music aptitude, 24, 26, 206–7

music educators, 25, 52–54, 157, 183, 188, 194–95, 197, 198, 221
music for now, music for later, 81, 108, 169
music lessons, 68, 146–47, 167, 194–97
music listening,
    before birth, 115–16
    connection to child's life, 39–40
    cultural context, 77, 151–52
    emotional regulation, 33, 71–72
    finding new music to listen to, 37–38
    global music, 36–37, 39
    identity development, 72
    in the family vehicle, 31, 37–38, 74–75, 127, 146, 150
    kids' music, 37
    joint music listening as a family, 40, 87, 170
    listening journal, 75–77
    musical preference or taste, 35–36, 37, 72
    repeated listening, 72, 146
    use of playlists, 33, 37–38, 116–17, 131, 169, 218, 221–22
musical babble, 121, 124, 134, 141
musical family, 24–26, 27, 28
musical home, 24–26, 196
musical hopes and dreams, 49–57
    connection to decision making, 51
    connection to general hopes and dreams for child, 50
    for family, 50–51
    mismatch between child/adult or parent/teachers, 49, 52–53
Music Learning Theory, 157–58
musical memories, 32, 33, 73–74, 155–56
musical parenting, 13, 14, 17–18, 21, 25–26, 50, 52–53, 66, 103–4, 130, 148, 178, 207, 214–16
musical play, 102, 124–26, 136, 142–43, 148–49, 154, 179–180
musical role models, 44, 54, 81, 92, 98, 102, 107, 108, 117, 155–56, 158, 195, 202–3, 218–19
music therapy, 19, 134–35, 141, 178, 183

musical toys, 128
musicking, 13, 15–17
mutuality, 42, 43, 47, 95, 176

Nathan, Amy, 215
neurodiversity, 72, 203
not one right way, 5–6, 36, 191, 201

Ochenduski, Nicole, 45–46
O'Connell, Patrick, 197
online music learning, 68, 106, 146, 151, 161, 164, 165, 194,196
Orff, Carl, 158
Orff–Schulwerk approach, 83, 158–50
Otis Redding Foundation, 103

Palkki, Joshua, 66, 188
Palmer, Katherine, 159
parenting for the "long game", 32–34, 205, 213–16
parenting musically, 13, 14–15, 31–32, 50, 51, 66, 72, 73–74, 75,94, 117, 130, 148, 149, 178, 207, 213–14, 215
Parenting Musically podcast, xiii, 7, 8, 13, 15–16, 31–32, 40, 45–46, 67, 74–75, 77, 103, 121, 134–35, 140–41, 164, 165, 195
parental decision making, 51, 154, 207
Parker, Elizabeth, 164
Pèa, Kailani, 134–35
Pèa, Pua, 134–35
Peanuts theme song, 49
perfectionism, 202–3
Perri, Christina, 64
picture books, 69, 83, 127–28, 141–42
places to musick, 148
  acoustically interesting spaces, 69–70
  family vehicle, 74–75, 169
  outside, 85–86, 89–90, 104–5, 211
playing by ear, 5, 17, 154, 163–64, 195, 196
playing instruments
  body percussion, 82
  choosing an instrument, 166, 181–87
  cultural context, 82
  found sounds, 84–86, 160–61, 167
  instrument classification, 83, 168
  logistics, 82
  playground instruments, 89–90, 104
  rhythm instruments, 82–83, 154
  recorders, 88–89
  timbre (sound quality), 185
practical musicking, 17–18, 20, 168–69, 193, 214–15
practice
  maintaining relational equilibrium during, 210–11
  parent involvement, 147, 201–8, 211
  principles, 201–3
  strategies, 208–10
presentational and participatory performance, 219–20
privilege, 21, 72
Puerto Rico, 83

Ramirez, Abner, 67
Redding, Otis, 103
recording children's musicking, 67, 85, 117
regret, 216–17
relational musicking, 17, 127–28, 140–41, 150–51, 155–57, 168–70, 193
research on children's musicking
  early childhood music research, 173–74
  correlation does not imply causation, 6, 112
  evaluating research, 111–13
  instrument choice, 184
  music and the brain, 116, 122
  reporting research, 112
Reynolds, Alison M., 225
Rhodes, James, 195, 196
"Right Hand Man," 73
Roberts, Kenitha, 31–32, 140–41
Roberts, Reyna, 31–32, 140–41
Rock & Roll Hall of Fame and Museum, 40, 73, 77
routines, musicking during, 123–25, 136–40, 149–50, 168–70
Ruthman, S. Alex, 107

school music
  access, 53

competition in program, 53
elementary music offerings, 157–59, 197–99
family support of school music teachers, 54
performance venue, 53
vernacular music, 53
Scott-Kassner, Carol, 225
secure attachment, 135
self-efficacy, 2, 19–20, 45–46, 51, 85
singing, 61–70
    adults improving singing, 63–64
    importance of hearing caregivers' voices, 61, 62
    karaoke, 140–41, 218
    "little songs," 132, 133–34, 149, 150
    lullabies, 119–20, 135, 180
    private vocal lessons, 61
    singing ranges, 64–65, 153–54
    vocal injury, 68
    voice change (adolescent), 65–67
Small, Christopher, 13, 15–16, 23, 91
Smith, Mandy, 40
social media, 28, 37, 83, 85, 97, 112, 175, 178, 183, 186
Sole, Meryl, 133
"Songs for Carmella: Lullabies & Sing-Alongs," 64
songstress jo, 45–46
soundscape, 85–86, 159–60
sound sensitivity, 160
South Africa, 82

spirituality, 157
"Star-Spangled Banner," 147
Star Wars, 51–52, 117
Stomp, 84
Sudano, Amanda, 67
Suzuki method, 2, 51, 146–47, 195
Suzuki, Shinichi, 25–26, 146–47
Sweet, Bridget, 65–66
Swift, Taylor, 64

Taggart, Cynthia Crump, 26, 178, 225
Tate, Kimberly, 136, 137*f*
technology, 106–7, 135
"This Little Light of Mine," 140–41
tidying, 86, 95, 137, 138
Thompson, David, 106
Topp, Dale, 205
transgender and gender expansive, 66, 70
Trehub, Sandra D., 121, 140
Turino, Thomas, 219–20

Uno, 209–10

Valerio, Wendy H., 225
van Laban, Rudolf, 92–95
Volk, Terese M., 36–37

Western classical music, 5, 6–7
Williams, John, 117

youth orchestra, 2
you're doing more than you realize, 2, 7, 24

Made in the USA
Monee, IL
28 April 2026

49136499R00171